D1142084

The Story of Michael

By the Same Author

Novels include:

The Lady in Waiting (Century)
Deal (Michael Joseph)
Reflections (Michael Joseph)
Ripples (Michael Joseph)

Business books include:

Starting a Small Business (Sphere)
The Business Handbook (Sphere)
Putting Your Money to Work (Sphere)

THE STORY OF
MICHAEL

A child rescued from Romania

Deborah Fowler

EBURY PRESS
London

Published in 1991 by Ebury Press
an imprint of the Random Century Group
Random Century House
20 Vauxhall Bridge Road
London SW1V 2SA

Copyright © Shepherd's Keep Studio Ltd 1991

The right of Deborah Fowler identified as the author of this book
has been asserted by her in accordance with the Copyright, Designs
and Patents Act, 1988.

All rights reserved. No part of the publication may be reproduced,
stored in a retrieval system, or transmitted in any form or by any
means, electronic, mechanical, photocopying, recording or otherwise,
without the prior permission of the copyright owner.

(CIP data to follow)

Typeset in News Gothic and Sabon by 🐦 Tek Art Limited,
Croydon, Surrey

Printed and bound in Great Britain by
Mackays of Chatham PLC

Jacket photographs: Bill Dodwell

Front cover (left): Michael, July 1990 (right): Michael, September 1990

For the children of Romania.
Please God, may the world never forget them.

'Love is the same whichever country it is given in.'

Dr. Liliana Bacila, Orphanage No. 1, Bucharest.
January 1990

CONTENTS

ACKNOWLEDGEMENTS

The Story of Michael spans a period of about nine months. During that time, we have had reason to be grateful to so many people, who, to a greater or lesser degree, have made it possible for this tale to have a happy ending.

On the home front, we would like to thank particularly Margaret Wiltshire, Viola Niness (Aunty Vi), Fran Swanson, Sue Timms, Tom and Anne Reeve and daughters Sarah, Karen and Vickie, Sally Drummond-Hay, and Lesley Burt. In addition many people whose job it was to assist us went far beyond the call of duty on Michael's behalf – Jane Allan, Dr Adrian Young, Dr Unescu, Dr Magdalena Dragon, Nicolae Ivan, Bob House and, of course, Dinu Ianculescu. We are extremely grateful for the advice and guidance we received from Caroline Martin, Suzy Gale, Harry McCormick, Ion Mazilu, Kerry Male, and Miranda Cavill.

A special thank-you to Alan's partner, John Runacres, and my agent, Vivienne Schuster, for being so long-suffering about our having to give up work for such a protracted period. Finally, and most important of all, are the thanks due to Adrian and Marianna Gligor, "Granny and Grandpa" Carstulescu and Cristian Filip (Christie) whose loving and reliable care of Michael in all probability saved his life.

Alan and Deborah Fowler

Oxford, 1991

FOREWORD

I never intended to write this book. In fact, early on in our bid to adopt a Romanian orphan, I decided quite definitely that although I am a writer by trade, this was one story I would never tell. It was too emotional, too personal, the experience such a jumbled mess of sadness and joy, hope and hopelessness, I could not see myself standing back from it sufficiently to put my thoughts on paper.

What changed my mind was the realisation that while we had gone to Romania with the express intention of adopting a child, we came home having adopted a country. As one mother said to me, having herself successfully adopted three tiny children, 'However many children you bring out of Romania, you will always remember the one you left behind.'

Arguably, if we raise Michael to be a happy, well-balanced, healthy child we will have 'done our bit' for Romania. If only it were that simple. We cannot let the matter rest there because the scale of the problem is so vast and the suffering so great. I do not believe that anyone who has been to Romania and seen the orphanages for themselves can come back the same person, or, indeed, leave the country and its problems behind them and simply get on with their lives. I am not ashamed to admit that sometimes I wish that we could.

Neither Alan, my husband, nor I have any medical training, and with a very young family to care for it is simply not practical for us to spend any length of time in Romania at the moment. It was while we were searching our minds for a way to help, we realised that telling Michael's story – our story – might be the answer. For what is important now is that Ceauşescu's children are not forgotten. In recent months there have been many reports that much of the foreign aid has been pilfered from the orphanages, that aid trucks have been hijacked and that medicines and baby food are readily available on the black market, not only in Romania but also in Hungary. This is true, and inevitably the backlash is going to make fund-raising for the children far more difficult in future. Several orphanages which have been equipped with new cots, play areas, toys and decent plumbing have been stripped within days of the relief workers leaving. There are instances of children having their new clothes taken off them and their old rags replaced, of toys removed from cots, food almost from their very mouths. I know these reports are not exaggerated for I have seen it happen myself. It is desperately disheartening for all the people who have given time and money they can often ill afford to know that, on the face of it, their efforts have been largely in vain.

The object of this book is to ask you not to give up on the children – because they need you, they need you so much. It is easy to blame the Romanians, to say that there must be something wrong with a nation who would steal from sick and dying children. Such criticism is harsh and unfair. What is important to understand is that the orphans and abandoned children are only one symptom of a sick nation. The people of Romania have nothing; life is a perpetual struggle. Yes, they are tough on their children, bringing them up in much the same way as the Victorians brought up our great-grandparents. No concessions are made for children, they have to fit in, they are expected to work hard, to be disciplined – and so they are. For this reason there is no sentimentality about the abandoned children. They are the bottom of the heap; it is bad luck, but then somebody has to be. Romanian people cannot afford to waste their energy – emotional or physical – on other people's children, and I wonder how many of us would steal from the mouths of orphans to feed our own starving children. Most of us, I suspect.

In practical terms, 50 per cent of the profits of this book are being given to the Romanian Orphanage Trust, to be used to set up family housing for small groups of children. But I hope, too, that *The Story of Michael* will encourage others to consider adopting a child from Romania. Improving the state of the orphanages is only half the answer. You can put in as many bathrooms as you like, with gold-plated taps and marble finishes; you can put in cots from Harrods and dress the children in designer clothes; you can provide a well-balanced diet served from a hygienic and properly run kitchen, but still an institution is not the right place for a child. Children need families, children need mothers and fathers, and if the telling of Michael's story helps one child find a family of his or her own, then this book will not have been written in vain.

What is important now is for the world not to forget that, while the conditions in many orphanages have improved and many of the orphans have been adopted and given the chance of a new life, there are still tens of thousands of children in Romania whose bleak lives are no better than on the day Ceauşescu was shot. We pray that the story of one little boy's suffering may help keep alive the realisation that most of Romania's abandoned children are still locked in hell.

1
THE CHILDREN OF THE FALCON

O<small>N</small> the day they shot Ceauşescu, 25 December 1989, I was blissfully unaware of Romania's struggle to free herself from her mad dictator. Exhausted from Christmas catering, and coping with an extended family, it was not until the news came through at nine o'clock in the evening that I realised what had happened. Clearly there was considerable justification for putting Nicolae Ceauşescu to death, along with his wife, Elena, for the atrocities that they had both performed. Yet listening to the news that Christmas night, both Alan and I were shocked by the violence. Thirty-six hours later, the story dominated the newspapers. 'The Tyrant is Dead', screamed the headline in the *Daily Mail*, followed by a horrific account of Romania's persecuted people. We read the article carefully and discussed it as a family at some length, almost as if we sensed Romania was to have some special significance for us. At times during that day I remember thinking about what I had read. Born in 1947, bloodshed in Europe was only hearsay to me, and perhaps it was for this reason I found the Ceauşescus' death so unsettling. Like everyone else, I had watched the collapse of Communism in the weeks and months leading to Christmas, marvelling at the speed with which a regime – once so dominant – could fall apart so quickly. Yet the situation in Romania seemed different. It was more bloody, of course, than its neighbours but it was not as simple as that. I can only describe it as it seemed to me then – somehow sinister, menacing. Months later, a desperate American woman clutching an abandoned two-month-old baby in a hotel room in Bucharest was to say to me, 'Romania frightens me'. I knew what she meant then and something of that fear seemed to touch me as I read the reports of Romania's struggle, secure as I was, surrounded by family, cushioned and protected from the violence of the world.

The following day Alan and I started to clear the debris of Christmas and the family began to disperse. By lunchtime there were just the four of us – Alan and I, our daughter Lucy, known as Locket, newly turned fifteen and becoming frighteningly grown-up, and Charlie, eleven months, his good humour restored along with his routine following the Christmas high jinks. After lunch Locket took Charlie for a walk and Alan and I collapsed in the playroom with the newspapers. It was a lovely afternoon, the air bright and fresh after two miserable damp days. The view from the playroom is quite unique, for it overlooks fields where once there stood a thriving Saxon village, and beyond to a ruined Elizabethan manor house, past which the River Cherwell makes its way towards the Thames. A tranquil, very English scene. I can remember the precise moment when I opened the *Daily Mail* and read for the first time of Romania's children. It was an article by Anne Barrowclough entitled 'The Lost Children of the Falcon'. It was early, much too early for any journalist to have uncovered the full horror of the orphanages, but Anne was on the way. She had learnt that children were being raised in a kind of Orwellian fashion, to feed the Securitate, the secret police. The children were brought up without love, with inadequate food and the very minimum of basic care. At fifteen they were recruited into the Securitate and trained, quite literally, to be killing machines. If you have never known love, compassion, comfort and kindness, then you cannot give it. Ceauşescu's great hero, it appeared, had been Adolf Hitler, but even Hitler had not gone to these lengths. Hitler had allowed his youth a normal family upbringing, had allowed them girlfriends, wives, sisters. This was different. The Children of the Falcon, as they were known – taking their names from the national symbol, the Carpathian Falcon – were taught to recognise only one father and one mother: Nicolae and Elena Ceauşescu. They were taught to kill without emotion, they were slavishly loyal to the regime and learnt their skills in the latest terrorist techniques from recruited Libyans lent by Colonel Gaddafi. They were lethal, little more than robots, subhuman . . . It was an appalling idea.

I read the article to Alan and his prolonged silence when I had finished was indication enough that he was as shocked as I. We have our faults, Alan and I, like everyone, but we are very strong on family. We love our children dearly and despite the fact that ours is certainly not a conventional family, we are all very close and see each other regularly. The idea of children being raised in this cold-blooded, loveless way was not the sort of news story we could simply set aside and forget.

Alan and I have been married for ten years. We have both been married before, Alan to Sonja, with whom he had two sons, Russell and Murray, and I to Alastair Mackillop, who already had two sons, Lorne and Innes, and by whom I had a daughter, Lucy. After years of unsuccessfully trying to have a baby, we were blessed with Charlie, who was born on 29 January 1989. The result was that our rather odd family profile at the time looked like this: Lorne, thirty-seven; Innes, thirty-two; Russell, twenty-nine; Murray, twenty-three; Lucy (Locket), fifteen and Charlie, eleven months. At some point during the early months of our marriage we banned the prefixs of 'step' and 'half' – it was just too complicated. Everyone was someone's brother or sister, mum or dad. It worked well then, it still does.

We could not be more different, Alan and I. Alan trained as a chartered accountant and then rose to dizzy heights by becoming managing director of a public company. After a confrontation with his chairman, he decided to give up working for anyone but himself and in the last twelve years has gone into partnership with a number of people, helping them to establish their businesses. Together we have written a number of books giving advice on how to start in business. Alan is thirteen years older than me, though I do not think either of us notice the age difference. What I do notice is that he is considerably brighter than I am, and he is also much more efficient – a very tidy, organised person. How he puts up with my controlled chaos I will never know, but I daily thank God for it.

After an early, brief and unsuccessful marriage, I battled away on my own with Locket for some years. Anxious not to have someone else bring up my daughter, and yet needing to support us both, I started a mail-order business selling children's clothes so that I could work flexible hours. The business grew like topsy – we moved from crisis to crisis, usually financial, and it was not until I was introduced to Alan, who came into partnership with me to help stabilise the business, that we made any real commercial progress . . . and also found each other. At the time we met, our respective homes could probably demonstrate more clearly than anything else how incredibly different we were. Lucy and I were living in a dilapidated, though beautiful, Cotswolds farmhouse, awash with toys, dog hairs and the trappings of my business – fabrics, sewing machines, mail bags. It was a cheerful and friendly place – coffee was always on offer if anyone could find a clean mug. We lived in the kitchen, burning half trees in a huge open fireplace. Alan, by contrast, lived in a very skilfully converted village school. It was like a show house, scrupulously clean and tidy, not a cushion out of place, no washing-up cluttering the sink. The spartan order and cleanliness both impressed and terrified me.

So how could such an unlikely pair get together? A good question. We both lived alone and hated it, both loved our work and were very committed to it. We enjoyed each other's company, liked the same sort of people, but, of course, none of that is enough. Sitting at my desk now, I cannot find the words to describe that special spark which, once lit, makes you realise that you have to spend the rest of your life with someone in order to be happy. I am a little self-conscious I think, reluctant to describe something which after all is not the subject of this book. It crept up on us insidiously – we had both been hurt and were very wary of committing ourselves again. In the end, Alan took me away to Jersey for a long weekend and gave me the ultimatum. 'Either we get married or live together, we have to do one or the other,' he insisted. I tried to imagine myself, Locket, our scruffy mongrel, Bentley, and demented cat, Jessie, moving into Alan's immaculate house. I just could not – it seemed unlikely that our relationship would last a week. But he was right, there was no alternative. By then we knew we had to be together, and miraculously a combination of the great British art of compromise and an absolute commitment on both our parts not to have another failed marriage, won the day. The children all gave us their blessing and we could not believe our luck.

An odd family, perhaps, but right from the beginning of our marriage, a very stable one. Looking back on it now, though, I see us as being very much a product of Thatcher's Britain, relatively successful, middle-class, comfortable, complacent – much too complacent, and in such stark contrast to the people of Romania. In truth, we were dreadfully shocked when we read of the Children of the Falcon, but the situation held no reality. Neither of us at that time had ever been to an Eastern bloc country, we had never stared Communism in the face. Although we had both known times of hardship in our lives, we had never gone without a meal, warm clothes to wear, a roof over our heads or hope for tomorrow. We read of Romania's suffering and grieved for her people, but never in our wildest dreams c said.

There was a silence for a moment. 'The way I see it,' Alan said, at last, 'we don't really have a choice now, do we?'

'No,' I replied.

2

THE DECISION

THE village of Hampton Gay is, by anyone's standards, small — very small. We moved here five years ago and with us, the number of families in the village now totals three, the other two being the Reeves, who farm the land around us, and Mrs Dunn, who lives halfway down the track which leads to the next village. The Reeves have three girls, all within a year or two of Locket's age. Living as we do in this isolated spot, we rely very heavily on one another, not only in moments of crisis but also for companionship. We are all busy people, we do not crowd one another, but the other residents of Hampton Gay feel to us like extended family.

The getting of Charlie was quite an ordeal, something of a miracle. Before we met, Alan had had a vasectomy and when we decided we would like to try and have another child it had been necessary for him to endure three reversal operations before finally the 'plumbing' was said to be in working order again. Then I had a miscarriage. When, finally, Charlie was conceived, I was forty-two and Locket was fourteen — a much bigger gap between the children than we would have liked. The pregnancy was a dreary affair, much more so than I remembered with Locket. I felt wretched for most of the time and then at twenty weeks I went into premature labour, and only our quick-thinking GP and the brilliant staff at the John Radcliffe Hospital saved Charlie's life. I spent the second half of the pregnancy on the asthma drug called Salbutimol, with all its ghastly side effects and although we found it difficult to talk about, Alan and I kept wondering why I had nearly lost the baby halfway through the pregnancy. Was it because there was something wrong with it? When Charlie was born, hale and hearty, the joy and relief were enormous.

It was some months, therefore, before it began to dawn on us that, although we were lucky enough to live in what many people would consider a country idyll, the fact remained we were condemning Charlie to a lonely childhood. By the time he went to school Locket would already be at university, the Reeve girls, too, grown-up and leaving home. He would be the only child left in Hampton Gay. Yes, of course we would import friends for him and he was bound to make friends at school – he was a gregarious chap from birth – but it would not be the same as having siblings. With doting, older parents there seemed every likelihood that he would grow up to be a spoilt brat, the baby of the family, the apple of everyone's eye. Perhaps another baby was the answer, but at our ages?

We sought advice, starting with Locket. Yes, she thought another baby was a lovely idea but the thought of mother being pregnant again was truly appalling. I had been impossible to live with, she assured me. I knew she was right. Next stop was the gynaecologist. He saw no reason why I shouldn't have another healthy baby, so long as I became pregnant quickly as time was running out. The labour would be easy, he assured me, but the pregnancy as difficult as the last time, probably more so, and the likelihood of needing Salbutimol again a very strong possibility. We talked it through from every angle. Alan was keen to have another child but felt the cost to me, and the child, might be too high. From my point of view the risks were acceptable – I knew I was going to have a very difficult nine months but what were nine months out of a lifetime? There was also an added risk of having a Down's baby, but then life was a risk. I got pregnant very quickly and nine weeks later, on the first Sunday in March, I lost the baby.

The miscarriage hit me hard. If asked many women will admit to having experienced an early miscarriage at some point in their lives. The popular myth is that, while everybody recognises a late miscarriage is a dreadful experience, an early miscarriage is seen to be little more than a slight interruption to the monthly cycle. It is not true, at least it was not true for me. I felt I had lost someone I should have known. I mourned, I moped and I knew the pain would not go until I could conceive again, and even then . . . The gynaecologist was most encouraging. 'As time is short, just give it a full month's cycle and then try again,' he said. 'I'll give you some hormone injections next time, that should help keep it on board.'

I wanted to try again, I wanted to have another baby and yet slowly, insidiously, another thought was coming into my mind. Maybe we were not supposed to have another child of our own. Between us, Alan and I had been responsible for bringing four, happy, healthy children into the world, and we had the additional pleasure of knowing that Lorne and Innes, my elder stepsons, considered us to be family. Were we justified in having yet another baby when there were so many undernourished, unloved children in the world, without homes or parents? The thought, when it first came, was not directly associated with Romania. It was just a recognition of the fact that we had room in our hearts and, in a practical sense, in our home for one more child, and I wondered whether perhaps it was selfish and egocentric to be trying to make another child in our own image.

For some days the thought did not develop beyond that point, and we waited patiently for the month to pass so that we could try again. I did not share my thoughts with Alan at that stage, for I was afraid he might misunderstand them. He knew the miscarriage had hit me hard and I did not want him to think it was because of that I was losing my bottle, chickening out of another pregnancy. I am sure that was not the case. I knew the only way for me to become my old self again was to move ahead. It was just that the miscarriage had shaken me up, made me look at what we were doing and wonder whether we were right to be doing it. I do not know whether I would have ever told him of my feelings, had it not been for a family Sunday lunch in late April.

After lunch, on what had been an extraordinarily beautiful day for so early in the year, I was sitting beside the paddling pool with Mitch, Russell's wife. In the pool were Charlie, Russell and Mitch's daughter, Madi, who is just six weeks younger than Charlie. As we watched the children play, we both agreed we ought to get them together more often. We live only twenty miles apart but such are life's pressures we never seem to meet often enough. I explained to Mitch some of the problems of being an older mother. All my friends have children of Locket's age and at the time I knew no one else with a young child, which made it even more important that Charlie should spend some time with Madi.

'Why not have another baby?' Mitch asked. I found myself admitting to her that I had lost one just weeks before, and then, almost as if someone else was putting words into my mouth, I told her, with absolute conviction, that in any event I was not sure we should be having another baby, that perhaps we should be thinking of adoption.

Until I spoke the words I did not actually know this was how I felt, yet the moment I voiced my thoughts my words seemed to gather momentum. I found myself telling Mitch how I believed we had much to offer a child, that so many people talked about adoption but never did anything about it and that I did not want to fall into that trap . . . I was saying things that on the face of it were news to me. There was a long pause when I finished speaking.

'So, are you talking about a baby from Romania?' Mitch asked, and as she spoke the words I suddenly knew that I was. Since Christmas I, like everyone else, had watched with mounting horror the unfolding of the truth about the terrible suffering of Ceauşescu's children; of how women were forced to have five children they could not support and did not want, and how those children were condemned to live in orphanages, whose conditions were worse than anything Oliver Twist had ever experienced.

'I'm not sure,' I lied, still reeling from the knowledge that I was indeed very sure – sure that yes, I did want to adopt a Romanian baby, and no, I did not want to have another baby of my own, and that all of this was so certain and so sudden that I could hardly take in what was happening.

Mitch was staring at me oddly and it was then that she told me her story. There was no reason, no reason at all, why she and Russell should not have another child. Although Mitch is very small and slight, the pregnancy and birth had been relatively easy. She and Russell were fit, healthy and above all young, yet they had been hit by more or less the same qualms that I myself felt. Were they really justified in bringing another child into the world when so many were suffering? Completely independently of us, they had come to the conclusion that instead of having a second child of their own, they would offer a home to a Romanian orphan. They had already put the wheels in motion. They had been in touch with the Romanian Embassy and had received a great deal of paperwork. They were also in contact with a couple in Oxford who had just brought two little girls home from Romania, and they were planning to see them the following week.

Still shocked by the sudden realisation of what I wanted to do, I felt as if I was on a roller-coaster. 'Before we take this conversation much further,' I said, 'I'm going to need to talk to Alan.'

I waited until Locket and Charlie were in bed and for the first time raised with Alan the idea of adoption, and in particular a child from Romania. Instantly we were wary with one another, recognising how desperately important it was that both of us should express our views openly and honestly, yet equally afraid of hurting each other's feelings. If the idea had merit, then it was vital that we both felt committed to it, rather than simply agreeing because it was what the other wanted. Even at that early stage, I do not think for a moment it occurred to us that we would have any difficulty in loving an adopted child as much as our own. We were veteran step-parents by then; we had coped at one end of the scale with a succession of teenagers and at the other with Charlie's colic and general disinterest in sleeping. 'We have such a lot to offer,' I said, when I had finished telling him how I felt, 'a loving home, a child's paradise to grow up in.'

'But we're so old,' Alan replied, 'surely it's not fair on the child. I mean, let's face it, you're no spring chicken at forty-two, but at fifty-five I have to be over the hill!'

'Nature didn't think we were too old. Nature gave us Charlie,' I said.

Late into the night we continued to discuss the pros and cons, not just of trying to adopt a Romanian orphan but of adopting at all, of making room in our hearts and our home for another child. Primarily our thoughts were for the child – any child coming out of a Romanian orphanage would be bound to be disturbed. Were we equipped to cope, and was ours the right sort of home? Our household is never calm – it is always busy and there are always a great many people about. The fact that both of us work from home does generate a considerable amount of activity and Locket's social life has to be seen to be believed – there is a constant stream of teenagers through the house. A calmer atmosphere seemed preferable for a child so heavily scarred by life, and yet again, a child used to an institution might find an intense and insular relationship with doting parents too much of a contrast, and, despite our shortcomings, we were at least experienced parents, and many – probably most – adopted children go to couples who have not been parents before.

We thought, too, of our other children – of Locket just embarking on her GCSE year. Was it fair to turn the house upside down at such a time? Of Charlie, who was so used to being the apple of everyone's eye – how would he cope? Yet we could not help feeling their lives would be richer for the experience, and that the benefits would far outweigh even the most difficult adjustments. Eventually it was Alan who said: 'Let's find out more about it. Actually, Russell did mention it to me this afternoon and he's offered to drop in copies of the papers he received from the Romanian Embassy tomorrow. As I see it, there's no harm in finding out what's involved.' Alan is not the sort of person who likes rushing into a commitment and the fact that he had already agreed to Russell giving us the initial information made me realise just how serious he must be.

Things started to move very quickly. Russell and Mitch went to see the couple in Oxford and met their two small daughters. They were most helpful and gave Russell and Mitch a list of what was required in terms of paperwork, as well as the names of two lawyers in Romania who specialised in adoption. They had used a man named Poenaru, whom they recommended. It became clear that before even attempting to go to Romania, it was necessary to put together an enormous file of documentation – medical reports, police reports, references from employers, friends and bankers, birth certificates, marriage certificates and so on. The main feature, though, as we discovered, was the infamous home study. A home study, as explained to Russell and Mitch, was something normally carried out by the Social Services, to assess whether parents were suitable for adopting a child. However, in general terms, it appeared that the Social Services were not inclined to carry out a home study for the adoption of Romanian children, or indeed any foreign child, because social workers were already overworked coping with British children. This sounded like a dead end, but there was an alternative: a private home study, which would cost, we were told, upwards of £1,000. Russell and Mitch were given the address of Pamela Dowling, who runs an inter-country adoption agency and who has on her books qualified social workers able to undertake private home studies which the Romanians were prepared to accept so that the child could be adopted in Romania. However, the British Home Office did not recognise them, which explained why so many children had already been brought into the country illegally.

We discussed the implications of all this over supper on Thursday evening. We were daunted but oddly elated, too. It was clearly not easy but perhaps it was possible. On Friday morning Alan rang Oxford Social Services and spoke to Jane Allan, acting head of Adoption and Fostering for the area. She was not encouraging. She confirmed that the Social Services could carry out a home study but were under no statutory obligation to do so. The compiling of such a report was a lengthy process, she said, and she could not see how she could give any application much priority, bearing in mind that there were sixty children in Oxfordshire looking for permanent homes. As yet, she said, she had had no request to undertake a home study in connection with a Romanian child, although she understood that there were several children in the county already. Clearly this flouting of authority did not please her – understandably so. Alan outlined our family profile. 'You sound ideal adoptive parents,' she said, 'but why a Romanian, why not an English child?'

'We're too old to adopt in this country,' Alan said, confidently.

'You're not. For a newborn baby, yes, or even a toddler, but a school-age child would fit perfectly into your family profile. Don't you think you should be considering an Oxfordshire child?'

'But aren't they all problem children?' Alan asked.

'At least you know what the problems are,' Jane countered. 'Heaven knows what kind of trouble you're building up for yourselves, taking on an unknown Romanian baby.' She had a point. 'Look,' she said, 'why not come to an adoption meeting. The next one is on Thursday 17 May at County Hall. I'll send you an invitation.'

The telephone call with Jane Allan flummoxed us. 'She's a nice woman,' Alan said, 'and clearly knows her business. Maybe she's right, maybe we've been duped by the media into thinking the only children who need help are the Romanian orphans.'

I was not convinced. Since my talk with Mitch I had been haunted by those rows of cots, those desperate faces craving love, craving any attention. Alan instantly understood but felt we should go along to the meeting at County Hall, if only to dismiss it as an option.

It was raining when we arrived at County Hall and Alan and I had an argument on the way. I can't remember what it was about, it was so trivial, but I remember we were early and we sat outside in the car, bickering. Looking back on it now, I'm sure it was just tension. We felt uneasy and out of place. Still, whatever our differences, we managed to reconcile them before we were shown into the Committee Room and met Jane Allan, face to face for the first time. She made us welcome and seated us round an enormous table at which there were eight other couples. We were handed some information on fostering and adoption, and shortly after we arrived the meeting began.

'I think I should explain my position first,' Jane said, 'or rather that of my department. I realise that many of you will have travelled down a very long road to reach this point, one which will have been painful and plagued with disappointment. Don't feel I'm unsympathetic to what you have been through, but I must stress that this is not an agency for finding children for childless couples. Our responsibility is to the child. What we are trying to do is to find good homes and parents for our children – that is our priority.'

I looked around the table. I had not thought of this aspect of adoption until now – the awful desperation of the childless. I thought back to the feelings of despair and disappointment that we had experienced during the years we had tried to have a child, and those feelings had been set against a background of already having children. What must it be like for these people? Their faces told the story – gazes fixed on Jane Allan, who for most represented their last hope.

Jane went on to explain the position in Oxfordshire. On average, four newborn babies a year became available for adoption and, in view of the small number involved, very strict rules applied to the eligibility of couples wishing to be considered. Those seeking the adoption of a newborn baby had to be unable to have children of their own, and at the time of adoption both partners had to be under thirty-five. As there was a four-year waiting list, it was pointless for anyone over thirty to apply. At that time there were forty-seven children of various ages waiting to be adopted in the county, although over a third of these were black and therefore not available, so far as the people at this meeting were concerned. The rest, Jane explained, were almost entirely school-age children with some sort of physical or mental handicap, or deep psychological scarring. The exception to this tended to be sibling groups who would not be parted and therefore were not easy to place.

It was not a promising picture for any of us. I desperately wanted to protest about the ruling so far as black children were concerned but I did not dare, not wishing to make an enemy of Jane Allan. It seemed crazy. Here was a group of people desperately wanting to adopt a child but because they were all white it meant that no black child on Jane's register stood a chance of finding a family. If the civilised world is to make progress then colour prejudice has to be overcome and surely the nation's children are the best way to move forward. If white children are adopted by black families and vice versa, they will grow up understanding one another. Perhaps I have an oversimplified view of it, but years ago I employed in my business a black girl called Lyn, who had been adopted by white parents. A more outgoing, happy, well-balanced person it would have been hard to meet and I knew her during her turbulent teenage years when she should have been at her worst. What does colour matter, what do race or religion matter to a child needing a loving home, and here in Oxford we have a big black population in Cowley who would surely benefit from a more liberal policy. I kept quiet with difficulty.

The meeting dragged on. Jane explained the procedure for adoption and then concluded by asking if anyone had any questions. No one had. They all looked stunned, shell-shocked. Perhaps some of the couples there that day have since found their special child; I hope so. Certainly, though, there was no obvious enthusiasm, no quickening of interest. These people were not saints, not Mother Teresas, they were just ordinary people who desperately wanted children of their own. Perhaps they were at fault, or perhaps society as a whole gives us too blinkered a view as to what makes happy families, but a seven-year-old Down's syndrome girl, or a family of three boys who still had access to their mother, or a child with severe cerebral palsy were not going to fulfil these people's dreams. And that, of course, was what Jane Allan was saying. It wasn't her job to do so. Her job was to find good homes for her children, whatever their problems.

Tea was passed round, and revitalised by this, one or two questions were asked. It was then left to us all to decide whether we wished our names to be put forward on the register for either fostering or adoption, or both.

We left. It was still raining outside and it seemed appropriate. 'It's not for us, is it?' Alan said.

'It should be, if we had big enough hearts,' I said.

'I can't see how bringing a child with severe problems into our home is going to help anybody,' Alan said. 'I know it should, I know that helping a child overcome enormous difficulties should make us all better people, but for us it just doesn't feel right.'

'Then should we be thinking of adoption at all?' I asked. 'Any child we bring out of Romania is likely to be very disturbed, at any rate initially. Perhaps we're not strong enough or unselfish enough to take on such an enormous responsibility.'

It was our lowest point in those early days. We suddenly felt hampered by our own inadequacies, feeling that in order to be good adoptive parents we should be prepared to take any child, whatever the circumstances, to give him or her the best possible chance of a decent life.

That night, as I was giving Charlie his bedtime bottle, I remembered the faces of those other couples at the meeting. I couldn't be sure, of course, but I was fairly certain that we were the only couple present who already had children. I hugged Charlie tighter to me, recognising how lucky we were and wondering why it was we were putting our family's happiness on the line by our plan to bring into the family a little stranger who might well destroy our secure structure. It seemed madness . . . but that was before we met the Martins.

On the same day we were at County Hall, our secretary, Vi, known as Aunty Vi in the family, brought us a press cutting. Russell and Mitch had 'gone public' about their desire to adopt a Romanian orphan and had made the front page in the local paper, *The Banbury Cake*. They felt that the publicity might help their case with the Social Services by bringing pressure to bear on them. There was a big picture of Mitch and Madi, but it was not just that which caught our attention. In the same article the journalist mentioned James and Caroline Martin, who had successfully brought home three Romanian children. James was a doctor and they lived in Bloxham, just a few miles from our old home at Adderbury.

I telephoned Caroline Martin, feeling very guilty about disturbing her when she had three tiny children to look after. 'Of course I'll help you,' she said. 'I'll tell you everything I know. Come over next Monday. Have you any children?' I told her about Charlie and Locket. 'Bring Charlie with you,' she said, 'one of the children I've brought home is eighteen months old. I'd like to see the sort of development she should have achieved. Seeing Charlie will be very useful.'

Caroline Martin lived in a rambling old Cotswold house. I knew she had a stepdaughter of Locket's age and she was much younger than I had expected, blonde, pretty, tired but triumphant. She introduced Alexandra, eighteen months old, tiny and dark like a sparrow, shuffling around on the floor, still trying to learn to crawl. Then Toby, four months old, who had already spent nearly four weeks in England by the time we saw him. He lay in a big old pram in Caroline's dining room and on first glance was the picture of health: chubby cheeks, a happy, gurgling, contented child — until Caroline drew back the covers and we saw his tiny, wasted body. And Emily, little Emily . . . covered from head to foot in mosquito bites, her face like a teenager with a bad case of acne, crying wearily, desperately. 'We have a long way to go with her,' Caroline said. 'She is very weak; James is very worried about her.' She in no way resembled the three-month-old baby she was — I had never seen a child look so ill.

In contrast, Charlie marched around the house the picture of health — sturdy, pink, fresh-faced. It almost made me feel ashamed. The babies had so newly arrived, the house was not adapted for tiny children. Alexandra watched in wonder as Charlie tried to negotiate the stairs, pick up precious ornaments, knock over books, rifle his way through a pile of newspapers on the floor . . . It had not occurred to her to do any of these things.

Caroline had a girl from the village to help her but these three sick, disorientated children needed every moment of her time. Still, she made time for us, sitting down with Alan, telling him everything she had learned about Romania – about crooked lawyers, awkward officials, the very unsympathetic British Embassy . . . It sounded increasingly daunting. We learned a little of the problems of the Romanian people, who had nothing and could get nothing, even if they had money. Bribery was rife. We needed to take brandy, whisky, cigarettes, perfume, soap, toiletries and American dollars. 'You will get nowhere without bribery,' Caroline said, 'and it has to be on a continuing basis. You give someone a packet of cigarettes one day in order to get something done. The next day if you have no cigarettes, they'll pretend they don't even know you.' It sounded hostile and very alien.

She gave us a series of contacts; again the name of the lawyer Poenaru was mentioned. Then she gave us the name of a man named Mazilu. 'He is a member of the Government,' she said, 'in charge of adoption. I have been told that he is the only honest man in Romania and certainly from my dealings with him, that would seem to be the case.' She gave us his home and office telephone numbers.

Halfway through our meeting I took Charlie upstairs to change his nappy and Alexandra came with us. She sat, placidly watching while I set about Charlie's toiletries, and as she did so her tiny fist began banging rhythmically on the side of the bath. I bent down to stop her. Already her knuckles were bright red. She had spent all her life in an orphanage and it seemed that even pain offered a diversion from boredom. The realisation shocked me for it gave me an insight, a sudden glimpse of what the orphanages must be like, what this child must have suffered.

When I returned downstairs, Alan and Caroline were concluding their discussions. 'Is it as bad as the media suggests?' I said, still troubled by Alexandra.

'Worse,' Caroline said, 'much worse. There was a little boy in the orphanage – he was seven years old according to his records but he looked about two and was in a cot with other two-year-olds. I can't get him out of my mind. James says we'll go back and fetch him if I want, but I can't cope with any more, it wouldn't be fair on anyone.' She fixed us with a sad smile. 'That's the trouble with Romania,' she said, 'it doesn't matter how many children you bring back, you'll always think about the one you left behind.'

We drove home slowly. Charlie, in his car seat, fell instantly and deeply asleep. We began talking around the subject. We agreed that we liked Caroline very much, that her help was invaluable, and how much we could benefit from her experience. Alan slowed right down to turn left at Bletchingdon. 'So, what are we going to do,' he said, 'shall we go ahead?'

'I think you know how I feel,' I replied. 'From the beginning it's been something I've wanted to do, but I don't know whether it's fair to expect you to feel the same. Because of having Charlie and Locket to look after, it's you who is going to have to carry the brunt of this thing, it's you who is going to have to do all the paperwork, chasing up and shouting and screaming at officials. Probably you, too, who is going to have to go out to Romania more often than me. I can't keep leaving Charlie and it doesn't sound as though I can take him. It's going to mean an awful lot of hard work and hassle for you.'

Alan laughed. 'Charlie involved quite a lot of hard work and hassle for you, I seem to remember. You could say it's only fair that it's my turn this time.'

'You're very nice,' I said.

There was a silence for a moment. 'The way I see it,' Alan said, at last, 'we don't really have a choice now, do we?'

'No,' I replied.

3

TO BUCHAREST

I did not want to go. It was nearly midnight as I stood at the end of Charlie's cot, watching him while he slept. Alan had flown out to Bucharest earlier that day and Locket and I were due to follow him the next morning. I had never left Charlie before – his world up to that point had been totally secure. Not surprisingly, I was full of fear, imagining something happening to Alan and me, that in going out to Romania to save an orphan we would perhaps create one. It was a mother's instinct at its most basic – afraid to leave her child. While we were away Charlie was going to be looked after by Margaret Wiltshire, who he knew well and loved dearly. Since he was four months old Margaret had looked after him every weekday morning to that I could write, and in order that his routine should be disturbed as little as possible, she had made the magnificent gesture of offering to move her entire family into our home while we were away. I knew he would miss us but I knew he would be well looked after.

While there might be no reasonable justification for worrying about Charlie, I thought my fears for Locket were valid. There was no problem at all so far as her attitude to the proposed adoption was concerned. She was extremely enthusiastic and determined to be very much involved, but were we right to take her? In the weeks that had elapsed since our meeting with Caroline Martin, Romania had been subjected to two more devastating blows, the first in the form of an earthquake and the second in the miners' march on Bucharest. Alan and I had read with horror the reports of miners indiscriminately beating up people on the streets of Bucharest. There was talk of rape, assault. Were we crazy to be taking our fifteen-year-old daughter to such a city, at such a moment? We knew, however, that we could not go without her. Finding a child to adopt involved her as much as ourselves; she had to come if we were to go at all. We had sought advice and Ion Mazilu, 'the only honest man in Romania', had been very helpful. He had promised to help us if we had any difficulties while we were in Bucharest and he had assured us that we would be in no danger physically. The Foreign Office was not so encouraging. Alan had telephoned the previous day and asked, 'Would you take your fifteen-year-old daughter to Bucharest at the moment?' 'Good heavens, no,' was the reply. We had therefore devised the plan whereby Alan travelled ahead of Locket and I, so that he could see the city for himself and decide whether it was safe for us to follow him. He had just telephoned to report the most dreadful journey in a dilapidated plane which had been delayed for hours. To add insult to injury, his luggage was still at Heathrow. Having left us at nine o'clock in the morning, it had taken him until midnight to reach his hotel. Still, the good news was he was sure it was safe to come. The city was calm, much of the hysteria about the miners, Alan felt, had been media hype. He had talked to a lot of people, he said, including Kerry Male and the girl with whom she was sharing a hotel apartment, an American named Karen. They both felt it was safe to come.

We had known Kerry Male only a week but somehow, because of the circumstances, it seemed a great deal longer. She and her husband Steven lived in Abingdon. We had been given her name by a social worker. Kerry could not have children and a fortnight earlier she and Steven had gone to Bucharest and found a four-day-old boy, Alexander. They had been visiting a maternity hospital in the country, about sixty kilometres from Bucharest, where they had been told that there were children available for adoption who would be placed in orphanages if homes could not be found for them quickly. Before they had even entered the maternity hospital building, a young woman had flagged down their taxi and offered them her son. Their initial reaction had been one of horror that an apparently healthy young woman should be wishing to give up her child to the first strangers she met, but when they heard her story they began to understand.

Alexander was the woman's third child. She was married to his father but, incredibly, she was still only seventeen years old. There was no way she could support the baby, no way she could cope with yet another mouth to feed. Kerry and Steven met Alexander's father and the other children. The young couple were desperate; they did not want their baby to go into an orphanage but neither could they keep him. They begged Steven and Kerry to take him, and for the Males it was no big sacrifice – one look at Alexander and they loved him. They had spent a long time talking to the family and liked them very much. Kerry had agreed to send them regular photographs of Alexander as he grew, and would make sure that he knew of their whereabouts when he was old enough to decide whether he would like to meet his birth parents. It was desperately sad that a child could not be brought up by his natural parents, but at the same time it was at least a relief that baby Alexander had cheated the harsh reality of orphanage life. The only way Kerry and Steven had been able to keep him out of an orphanage had been to take him back to their hotel the following day. They had no equipment, no food, no nappies, nothing, but luckily they had met Karen, an American girl who had also found a baby at the same orphanage, and being an American was wonderfully equipped with every conceivable type of baby requirement, which she had generously shared with them. Locket and I were taking out a suitcase full of milk and supplies for Alexander.

Charlie woke on the dot of five the following day and for once I was pleased. It gave me plenty of time to be alone with him before Russell came to collect us at eight o'clock to take us to the airport. In view of the uncertainty in Romania – the miners' violence and the earthquake – Russell and Mitch had decided to postpone their plans for adoption until they saw how things went for us. It seemed a sensible move.

I gave Charlie his bottle and on the spur of the moment took some Polaroid pictures of him. He was in an excellent mood, full of laughter. For some reason, it made it all the more difficult to leave him. I ran a bath and climbed in. I had already dressed Charlie for the day but while my back was turned for an instant he managed to do a neat swallow dive over the top of the bath to join me . . . complete with socks and shoes. We had a hilarious time and that too made it worse. Once we were both dressed and dry things moved very quickly. I woke Locket who, like me, had spent a restless night, and when Margaret and her family arrived, Charlie was thrilled to see them. He did not give me a backward look when he ran to them. It was how it should be. When Russell arrived I suddenly knew that I had to get away quickly or I would never leave. We bundled our cases into the back of the car and I said a hasty goodbye to Margaret. We had spent days planning this moment. She had copious notes on every conceivable trauma that might hit Charlie, and a freezer full of food. We were totally organised and yet . . .

We spoke very little on the way to the airport. Locket was tired, I was miserable and Russell had been working very late the previous night and so was more than a little jaded. We had packed very little for ourselves, just a couple of changes of clothes, for we were all planning to return on the following Wednesday. The rest of the luggage was baby supplies for Alexander Male and our own baby. It seemed unreal. Our file was complete, including a private home study, and we had spoken to Poenaru, the lawyer, who had agreed to help us. We had just three days to find a baby.

So far as the child was concerned, we all felt it was important to keep an open mind as far as we could, but we were agreed in principle that we were looking for a little girl, as young as possible and certainly under nine months. We felt it had to be right to look for a child with a natural age gap between her and Charlie, and Locket was adamant that five brothers was enough and what she needed now was a sister. If we had a preference, Alan and I favoured a girl for practical reasons. Charlie is a bright child and physically very advanced. A child who had spent months in an orphanage was likely to be very behind in development and we could not help feeling that the obvious differences between them would be particularly unfair on our adopted child if they were highlighted by the children being very close in age and of the same sex. I suppose in our minds we were inspired by Kerry and Steven's story, and saving a newborn baby from having to go to an orphanage at all was a lovely idea. Looking back on it now, I wonder whether in fact I was trying to replace the child I had lost in my miscarriage, and that was why the idea of a very young baby had such an appeal. I do not know, but whatever our individual views, we all agreed that when we found our special child we would know. It was possibly a rather naïve thought, but the whole idea of visiting the orphanages and selecting a child was so abhorrent that we had to create some sort of mystique about it, otherwise I honestly do not think we could have coped with the concept of going to Romania at all.

At Heathrow, Russell left us at Terminal 2, in a chaotic queue. The previous day when I had delivered Alan to the airport I had collected our tickets from Harry McCormick, a delightful man with, despite his name, a heavy Romanian accent. We got to know him quite well in the months that followed and it emerged that his father had been Irish and his mother Romanian. Harry runs a business called Friendly Travel. He had begun the business some years previously in order to assist church members to visit Romania. The Revolution changed everything; his whole house has virtually become an office now and he employs several members of his family to cope with the volume of work which is a result of the Revolution, and more particularly of the plight of the orphans.

You can travel to Romania in a number of ways but the way most people travel is direct, by Romanian Airways, which is known as Tarom. There are plenty of stories about Tarom. We were told that Tarom pilots are the best pilots in the world – they have to be to survive flying planes in such a state of collapse. In fairness, many of the pilots are seconded from the virtually non-existent Romanian Air Force and are therefore highly skilled. The planes are terrible . . . none of the seats match, many of the lights do not work, the carpet is stained and the food is unbelievable – a piece of dried-out salami, some soapy cheese and a stale bread roll. Little did we realise the first time we flew by Tarom that this is the standard fare of most hotels in Bucharest – there simply is nothing else.

Ahead of us in the queue for the check-in were three doctors with boxes of medical supplies for the orphanages. When it was their turn, the Tarom representative came downstairs and let their excess luggage through free of charge on compassionate grounds. We had an enormous suitcase full of milk for Alexander, which we knew put us well over our weight limit. Taking our lead from the doctors we simply said it was for an orphanage and were also not charged excess baggage. It was a kindly gesture I saw repeated again and again on our various trips. Tarom could have been making a fortune out of charging for excess freight as desperate would-be parents carted out huge supplies of baby food, nappies and milk, but they rarely made any charge at all.

Once through check-in we went to the departure lounge where we found that, unlike poor Alan, our flight was only delayed an hour. We bought some breakfast and I accompanied it with a large brandy – I was trying not to think about Charlie. While we were waiting, I bought some Sunday newspapers. On the front page of the *Sunday Times* there was an article about the miners' march on Bucharest. 'They have left behind a city tingling with fear,' the article warned. I hid the paper from Locket. It was too late now; I knew that I could not dissuade her from going. We had made our commitment; we were on the way.

The plane was full and, once settled, Locket and I looked around in the hope of spotting other would-be adopters. Sitting across the aisle from us was a woman about my own age who introduced herself as Marie. She was Irish and we were soon in deep conversation. Four weeks earlier she had found a nine-month-old baby girl in an orphanage and was trying to adopt her. She had only seen the child once and was having enormous difficulty getting her papers signed in Romania. She was desperate, and there were tears in her eyes as she talked. 'It's bad enough when you see those pictures on television,' she said, 'but when you put a name to a face and make a commitment to a particular child, it's so much worse. She may die before I can get her home.' The Irish adoption procedure is much simpler than ours, I learnt. The Social Services there are quite happy to conduct home study reports on foreign children and if the couple is found to be suitable, the report automatically gives the right to bring a child into the country. In the case of the UK, we have to find a child and then wait an unspecified time for a home study report to be completed on that particular child, which, of course, prolongs the agony. As far as Marie was concerned all her paperwork was now complete, but there was talk of a change in Romanian law and she was having difficulty getting her adoption papers approved. This was not the first time we had heard rumours of a change in the law, and it was unsettling.

Marie introduced us to a couple sitting in front of us, Jane and John McGuire. They already had a ten-year-old son and had decided that rather than have another child they should adopt. John himself had been adopted and loved his adoptive parents very much. Clearly this had greatly influenced their decision.

We began talking about the plight of the orphans and in a very short space of time Jane began to cry. It was an extraordinary situation and a very emotional one, all flying into the unknown, all looking for a special baby. However, such was everyone's commitment to try and save at least one child, that there was no feeling of unease about what we were doing. The media have on occasions attempted to downgrade and criticise couples flying to Bucharest to adopt Romanian orphans, suggesting it is not unlike a shopping trip. Perhaps there are couples who simply jumped on the bandwagon because it seemed a fun thing to do. If so, we never met them. Everyone we ever met had a single common aim: to help a child climb out of hell and into a better life.

At the duty-free shop Locket and I had bought Kent cigarettes and whisky, as Caroline Martin had suggested. We had also bought a bottle of champagne on Alan's specific instruction. 'I think we should open the champagne right now,' said Locket, seeing the tears flow. We did so, sharing it with our three new Irish friends. We toasted our success and then, inspired by the champagne, we began drinking the truly disgusting, warm red wine which was served along with the stale salami. There were more tears, but at least it passed the time.

It was still daylight when we circled over Romania and straightened out to land at Bucharest. Our immediate impression of the country was one of drab greyness, and it also seemed a very flat landscape. When we landed we were bundled out of the plane and into coaches and the first thing that hit us was the incredible heat, which we had not expected. At the airport, as we climbed concrete steps to what could laughingly be described as the arrival lounge, a soldier suddenly stepped out in front of Locket and me. He had a machine-gun casually draped over one shoulder. He was very young, almost a child, but his age was far from reassuring for I could not help remembering what we had read of the Children of the Falcon, Ceauşescu's army of juvenile killers. Surely under the new regime, they no longer existed . . . did they? He smiled suddenly. This was no sinister robot. 'Do you have a cigarette?' he asked politely.

'No,' I lied, 'I don't smoke.'

'OK.' He stepped aside and let us pass.

'Poor chap, you should have given him some,' Locket said, reprovingly.

'Look around you,' I said, 'there are soldiers everywhere. Once we start we'll lose all our supply in seconds.'

Ahead of us queues were forming to go through passport control and suddenly we saw Alan waving frantically from the other side of the barrier and pointing us to an entrance where there was no queue at all. I have never been so glad to see anyone in my life. Locket and I went up to the desk. A dark, good-looking man I judged to be in his early thirties pushed ahead of Alan. 'Passport diplomatic,' he shouted, and grabbed at our passports.

'It's all right,' said Alan, 'I'll explain in a moment. This is Adrian.'

We handed over our passports, to which Adrian added a packet of Kent cigarettes. In a matter of seconds we were through passport control while everyone else on the plane queued patiently. This Adrian had to be good news. 'Who is he?' I whispered to Alan, as he bustled ahead of us, insisting on carrying all our luggage.

'He's a taxi driver Kerry found. In fact he works here too as an air traffic controller, but it pays him to get his boss to work his shifts while he works as a taxi driver. He's a great "fixer", as you saw, and best of all he has a lovely wife called Marianna and they have agreed to be foster parents if we find a baby.'

'That's marvellous,' I said. It was indeed. It was something that had been worrying us. If we found a baby in similar circumstances to Kerry, the child either had to be in our care in Romania or run the risk of being sent from the maternity hospital to an orphanage during the period it took us to finalise the adoption. Most of the couples coming out to Romania were childless and therefore it was possible for the wives to stay on in Bucharest with their babies in hotel rooms. It might not be very comfortable, but it was a far better alternative than risking their babies to an orphanage. Because of Charlie, we clearly could not do this, and not only Charlie – there was Locket to consider. Her school had kindly given her special dispensation to come with us on this one trip but she had to get back to work within a few days. 'Are you sure they're suitable?' I asked Alan.

'Yes, they are a terribly nice family. I spent part of yesterday with them. I'll tell you all about it later.' He introduced us formally to Adrian whose English was very good. He was very loud and full of himself but immediately likeable.

For the first time I looked around the airport. It was terrible, a ghastly concrete building and filthy dirty. By now we were at the baggage carousel, which appeared to have broken down. Everyone was shouting, but in a weary way, and the people looked so poor, so drab, so downtrodden. The heat was stifling. Alan handed round bottles of water. 'We're going to need these,' he said, 'it will take at least an hour for our luggage to come up. I'm just hoping mine's with yours or Kerry will be short on her supplies.'

He was right, it took a good hour for our baggage to arrive but mercifully all of it was there, including Alan's. Again, Adrian worked his magic. Dashing backwards and forwards, he moved our cases to customs. Another packet of cigarettes passed hands and in seconds we were outside the airport building, taking great lungfuls of fresh air. It was still stifling, but infinitely better than inside.

As we drove into Bucharest it was raining quite hard. Adrian drove at breakneck speed, his radio blaring. Once he skidded so badly in the wet that we were nearly concertinaed between a car and a lorry. Alan asked him to slow down, and to take our mind off Adrian's driving he began to tell us what he had been doing in the last twenty-four hours. He had spent some considerable time with Kerry and her American friend Karen, who, with her premature two-month-old baby named Emily, was sharing a hotel flat along with Kerry and Alexander. The situation did not look good. President Iliescu had apparently stopped signing adoption papers and no one quite knew why. I thought immediately of poor Marie and wondered if she would ever have her little girl. Kerry and Karen at least had their children with them, but they could not leave Romania without the President's signature. He'd had their papers now for over a fortnight, yet nothing had happened. They were becoming increasingly disillusioned with Poenaru, which was also unsettling.

'I've arranged a meeting for nine o'clock tonight with Daniella,' said Alan. Daniella was Mr Poenaru's assistant, and it was she who had helped Kerry find Alexander.

I felt a glimmer of hope. 'Perhaps she could take us to the same maternity hospital as Kerry.'

'That's the idea,' said Alan. 'Adrian knows the way. He was there too when Kerry and Steven found Alexander.'

We had been told by Harry McCormick that the Hotel Bucuresti was probably the best hotel in Romania. All one can say is that we were extremely glad not to be in the worst. It had been growing dark as we had driven through the city streets and, apart from spying the shadowy forms of one or two fine buildings, it was not possible to see much for there were very few streetlights. And, interestingly, practically no one about although by Bucharest time it was still only seven o'clock. The hotel had a faded, neglected look. It was big and the hallway area quite impressive, but the bedrooms were dreary in the extreme. The first problem came when we tried room service for some supper. All that was available was bread, soapy cheese and salami, bottled water and the same filthy red wine we had drunk on the plane.

We were hot and exhausted. Locket and I showered while Alan laid out the 'feast'. We ate hastily and then trooped over to Kerry and Karen's flat, which involved walking round the back of the hotel to a separate block. Adrian joined us. 'I don't want him at the meeting with Daniella,' Alan whispered, 'but I don't know how to get rid of him.'

'I expect we'll just have to put up with him,' I said. Adrian was being very attentive to Locket and it worried me slightly. He suggested he should show her the town, which we quickly but politely refused.

Kerry and Karen's flat was tiny, cramped and airless. Both babies were screaming. Karen had already been there for two and a half weeks without a break and Kerry had been home only briefly to complete her home study and then return hastily to Alexander. They both looked tired and pale. Kerry, I noticed, had lost a great deal of weight in just a week. She appeared very nervy and was chain-smoking. Locket and I picked up the babies and began rocking them, to give the girls a break.

They were very different. Alex was by then ten days old. Despite being such a young baby, one would never imagine he was anything other than a boy; he had a thick thatch of dark hair, slanting, slightly slavic eyes and a determined little frown. A lovely baby, who, thanks to Kerry, would now never know orphanage life.

Karen's Emily had come from the same hospital. She had been kept in because she was born two months prematurely. She was not a pretty baby but there was something very special about Emily – a determination and, even at such a young age, a glorious sense of humour. She looked like a little elf, desperately undersized but alert, bright and grinning from ear to ear.

'When the nurses finished feeding the babies, they just chucked them into a cot in a big pile,' Karen explained, her eyes misting at the memory. 'I dug through the pile and there she was at the bottom. I didn't pick Emily – she picked me.'

Sorting through a pile of babies, it sounded a nightmare, impossible to believe but for the conviction in Karen's voice. I hugged Emily very tight. 'Still, they're safe now,' I said.

'I'm not sure,' said Kerry. 'Poenaru says the papers aren't signed yet and we have to wait, but as we understand it, Iliescu has stopped signing papers and if they're not signed now, it could be that they never will be. If it's OK with you, I'll come to your meeting with Daniella and find out what's going on.'

At nine o'clock we left Karen with both babies. Alan, Locket, Kerry and I, together with Adrian, went down to the hotel lobby. It got to ten, half-past ten, eleven o'clock. We were all exhausted and we were almost at the point of giving up when suddenly Daniella came through the swing doors. 'There she is, the bitch,' said Kerry. She was well past being subtle.

One could see immediately that Daniella was a hard woman. She looked rather like a younger version of Edwina Currie only much, much tougher. She was crisply dressed and did not even look slightly tired, despite the hour. Her appearance also suggested she was in a very different income group from most of the population.

Alan quickly explained our position. We had already spoken to Mr Poenaru, who had agreed to take on our case and Alan had sent ahead a full copy of our file. He had the original file with him. 'We are looking for a baby girl,' he said, 'preferably under nine months old. We thought perhaps our best bet would be to go to the same maternity hospital as Kerry and Karen.'

'It's not possible,' said Daniella, 'no more babies can be adopted in Romania at the moment.'

We all stared at her, shocked to the core by her words. 'What do you mean?' I stammered.

'There is no law,' she said. She seemed to be enjoying the impact she was making.

'But we spoke to Mr Poenaru on Friday,' Alan said, 'and Mr Mazilu. Neither of them mentioned this. Do you know Mr Mazilu?'

'Yes, I do,' said Daniella, 'and I do not think you should trust him.'

'All right, but Mr Poenaru is our lawyer, why did he not tell us about this?' Alan asked, sounding very calm. 'Why did he let us come all this way for nothing?'

Daniella shrugged. 'No one knows whether there will be any more foreign adoptions. We have so many problems in Romania, it is not a priority.'

'As I understand it,' I said, 'there are 450,000 children desperately needing care. Surely that's some kind of priority.' I could not bear the woman and her cold indifference.

'The whole economy is in chaos. This must be resolved first, then the children.'

Adrian interjected with a barrage of Romanian. Their conversation became very heated. 'I wish he wouldn't do that,' said Kerry. 'He's always interfering at meetings. You never know what he's saying and whether he's getting it right. Adrian what are you saying?'

'One moment.' Their conversation continued for some time, then Adrian turned to us. 'She says she believes that there will be a new law but she does not know how long it will take. I have told her that we will look after your baby however long it takes – it's not a problem.' This was a favourite expression of Adrian's: according to him, everything could be solved – it was not a problem.

'If this is so,' I said to Daniella, 'could you help us to find a baby and then Adrian and his wife will look after it until the new law is passed?'

'But the law may never be passed,' she said, 'and what happens then?'

I looked at Alan. 'I suppose in those circumstances we would sponsor the child and help Adrian and Marianna to keep it, if they would be willing.'

'We would certainly be willing,' said Adrian, 'but there will be a law, I know it.'

'You cannot know it,' said Daniella, 'no one knows what will happen and you cannot take a baby from a maternity hospital when there is no law.'

'Wait a moment,' said Alan, 'I spoke to the British Embassy as well on Friday to check whether it was safe for me to bring my wife and daughter to Bucharest. I told them the purpose of my visit and they said nothing about there being no law. Are you sure you have your facts right, because presumably the British Embassy would know if the law was changing?'

'Of course I have my facts right,' said Daniella. She was becoming angry now. 'The British Embassy have been told. They know as well as I do that there is no law.'

'So are you saying you won't help us?'

'I cannot,' said Daniella.

So there we had it, a wasted trip, and far, far worse, apparently the children of Romania were now imprisoned in their orphanages with no law to free them for foreign adoption.

'But what about me,' Kerry said, 'and Alexander?'

'Your papers will be signed – they were received in time.'

'But when?' wailed Kerry. 'You said that last week and the week before.'

'It will be in the next few days.'

'But we've been told that Iliescu is signing no more papers.'

Daniella sighed and began speaking with studied patience, as if to a stupid child. 'He is not signing papers for adoptions which occurred after the 10th June but your papers were handed in before the 10th June – that is why we were in such a hurry to complete them. Mr Poenaru is handling it, all will be well. Call me next week.'

'Next week,' shouted Kerry. 'I want to go home now. Alex is ill, he has very bad diarrhoea. I must get him away from this city and this godforsaken country.'

Again Daniella shrugged, apparently indifferent to Kerry's outburst. 'You must wait.' She stood up to go. 'I'm sorry I cannot help you,' she said, looking directly at us for the first time. It was a platitude; her eyes remained cold and bored.

Adrian began speaking to her in rapid Romanian, then he turned to us. 'I will take Daniella home and speak with her on the way. I will see you in the morning, yes?'

'Yes,' said Alan. 'I suppose our first port of call had better be the British Embassy, to find out what's really going on.'

We returned to Kerry's flat. Climbing up the stairs we heard the wails of babies three floors above. 'Oh God,' said Kerry, 'I bet Karen's freaking.'

She was. 'I think Alex is having convulsions,' she said as we walked in, and then burst into tears. 'Alan's been on the phone [Alan is also the name of Karen's husband]. He doesn't seem to understand we're rotting away here, he just tells me to be patient. Jesus! What happened with Daniella?'

'Nothing,' said Kerry and told her the story, 'and she's not going to help the Fowlers.'

'Well, I guess the best thing you can do is to get hold of Ivan,' said Karen, calming a little.

The name rang a bell. 'Nicolae Ivan is the name of the other lawyer Caroline Martin told us about,' Alan reminded me. 'That's a good idea.'

'Use our phone,' said Karen.

'Only for God's sake don't mention Poenaru,' said Kerry. 'I tried to persuade Ivan to represent me when I first hit problems with Poenaru but as soon as I mentioned the guy's name Ivan hung up. You must make sure Adrian doesn't tell him either. Sometimes I'm not sure about Adrian's loyalties. Look at the way he's gone sneaking off with Daniella. This place gives me the creeps, you just don't know who you can trust here.'

'Romania frightens me,' said Karen

We were all silent for a moment, digesting her words. She was sitting nursing fragile little Emily, mercifully asleep now, while tears poured down her face. 'Why the hell did we come?' she asked no one in particular.

Karen's story was different again. She had married extremely young and had a son who was now a teenager. When the marriage had broken up she had married Alan who could not have children and they had therefore adopted a little American girl, Stacey, who was now four. The plight of the Romanian children and the fact that they felt Stacey needed a brother or sister had brought them to Bucharest. As Karen was the first to admit, she had gone from the security of her parents' home to her first marriage, and then to her second marriage, so she had never really had the chance or the need to be an independent person. Now that Alan, because of business pressures, had been forced to return to New York, she was left literally holding the baby, and for the first time in her life was trying to cope on her own. She was not coping – at least she wasn't that night.

In the end we left them. Alex did not have convulsions, he was just suffering from the heat and from the tension in the room. Kerry and Karen could not stop bickering, which was hardly surprising, and now it seemed possible that they still faced weeks before they could go home. Neither Alan or I trusted Daniella – something was wrong.

Back in our hotel room we forgot for a moment about Kerry and Karen and their problems, and thought of our own. On the face of it we had come out to Romania on a wild-goose chase. On the other hand, while Locket and I were nursing the babies and trying to calm Kerry and Karen, Alan had managed to get through to Nicolae Ivan, who had agreed to see us the following evening.

'You told him what we wanted to do?' I asked.

'Yes,' said Alan.

'Did he mention the fact that there was no law?'

'No,' said Alan, 'and neither did I. I didn't want to give him an excuse not to see us. I thought if we met, we could talk it all through then. He's coming at eight.'

'Or nine, ten or eleven,' I said, bitterly.

'He sounded a nice man, very businesslike, different somehow from Poenaru.'

'We must be careful not to mention Poenaru's name.'

'Yes,' said Alan. 'I think I'll ring Poenaru tomorrow and tell him to return the file since they can't help us. We'll copy a file for Ivan if he's going to do anything for us, and I don't want any further association with Poenaru. God, Daniella was a first-rate bitch, wasn't she?'

We spent a few minutes, the three of us, tearing Daniella to shreds. It was a relief, but then reality set in. 'So what are we going to do tomorrow?' I said.

'We'll go to the British Embassy as I suggested,' said Alan, 'and find out exactly what's going on.'

'And then?' I said.

'Perhaps there are some maternity hospitals in Bucharest,' said Alan. 'Certainly there's no point in going out to the country if the chances of adopting a child are slim. Still, we can't decide until we've spoken to the Embassy. The best thing we can do now is to try and sleep.'

We hardly slept at all, of course. We lay in our beds trying to come to terms with what we had heard. It was a personal tragedy for us, after the weeks we had spent getting our file together and planning the trip, but what haunted us most was the thought of all the children who, if Daniella was to be believed, would not now have a chance of adoption. Ceauşescu's children doomed to a lifetime of institutional care. It was not a thought conducive to sleep.

---4---
THE DAY WE FOUND
MICHAEL

B REAKFAST at the Hotel Bucuresti proved to be the only edible
meal of the day, and then it was only just. We were offered fruit
juice – orange or grapefruit. Whichever you chose you received the
same – banana. It was quite revolting. We ordered scrambled eggs,
which came with the standard-issue stale rolls (we had now discovered
that baking in Bucharest only takes place on Tuesdays, so Monday's
bread was a disaster), washed down with unexpectedly good coffee.

While we were still having breakfast, Adrian arrived. After Kerry's
suspicions of the night before I expected him to look shifty and sinister
in the light of the day. He did not. We ordered him a coffee, he smoked
a cigarette and munched his way through a roll. The bill came and
Alan paid it, telling the waiter to keep the change. Adrian was
appalled. 'You gave him too much. From now on I will pay your bills
– you give me the money.'

'Surely I didn't,' Alan protested.

'What did it cost?' I asked.

'The bill came to 280 lei,' Alan said, 'so I gave him 400 and told
him to keep the change.'

'What's that in English money?' I asked.

'About £2.50,' said Alan.

Adrian was angry. 'You must not think of English money here,' he
said, 'it is not relevant. You paid 400 lei for your breakfast, right?'
Alan nodded. 'I work as an air traffic controller, as you know. It is
one of the best-paid jobs in Bucharest, and I receive 3,000 lei a month.'
He shrugged his shoulders and grimaced. 'Seven breakfasts here at the
Bucuresti!' His words humbled us and for the first time we had an
inkling of the hardship of the Romanian people. 'It is impossible for
you to understand,' Adrian continued, 'we have nothing. Even if we
earn good money it is still a problem to feed our families – there is
simply no food to buy.'

We left the hotel chastened. Adrian drove us through the streets of
Bucharest to the British Embassay. It was a hot day, the sun was

shining but it was hazy, the air heavy with smoke and exhaust polution. Bucharest surprised us all. It is essentially a beautiful city – it was known as the Paris of the Balkans before Communism took its toll. Some of the buildings are truly magnificent, in an ornate, baroque style. There are large open squares and a surprising amount of trees and flowers, very well tended. Yet underlying this façade, one could sense the air of neglect and poverty. The city is quite frankly exhausted, drained of its lifeblood, and it showed itself in the tired masonry, in the bad roads, in the cracked pavements, in the empty shops and, above all, in the faces of its people. As Adrian drove he kept up a constant chatter, pointing out sights to us: buildings split apart by the recent earthquake, districts where there had been fierce fighting in the Revolution, leaving houses riddled with bullet holes and in some cases all but destroyed.

The British Embassy was in a quiet, leafy street and not at all imposing. We showed our passports at the gate, leaving Adrian in the car, as he was not allowed to enter. We asked to be directed to Kirstie Rowe who, we had been told, was the vice-consul and in charge of adoptions. Instead of going through the main doorway of the Embassy, we were shown round the side to a small waiting room. It was the first and last time we were ever fobbed off with having to use the 'tradesmen's entrance' at the Embassy – we learnt our lesson and thereafter only used the main front door!

The waiting room was crammed. There were a great many Romanians talking excitedly, showing papers, arguing, shouting – all clearly seeking visas to enter Britain. There were also a number of British couples sitting about, their eyes like dead fish, shell-shocked, desperate. It was all too obvious what they were doing. Already caught up in the nightmarish red tape of the adoption procedure, their expressions told it all – the frustration and hopelessness of their situation. Thank God, that day we could only guess at their problems. Adrian-style, we barged our way to the front of the queue and asked to see Kirstie Rowe.

'Would you fill out a form, please,' the receptionist said. She was separated from the waiting room by a large glass panel and behind her on the wall was a torn poster of the Prince and Princess of Wales with their two young sons. As a little piece of Britain, the waiting room was not impressive; even the token rubber plant had died. We filled out our form. 'You'll have to wait,' she said, 'there's a big queue.'

'We haven't time to wait,' I said, 'we only have two days in Bucharest. We just have one question to ask Kirstie Rowe, it will take two seconds. Could you fit us in?'

'I'll see what I can do,' she promised.

Five minutes later a couple were shown out of what appeared to be the inner sanctum. The receptionist beckoned to us. 'Quick,' she said.

We hurried through the door. A grey-haired woman, in her late fifties, early sixties, was standing in the corridor. 'What's going on?' she asked, angrily.

'These people have a quick question to ask,' the receptionist said apologetically.

'They'll have to wait their turn like everyone else. This really is most irregular.'

'Please . . .' I said, 'just one question, it won't take a moment.'

'What question?' she barked.

'We have been told by our lawyer, Mr Poenaru, that there is no longer any law to deal with the adoption of Romanian babies. Is this true?'

She met my eye. 'No, it is not true. We are processing applications at this moment.'

'Thank you. That's all we needed to know.'

In seconds we were out of the door, our spirits restored. For whatever reason, Poenaru, or Daniella, or both, had decided to spin us a story. Why, we would never know but it could not have mattered less. We were in Bucharest, the day stretched ahead, we had a date to see a new lawyer and there seemed to be nothing to stop us now from adopting a baby. It never occurred to us to doubt the word of a British Embassy vice-consul.

We told Adrian the news. 'I'm not surprised,' he said, 'I do not trust that Daniella.'

Alan and I exchanged a look. 'Will you be seeing her again?' Alan asked, casually.

'Maybe,' said Adrian, 'when I'm doing business for Kerry.'

'Please don't mention to her that we have stayed on in Bucharest and that we're going to employ Ivan instead' I said, anxiously.

'No, no, of course not,' said Adrian, 'I'm not stupid. So, where do you want to go now? You have only two days, right?'

'Right,' said Alan. 'Could you take us to an orphanage or maternity hospital, outside of Bucharest? We've been told that it is better to go outside the city, as there is less chance of the children being infected with AIDS.'

'No,' said Adrian, 'it is better here in Bucharest.'

'But why?' I asked.

'Outside the city people think because I am from Bucharest that I am a revolutionary – they will not help me. Here, a few packets of cigarettes, a few dollars, I will find you a baby. It's not a problem.'

We were in his hands, of course. 'Then what we would like to do is to go first to the maternity hospitals, rather than the orphanages,' said Alan. He explained again that we were looking for a baby girl, anything from newborn to nine months.

'OK, OK,' said Adrian, 'let's go.'

The first 'maternity home' he took us to, we later discovered, was not a maternity home at all, but the infamous Orphanage No. 1, the largest orphanage in Bucharest and the most highly publicised, for it was here that AIDS in the children was found for the first time. The exterior of the building was surprisingly pleasant. Gardens with seats dotted about, lush vegetation, an air of relaxation. We waited by the lodge gates while Adrian talked to a doctor. No, they had no babies available to fit our requirements. The answer at the second orphanage we visited was the same. This time, at his own request, Adrian went in alone leaving us outside a great heavy metal gate, which looked exactly like the entrance to a prison. The same negative response was unsettling. Later we learnt our mistake. Adrian, like us, was new to the orphanage business. To gain access to any orphanage you must have a gift (or several). There were plenty of children we could have seen, then as now, but very often the staff will not admit to it unless bribed in some way. The availability of children for adoption was already recognised as a valuable commodity, but we, poor mugs, did not realise it.

Our third visit was to an orphanage in a poorer part of the city. The building looked as if it was quite literally falling to pieces. We climbed the cracked stone steps, pushed open a creaky door where the paint had long since flaked off in the baking sun, and found ourselves in a reception area, which on first sight was not unpleasant. There were rugs on the floor and a huge central table on which there was a pile of toys being unloaded by what appeared to be two women voluntary workers. As they spoke rapidly to one another, we realised they were French. Adrian approached a nurse and within seconds he and Alan were taken upstairs to meet the principal. Locket and I sat down on the one and only sofa in the reception room and waited . . . and waited. When we arrived, we had been aware of the background sound of crying and wailing babies and as we sat there, conversation between us seeming inappropriate, as in a church, the wailing grew in momentum until it was so loud, with so many little voices raised in protest, that conversation was almost impossible anyway. 'They're hungry,' I said, recognising that sound anywhere.

One of the French women who was still unloading toys must have overheard me and looked up. 'Yes,' she said, 'they won't have had their breakfast yet.'

I looked at my watch; it was just after eleven o'clock. 'Will they be fed soon?' I almost shouted to be heard.

The Frenchwoman shrugged, her eyes full of sorrow. 'Some of them only have one meal a day – too many children, too few staff. They need changing and washing, it's all hopeless, there are so many of them.' There were tears in her eyes as she spoke.

At that moment the door to the reception opened and a little girl wandered in. Involuntarily, Locket and I gasped aloud. She was tiny in stature, no larger than a two-year-old, though her face suggested she was much older. She was completely naked, her belly grotesquely distended by malnutrition, her arms and legs stick-like, except at the joints, where they were hugely swollen. She turned away from us and we saw that her back and bottom were a mass of running sores. She walked a few steps and fell over. The French woman helped her up. She seemed dazed and then, turning back towards us, she ambled out of the door from which she had come. The shock was total. I reached out and took Locket's hand.

Nothing could have prepared us for the sight of that child . . . nothing at all.

The media have rightly made it their job in recent years to bring us regular pictures of starving children in the Third World. The droughts, the famines, the wars which cause incalculable human suffering are well documented. Most Western families give a little from time to time, to this charity or that, to salve their consciences. They moan about the craziness of a world which on the one hand has food mountains and on the other has half its population close to starvation. What made this little girl different – though of course, it should not have done – was the fact that she was European. Under the matted hair, the pinched white face could so easily have been that of a British child. Stories of the Industrial Revolution and Dickensian orphanages make emotive reading but today, in our so-called civilised society, such conditions for little children are unthinkable. Yet here, before our eyes, we had seen living proof that European children were starving and dying, for our untrained eyes could clearly see that even with the best medical help the child could not live for much longer.

Moments later, Adrian and Alan arrived. 'No luck, I'm afraid,' said Alan. 'Good heavens, what's all this noise?'

'They haven't been fed,' I said dully.

Once outside the orphanage, Alan told us that the principal had said she had no babies available for adoption because the children at this particular orphanage were only there temporarily, until their parents could afford to have them back home. I must have looked doubtful for Alan grimaced and said that he had not believed her either. 'I think she would have changed her mind if we'd offered her some money or something,' he said. 'I suggested it to Adrian, but he refused to do so. I'm sure he was wrong.' I could not bring myself to tell Alan at that moment about the little girl we had seen. Locket was very silent and pale and I sensed that she, too, was not ready to talk about it.

'We will go to my house now, for coffee,' Adrian said.

I did not want to go for coffee at Adrian's house. After what we had just witnessed, it seemed too normal – no, worse than that – it seemed immoral to think of our own needs while children starved, screaming in pain and misery. I did not argue but I kept thinking about the little girl as we drove. I still do. I wonder if she survived, whether medical help came in time. She is the child I left behind and I wish I had not deserted her. We were so naïve then. If only I had made more of a fuss, maybe a bottle of whisky, or a few dollars, or half a dozen packets of Kent cigarettes would have bought her medical treatment, the chance of adoption and life itself.

Kerry had already told us that compared with most Romanians, Adrian's flat was luxurious. He drove us to what can only be described as a tenement block, where we took a rickety, evil-smelling lift to the fourth floor. The door was opened by Marianna, a very pretty woman in her early thirties, slim as a wand, with a natural elegance, and the unusual combination of fair hair and brown eyes. She ushered us in and introduced us to her mother and to her daughter, Irena, who was seven. Her main sitting room was tiny, dominated by an enormous television, on which stood, in pride of place, a ghetto-blaster. Adrian explained that they were the only family in the block to have a television. We sat down, Irena beside Locket, whose hand she held. Locket tried not to look embarrassed. In a short while Marianna arrived with coffee and little open sandwiches of . . . cheese and salami. At the time we did not realise what a big hole in their budget producing this meal for us must have made. We did not realise that coffee was an almost unheard-of-luxury and that buying cheese and salami meant queuing for hours on end.

We talked, or rather Adrian talked, and we all listened. Marianna, smiling and nodding, said that she would be delighted to look after our baby, should we find one. She, too, was an air traffic controller but naturally . . . it was not a problem. Adrian assured us that Marianna could give up her job for as many weeks as was necessary. They had only had one child, he explained, because Marianna could have no more. She would love to look after a baby, and we agreed that on the following day we would deliver all our baby equipment to them. I tried not to remember Kerry's dire warnings about Adrian, but could not help wondering whether everything would eventually end up on the black market.

We were shown round the flat. There were two other bedrooms, one occupied by Marianna's mother and father, the other by Irena. There was a tiny bathroom and an equally tiny kitchen. Running the length of the flat was an outside balcony which was used mainly for storage.

The whole area would have fitted inside our sitting room at home and yet five people lived there, and by Romanian standards it was the height of luxury because they had running water and a television.

From the balcony we looked down on the street below. The transport system of Bucharest relies heavily on old trolley buses. Here, in a somewhat less smart area of the city compared to our hotel and the British Embassy, we saw ordinary people struggling to exist. Somehow the grey drabness of their lives was very much in evidence, although the sun was shining and the leaves on the trees were green and lush. We left after about an hour, Marianna and Irena waving to us from the balcony.

'You have a very nice family, Adrian,' I said.

'Yes,' he agreed, 'but I would like for them to have a better life – maybe one day.'

'Have you ever been to London?' I asked.

'I have never been anywhere,' said Adrian. 'You forget, until the Revolution we were twenty-three million people imprisoned in our own country. We were not allowed to leave at all.' I had forgotten and again I felt humbled.

'Well you must come to England to see us,' said Alan, 'and when you come, I shall be your taxi driver.'

Adrian laughed. 'And I shall pay you in lei,' he said, quick as a flash.

Adrian took us back to our hotel, where we had agreed to meet Kerry and Karen for lunch. Adrian insisted he had some important business to attend to. It was something to do with an expected load of black-market Coca-Cola. We agreed that we would meet again at three o'clock and visit some more orphanages.

Kerry, Karen and the babies were sitting in a little bar at the back of the hotel reception. The bars around the hotel were all different – this one served only beer and fruit juice and would only accept American dollars as currency. They were both looking better this morning and the babies were deeply asleep. They apologised for having been so fraught the night before. We asked if they had managed to make any progress with Poenaru. They had not and both admitted to feeling as if their husbands had abandoned them. Neither could imagine ever getting out of Bucharest, or ever getting their papers signed. Alan bought us all some beer and we told Kerry and Karen about our morning.

'So what are you going to do this afternoon?' Kerry asked.

'Press on, I suppose,' I said.

'Have you a list of orphanages to visit?'

'Yes,' said Alan, 'I have it here in my briefcase.'

'Let me have a look through it,' said Kerry. 'I might come up with an idea. I've spoken to so many people in recent weeks that perhaps I can remember where some of their children came from.'

Locket, not having had breakfast, was hungry, so she and Alan went off to the inappropriately named 'Snack Bar' to eat, while I stayed with Kerry and Karen and went through the list of orphanages. After Kerry had studied them for some time she shook her head. 'There's none here which ring a bell with me, but I would have thought it sensible to try Orphanage No. 4.'

'Why?' I asked.

'It's in Sector 2 which is where Adrian lives. He will know how to find it, obviously, and perhaps he may know someone who works there who might be able to help you. It's just a thought.' She shrugged her shoulders.

I shall be grateful to Kerry Male for that thought for the rest of my life.

I went and joined Locket and Alan for lunch. There was a choice of three main courses: beef steak, pork chop or beef casserole. We ordered a different dish each out of interest, but when they arrived, they were all pork. We tried to eat it, with little success, but we were given a surprisingly good bottle of Romanian claret which lifted our spirits a little and the whole meal, including coffee, came to less than five pounds. We agreed that we would try Orphanage No. 4, so when Adrian arrived we said goodbye to Karen and Kerry, who had decided to take their babies for a walk. They were very tense again; the day was dragging for them. They had tried telephoning Poenaru but he would not take their call.

Despite the fact that Orphanage No. 4 was close to Adrian's home, he had a great deal of difficulty in finding it. We were now in a very poor part of the city. Ragged children played in the streets, old women dressed in black watched from doorways and pointed at us. We had to ask four or five times before we eventually found it, by which time Adrian's temper was extremely short. We agreed that once again we should all go with him into the orphanage. After our experiences of the morning I felt sick with apprehension and, as we entered the grounds through a rusted gate of chicken-wire, Alan and Locket looked equally hesitant and apprehensive.

We walked up a broken concrete path. On the right of the path there was a play area and at first sight it did not look too bad – there were swings and a carousel, rusted but obviously in working order. On closer inspection, however, the scrub, for one could not call it grass, was covered in litter and broken glass. Could children really play here? I imagined not. On our left we passed a chicken run housing scrawny hens and smelling strongly in the heat of the afternoon sun, and then we turned a corner of the building and saw for the first time Ceauşescu's children . . .

Through dirty windows we could see cots, row upon row of cots packed tightly together. The windows were partially covered with grey net curtains but squinting through them we could just make out the faces of children sitting or standing, some impassive, some screaming, some banging their heads, some swaying. One or two of them noticed us and held out their arms begging for attention. We could not hear what they said through the glass, but their desperation was obvious. It was the scene so often portrayed in newspapers and on television, but this was real – we were seeing it for ourselves. Because of the extensive media coverage it was familiar, but nonetheless terrible for that. There were so many of them, their misery so apparent I wanted to tear down the barriers between us and take them all, all of them, away from that dreadful place. We lingered, smiling and waving, uncertain what to do. It was Adrian who eventually urged us on and as we turned to go, the animation left their faces, their hopelessness returned. It was heartbreaking, pitiful and we felt so utterly helpless.

We went through a side door of the building, up gloomy stairs and down a long, darkened corridor. At the end of the corridor we opened a door and entered a surprisingly sunny and pleasant room. There were French windows on one side, thrown open on to two small balconies, and a pleasant breeze blew through the windows making the room feel cool and airy. There were murals of Disney characters on the wall and several old sofas. In a corner, there was a huge pile of Mothercare baby-walkers. In the centre of the room there were several women sitting round a table, sorting through a card index. They were dressed alike in blue overdresses, presumably a sort of nurses' uniform, and they were full of chatter and laughter.

'This is a lot better than the conditions downstairs,' Alan whispered. 'I wonder why that should be? Perhaps they are in the middle of refurbishing this orphanage.'

For the first time since we had arrived in Bucharest, we all felt a sudden surge of optimism – things were happening, albeit slowly, to improve the lot of the Romanian children and here was clear evidence of it: the murals, the baby-walkers, the fresh air, the happy women in their uniforms. Adrian approached the group and spoke to them. One of the nurses disappeared and returned with a small, mousy-looking woman in a white coat and wearing an enormous pair of glasses which dwarfed her features. Adrian began talking to her. She raised her eyes to heaven and lifted her arms in a gesture of hopelessness. She looked at us and smiled. 'French, Italian, Irish' she said, in a tired voice. 'They all come, they all want a child.' She turned to Adrian and began speaking in Romanian again.

Eventually Adrian turned to us. 'This lady is a doctor and her name is Dr Unescu. She says she may be able to help us but she is going off duty now. She says that perhaps we could come back tomorrow at twelve o'clock.'

'We don't have the time,' Alan said, 'will you tell her that?'

Adrian spoke to her once more. She made as if to go and then paused. She turned, our eyes met and held for what seemed a very long moment. 'There is a baby,' she said, slowly, in perfect English. 'He only came here today. I have no papers on him, yet. His name is Marian, he is twenty-three months old and . . .' she hesitated, searching for the right word, 'he is special. Would you like to see him?'

No one spoke. I glanced at Alan but it was impossible to read his expression. 'Yes,' I said. 'Yes, please.'

She led us back down the dark corridor and gloomy stairs to the ground floor, and then through a door made of rusting mesh. The moment we went through that door all our preconceived ideas about improvements to the orphanage were destroyed. We simply passed into hell; there is no other way to describe it. The first thing that hit us was the stench – the stench of urine, stale milk, vomit, closely packed bodies, fear, illness. It was so stifling that our breathing was instantly laboured. Dr Unescu began leading us down a narrow corridor where at intervals there were dumped piles of dirty linen, looking more like rags than presumably what they were – babies' clothing. On either side of the corridor there were tiny rooms, each housing six cots, and from these rooms came a continual battering of noise – crying, moaning, coughing, shrieking – but not a single happy sound, no laughter, no chuckles. Misery was the king here. I did not want to look at the children as we passed – I was afraid to – and yet it was impossible to look away. Tiny fingers clawed at the bars of their cots, huge eyes in appallingly emaciated faces followed our progress down the corridor – chalk-white faces, stick-like limbs, running sores . . . These were children, children – what sort of world did we live in that could condone this suffering? I wanted to scream 'Get them out, get them out,' the horror of it was crowding all my senses, yet all we could do was stumble along, bleak with shock. The world we had left upstairs held no reality here. Upstairs where the women chattered, where the meaningless murals were daubed on the walls, where the baby-walkers stood (we were later to learn they were never used, for there were no staff to supervise their use), this was all a front. It fooled people as it fooled us that the orphanage was clean, well run, efficient. In reality, while the staff lived and worked in comparative comfort, the children were imprisoned in hell. I am very wary of the responsibility in making a comparison between the conditions in Orphanage No. 4 and those in the concentration camps of Europe during the Second World War. I do not want to sensationalise what we saw but neither can I trivialise it, and I believe such a comparison is valid.

Halfway down the corridor Dr Unescu stopped and consulted a clipboard. She opened a door on the left and we entered a tiny room. There were three cots along either side of the room and between them a small space just wide enough to take a single person sideways on. At the end of the room there was a tiny fanlight from which no air seemed to be coming. The heat was terrible. Despite the bright day outside, the room was in semi-darkness. She went to the second cot on the left and lifted a tiny body, little bigger than a newborn baby. 'This is Marian,' she said.

He had been asleep and as he rubbed the sleep from his eyes he regarded us solemnly over her shoulder. Big, brown eyes in a tiny, white, pinched face, a running nose, mousy hair shaved in a crew cut. 'Would you like to hold him?' Dr Unescu asked.

I took him in my arms. He was so light, so frail that I was afraid to hold him tight for fear something would break. It was impossible to believe this child was seven months older than Charlie. He was less than half the size in height, in weight and presumably in development. There was no way this child could stand or walk. He clung to me and as I held him I saw that the back of his head was a mass of running sores which had been left unattended. They looked very painful and there was fresh blood on the back of his jumper where clearly he had been scratching at them. Normally a fairly fastidious person, the running nose, the open sores, the nappy which had obviously not been changed in a very long time, did not worry me in the slightest. I held him tightly to me, desperate to give him some comfort, however briefly.

Adrian and Dr Unescu were talking rapidly to one another. 'He cannot walk yet,' Adrian said, unnecessarily, 'but he can almost stand. Mentally he is excellent, very excellent, and apart from his walking he is in good health generally.'

Good health – the words were obscene when applied to this child. He was clinging to life, his whole body must have been a torture to him – the sores, the malnutrition, and he was feverish too, I realised. His burning forehead pressed against my neck was not simply the result of the stifling conditions. Gently I prised him away from me and handed him to Alan. Alan took him. Again, Marian's arms shot round Alan's neck. I went and stood behind him so that I could see Marian's face – he was staring into space, his eyelids still heavy with sleep. 'Hello Marian,' I said. His eyes focused on mine and then, miraculously, he smiled – *smiled*. Not a gentle smile, not a pathetic, weary smile, but a huge mischievous grin which split his face in half, his eyes suddenly alight with humour and interest. It was so unexpected, so totally, crazily out of context with his terrible situation. I felt tears rush into my eyes. 'Look, Locket.' She came and stood beside me and began gently tickling him. The smile broke across his face again, this time accompanied by a deep, throaty chuckle. 'You hold him,' I said to her.

'I don't want to,' Locket replied.

'Why?' I asked.

'I don't want to make a commitment to him, not yet.'

'Please,' I whispered.

She took him in her arms. Marian liked her instantly. He was more alert now, smiling, flirting with her. Adrian gave him his car keys. He took them in a surprisingly strong grip, turning them over in his hands. I looked into his cot, grey, stained and evil-smelling. There were no toys. The cot had once been white but most of the paint had peeled off the bars, the mattress was lumpy and it seemed that at one end the base had broken for the mattress sagged dangerously. Dr Unescu must have sensed what I was looking for. She walked to the end of the room and picked up a cardboard box – inside there were three dirty squeaky rubber toys. She took out one and handed it to Marian. He held it tightly in one hand, the keys in the other. Dr Unescu looked at me and smiled sadly. She did not need to say anything, it was obvious that these toys were all the six children in this room had to play with.

Locket returned Marian to me and he settled down again in the nape of my neck, clinging very tightly. As I held him I could feel his chest vibrating against mine as he fought for breath; he clearly had bronchitis or something very similar. It made me look at the other children. Opposite Marian's cot there was a little red-haired boy who was so chalk-white that one could only assume he had leukaemia. He stood unsteadily, peering over the bars at the interest being expressed in his companion. He looked terribly ill. At the far end of the room were two also obviously very sick children: one appeared retarded as he lay hunched in his cot, staring into space, oblivious of everything going on around him. The other simply seemed ill – he wanted to be interested in us but he did not have the strength to move. By the door there was a dark baby, desperately thin. 'He's a gypsy,' Adrian said, contemptuously. The sixth cot was unoccupied. 'The child is in hospital,' Adrian told us as we looked in the empty cot. It was clear that all the children in the room were very ill. It was also clear that, with the exception of Marian, they had given up. But Marian had not, oh no – Marian could smile, Marian could laugh, and now I knew why Dr Unescu had said he was special.

'I think I'll have to go,' Locket whispered, 'I'm feeling very sick.'

I nodded and turned to Adrian. 'What happens now?'

Adrian spoke to Dr Unescu at length. 'She says that if you are interested in the boy, to come back tomorrow morning when she will have his papers. He was at Orphanage No. 6 and was only transferred here today. He may not even be available for adoption, but if he is, she will give you the details.'

'Thank you,' I said. I looked up at Alan. 'Do you want to hold him again?'

'Yes,' he said, much to my surprise. I handed Marian to him and as I did so I realised something had happened to Alan. It was clear the little boy had made an enormous impact on him. He held him very tightly, talking quietly to him.

'Please, let's go,' Locket whispered, desperately.

I put an arm round her to comfort us both. 'Just one last thing,' I said. 'Adrian, about his name. In England Marian is usually a girl's name.'

Dr Unescu heard me and began speaking in rapid Romanian. 'The doctor says that the English translation of Marian is Michael,' said Adrian, 'the boy's name is Michael.'

None of us spoke as we walked away from the orphanage. When Alan had handed Michael back to Dr Unescu we had not said goodbye to him, we could not. We did not know whether we would ever see him again and somehow none of us seemed able to make our parting official. We slunk away, avoiding his eyes. When she had placed him in his cot he had begun to whimper. When she told him to hush he stopped and watched us leave, quietly and with dignity. He handled the parting a great deal better than we did.

When we reached the car Adrian rested his head on the roof for a moment. 'What is it, Adrian, are you ill?' I asked.

He shook his head and when he looked up I saw that he was crying. 'I did not know,' he said, brokenly, 'I did not realise such places as this existed in Romania, that little children suffered so much. I am so ashamed of my country. I did not know, I did not know – I hope you understand.'

We stared at him. 'You mean you didn't realise that the orphanages were like this?'

He shook his head, wiping away his tears ferociously with the back of his hand, the gesture of a small child. Gone was our Mr Fix It, the man for whom nothing was a problem. He was clearly as shocked as we were by what he had seen, yet the flat in which he lived was less than five minutes walk from the orphanage. I thought suddenly of Germany during the last war, when ordinary people, the men and women in the street, had denied any knowledge of the concentration camps. In Britain, blessed with our free press, we found it impossible to believe. Yet here was history repeating itself: the world knew about the plight of Ceauşescu's children, yet the Romanian people themselves seemed to be in ignorance. I searched Adrian's face; I swear he was not lying. He made an effort to pull himself together. 'Michael, he is a lovely little boy, isn't he?' he said, inquiringly, hopefully.

'Yes,' said Alan, 'you can't easily forget a boy like Michael.'

We climbed in the car. 'Do you want to see any more orphanages?' Adrian asked.

'No,' the three of us replied in unison. We drove in silence. Now was not the moment to talk about what we had seen, nor to speculate on what we should do about Michael.

After a few minutes Adrian said, 'I am not taking you to your hotel, I'm taking you first to see Ceauşescu's palace.'

'No, please Adrian,' I said, wearily, 'we just need to get back to the hotel and have a shower and a rest. We have our new lawyer coming soon and I think we need a little time on our own before we meet him.'

'First you see Ceauşescu's palace,' said Adrian. It was not a suggestion, it was an order and none of us felt strong enough to argue with him.

He drove to the centre of the city and suddenly the houses fell away and we were driving down a straight, broad avenue with imposing buildings constructed of cream stonework on either side. 'There it is,' said Adrian.

Ahead of us, shining in the sun, was the most enormous and grotesque building I have ever seen. I suppose it was roughly twenty times the size of Buckingham Palace and built in a near semicircle. It hung over the city like a bird of prey. 'The houses on either side of the road used to belong to the Securitate,' said Adrian, 'and that building next to the main palace was hers.' He spat out the word.

'Elena Ceauşescu's?' I asked.

'Yes, a His and Hers palace.' His voice was full of bitterness.

He drove us right up to the palace wall and stopped. We got out. Although it was now late afternoon it was still very hot. A group of workmen were labouring with the masonry on one corner of the palace, which still seemed to be partially under construction. 'What is to become of it?' I asked.

Adrian shrugged his shoulders. 'I think it may become an art gallery or a museum, I do not know.'

I left Adrian talking to Alan and Locket and wandered on my own for a few yards along the perimeter wall. Adrian had been right to bring us here. The contrast between Michael's stinking cot and the obscenity of Ceauşescu's palace did more to make me understand the plight of the Romanian people than ten thousand words written in condemnation of this form of Communism. Months later, we asked Harry McCormick, our travel Agent, what Communism had done to his country. 'It has destroyed our soul,' he said, simply. Standing there that day, the image of Michael horrifyingly fresh in my mind, I knew exactly what he meant.

———— 5 ————
COMMITMENT

NICOLAE Ivan arrived in the lobby of the Hotel Bucaresti at two minutes past eight. His appointment had been for eight. This in itself was encouraging. A big, burly man, with thick dark hair and a swarthy complexion emphasised by impressive five o'clock shadow, he looked more like a bandit than a lawyer. His mode of dress was interesting, too: a dark suit, an open-necked shirt and, amazingly, navy canvas sailing shoes. Despite his bulk, he moved with enormous speed and even when he sat down with us he was restless, constantly on the move. It made one tired just watching him. We explained our position and said we had heard rumours that there was in fact no law existing at the moment for the adoption of Romanian orphans. 'This is true,' he said, cheerfully.

We reeled at his words. 'But the British Embassy told us today that it was not true,' Alan said.

Ivan shrugged his shoulders. 'And I am telling you that it is. Do not worry – there will be a new law, and soon. The orphanage problem is a big one and we cannot handle it. Most people in the Government are in favour of foreign adoption. A new system is being devised, it will be a judicial process and it will be much better than the old law.'

'Is it sensible for us to proceed with the adoption of a baby at the moment?' I asked.

'Why, of course,' said Ivan. 'As I told you, it will not be long – only a few weeks.'

In the space of twenty-four hours we had been given three totally contrary pieces of advice – it was unbelievable. Without the opportunity of discussing it, I glanced at Alan, trying to read his mind. He nodded imperceptibly. He clearly felt we should trust Ivan and so, instinctively, did I. It was not just that he appeared to be honest and straightforward, he was also authoritative and businesslike. This was not a man who had time to mess about. He told us he could help us and we believed him. As events were to prove, we were right to do so.

'So,' he said, 'you are looking for a baby girl. The best advice I can

give you is that you should adopt a child from a maternity hospital –
that way the child will be healthy. Go home to England and wait.
Within one week, or two at the most, I will telephone you when I have
found a mother who has recently given birth and who does not wish
to keep her child. You can then come and see the baby and if you are
happy with her then we will obtain the mother's consent and proceed
with the adoption.'

'We do have Romanian foster parents,' I said.

'That is excellent. Then I can see no problem at all.'

'What about Michael?' I looked at Alan.

'Michael, who is Michael?' Ivan asked.

'We went to Orphanage No. 4 today,' said Alan. 'There was a little
boy there called Michael. We do not know yet whether he is available
for adoption nor whether we should adopt him. We have not had time
to discuss it.'

'I think it is better that you adopt a newborn baby,' said Ivan. 'You
already have a son, you say, so now you need another little daughter.'

'I'd love a sister because I already have five brothers,' said Locket,
'at least that's how I felt before we met Michael.'

'I think you should still have your sister,' said Ivan, with a rare smile.
'Leave things with me, I will find you a healthy baby girl. This Michael,
how long has he been in an orphanage?'

'I don't know,' said Alan.

'He will probably be sickly, he may have AIDS. Forget him.' He
stood up, poised for flight. Alan handed him a copy of our file and
our address. 'You will hear from me very soon,' said Ivan, and before
we had time to thank him he was gone.

The temptation to start talking about our meeting with Ivan was
enormous, but Alan was adamant. We needed to eat and to sleep.
There was no way in his view we could sensibly discuss Michael that
night – it would not be fair to him, he insisted. We were emotionally
and physically exhausted; we needed to talk through Ivan's advice with
fresh minds in the morning. None of us was hungry, though we
recognised that we should try and eat. Although it was only nine, the
snack bar was closed as usual, and so we went back to our room and
ordered room service. It arrived, eventually – salami, soapy cheese and
stale bread. We ate a little, then Locket said goodnight and went to
her room and we prepared for bed. Under any circumstances sleep
would not have been easy, but the air-conditioning was not working
and it was stiflingly hot. Looking back on it, we had eaten so little we
were probably drained of energy as well.

For me, the image of Michael in his cot persisted all night. I could
not bear the thought of him being alone, so obviously unwell, hungry
and in the dark. I felt we should not have left him, that we should have

taken him with us. It was absurd, of course. Unlike children from maternity homes, children from orphanages are not allowed out until they have been adopted and for all we knew, Michael might not even be available for adoption. Yet I felt I needed to go to him, to give him comfort and reassurance. To reassure him about what? I thought about Ivan's advice. Michael, in theory at least, was wrong in every way – he was a boy, he was older than Charlie, there was not a natural age gap between them, and coming as he did from a Bucharest orphanage, it was highly likely that he would either be HIV positive or at the very least have hepatitis B. The closeness in the two boy's ages would not be good for either of them – not twins, but too close for brothers, competitive at school, competitive for attention, it would be a nightmare.

Although I had agreed not to talk about Michael that night, I certainly had no control over my thoughts. To say I loved him would be trivialising the word, for how can you love someone you have only met for ten minutes? Yet when I thought about leaving him in the orphanage, I felt sick with misery and it was not simply pity. Michael had lit a very special spark for me when he had smiled. He had such courage and warmth; miraculously he was holding on, and he had not lost his interest in life. He needed a chance, he had to have a chance . . .

I wondered for a moment how Locket felt. She had been very definite about wanting a sister and had been reluctant to hold Michael, but when she had, he had responded more positively to her than to anyone. And Alan? I turned to him in the darkness. He was awake, staring at the ceiling. 'Are you thinking about Michael?' I asked.

'Of course,' he said.

'What do you feel about him?'

'Like I said, he's not a little boy who's easy to forget.' His voice sounded bleak. 'Still, I – I imagine you'd rather stick with the original plan and have a baby girl. If we adopted Michael, it would be very difficult for both him and Charlie.'

In my mind I tried to summon up the image of us returning triumphant from Romania with a baby sister for Charlie – nothing happened. Michael . . . I could picture it immediately. My heart gave a lurch, we simply could not walk away from him, however impractical his adoption might seem. 'I think we should go to the orphanage tomorrow, see if his papers have arrived and, if so, whether we can trace his parents,' I said, unsteadily. 'Then and only then, we should make our decision.'

'I agree,' said Alan, with obvious relief.

At the orphanage the following day, Dr Unescu came to greet us like long-lost friends. She was far more outgoing and friendly than on the previous afternoon when, clearly, she had been very tired. She spoke rapidly to Adrian and he interpreted for us. She had received Michael's papers. His full name was Marian Aurel Trifan and he had been born in Bucharest on 8 July 1988. He had two sisters, Mirella, seven, and Christina-Daniella, three. Neither of the sisters was at Orphanage No. 4, although up until a few months previously Michael and Christina-Daniella had shared a cot in Orphanage No. 6, from where he had been transferred the previous day.

I stared at Dr Unescu in disbelief. 'You mean . . . the children have been split up?'

She understood my words and gave Adrian a long explanation. He grimaced and translated. As far as anyone could tell, it appeared that Michael and his sister had been together in a cot until Christina-Daniella had reached her third birthday. Once she was three, she had to go to a different type of orphanage which caters for older children, and so she and Michael had been separated just a few weeks before.

I tried to imagine it, the parting of this little brother and sister. My mind recoiled from it. They had shared a cot for how long? All their lives, probably. They had played together, given each other comfort, lain close together to keep each other warm and now they were parted. 'It's barbaric,' I almost shouted, close to tears. Alan took my hand and squeezed it. I thought for a moment of all the baby books I had read during Locket's and Charlie's early days, of the need to minimise dramas and changes in a tiny child's life. In the space of just a few weeks Michael had lost his sister and been transferred from one orphanage to another. He was half dead from lack of food, he had a raging temperature, and still he could smile.

Adrian was talking again, giving us more background on the family. The children's mother, it appeared, had left the family and gone off with another man shortly after Michael's birth. The father had struggled to bring up the children on his own and, not surprisingly, had failed. As far as Dr Unescu was aware, Michael had been in an orphanage more or less all his life.

This piece of news surprised me and at first I wondered why. 'Adrian,' I said, 'can you ask Dr Unescu again if she is sure he has always been in an orphanage?' That's what his papers say, the reply came back. 'But unlike the other children he doesn't seem to do any head-banging or swaying, he laughed, he . . .', I searched my mind for the right words, 'he hasn't given up.'

Dr Unescu's English was a great deal better than she was prepared to admit. 'Yes,' she said, 'that is right, that is why I showed him to you. He is a special child but I don't know why.'

We asked what we had to do next and it appeared we had to go and see the father to seek his consent. As the mother had abandoned the family, it was probably not necessary to have her consent also, but on this point nobody seemed clear.

'If the parents are willing for Michael to be adopted, then you must tell us and we will hold the child for you,' Adrian interpreted. It sounded terrible, like putting a deposit on a piece of furniture. Adrian looked at the file, recognised the father's address and we agreed that we would go and see him, at four o'clock, the normal time for Romanians to come home from work. We told Dr Unescu that if the father was prepared to give his consent then we would return the following morning before catching our plane home, to let her know if we wished to adopt Michael.

'Do you want to see Michael again?' Alan whispered.

I shook my head. I thought suddenly of Marie, the Irishwoman we had met on the plane. She had only seen her baby once, because she could not bear to see her again in case things went wrong. At the time I had thought her rather strange but now I understood perfectly. The idea of meeting Michael again and then finding we could not adopt him was more than I could bear.

Back at the hotel, Kerry and Karen were near to hysteria. Poenaru was still refusing to answer their telephone calls. They wanted to borrow Adrian for an hour or so, firstly to visit Poenaru's office and, if he was not there, to go to his home. Locket and I volunteered to look after Alexander and Emily, and they left immediately. They were back twenty minutes later, in a furious temper. Poenaru had been neither at the office nor at home – he was playing tennis and his wife had refused to say where. We invited the girls to come to lunch with us to try and cheer them up. They decided to stay by the telephone, so the three of us went down to the Snack Bar, ordered chicken and were of course served with pork.

We had arranged for Adrian to collect us after lunch, to take us to see Michael's father, but still we had not talked. Now we did so. The emotions seemed to pour out of us, like lancing a boil. None of us could bear the idea of leaving little Michael where he was, yet we were all worried for him and Charlie, that the closeness in their ages would be a disaster. We agreed that Charlie was an easygoing chap and we could see no problem with him adjusting to the concept of a new baby, whether a few days, weeks or months old. But this was different. Michael was a little boy who, once he'd regained his strength, would invade Charlie's space, in every possible way. Charlie would be bound to suffer a great deal. And what of Michael? He needed a great deal of love, reassurance and attention, a calm and relaxed atmosphere to help heal his wounds, both physical and emotional. A life shared with Charlie would certainly not be dull but it was hardly going to offer the kind of tranquillity that we thought Michael would need.

We took it in turns to air our views. Locket was very clear in her own mind. She had wanted a baby sister but now that we had met Michael we had to go ahead and see if he was available for adoption. 'And if he is?' Alan asked. 'Then I don't see how we can leave him there,' said Locket simply.

Alan's views were similar but more definite. Michael had made an enormous impact on him, and it was very clear that he wanted to adopt him for who he was, not what he was. In the orphanage I had been aware that Alan and Michael seemed to have bonded in some way, and this now became abundantly obvious. There was no way Alan Fowler was going to leave Romania without Marian Trifan, not without a fight, one hell of a fight.

Then it was my turn. Much to my surprise and shame I began to cry and once started, I didn't seem to be able to stop. 'It's so awful,' I sniffed, 'having to make this kind of decision, knowing that a child's life hangs in the balance. It's like playing God, no one should be expected to do it and no one has the right.' I blew my nose and tried again. 'Obviously it would be best for the family if we had a baby, and preferably a girl, but Michael is what Romania is all about.' I looked round the restaurant. 'This city's stuffed with poor, desperate, childless couples hoping to fulfil their dreams by adopting a baby. I don't believe that any healthy, newborn baby put up for adoption in this city from now on will want for a home. It's the Michaels who will remain forgotten, the true victims of Ceauşescu, and the older they get the less likely the chance of anyone helping them. Let's face it, it's because of children like Michael that we came here in the first place. I don't like Ivan's idea of hanging around, waiting for someone's unwanted child to be born, and yet I don't mind admitting it is difficult to give up the idea of a newborn baby. I think perhaps I may still be suffering from the miscarriage,' I acknowledged.

'So what do we do?' said Alan.

I took a deep breath. 'It has to be Michael, doesn't it?'

'I think so,' said Alan, quietly. 'What do you say, Locket?'

'Michael,' she replied, 'but only if Mum feels she can manage without her baby.'

'Can you?' Alan asked me.

'Yes,' I said, 'for Michael,' and burst into tears all over again.

We left the hotel in a jubilant mood now our decision was made, but it began to deteriorate as we drove across the city in search of Michael's father. The fine old buildings slipped away to be replaced by street after street of tenement blocks. Like the rest of Bucharest, the buildings looked exhausted. It was more than just the result of the earthquake. Repairs had not been carried out for years and it showed. At last we drew to a halt outside a particularly dilapidated block of flats. The road was bumpy and dusty, the grass outside the flats burnt brown by the sun and covered in litter. We followed Adrian up the stairs into a darkened hallway. He consulted his piece of paper. 'It's here,' he said, 'on the ground floor. It must be . . . yes, this apartment.' He rang the bell. We waited, desperately aware that our time was running out. *He had to be in*. Adrian tried the bell again. It echoed strangely. He peered through a tiny window in the dirty, stained door. 'It doesn't look like anyone lives here,' he said. As he spoke, the door to the adjoining flat opened. A man came out. The conversation was lengthy. I felt sick with nerves. At last, Adrian turned to us. 'The father is dead. He did live here with the children but they are now all in orphanages, as we know. The father was apparently shot in the Revolution and died several months later.'

'And the mother?' Alan asked.

'The mother is living with another man. These people do not know her address but she has a good friend who lives in this apartment block, on the seventh floor. I'm going to go up to see her now. She will be able to tell us the mother's address.' We thanked the family, who watched us out of sight as we went back to the front door. 'You wait here,' said Adrian, 'I won't be a moment.'

As we stood in the doorway of the building, a group of children began to gather – all ages, from toddlers to teenagers. They stood around staring at us, but it was not a hostile stare and we felt not even slightly intimidated. These people had nothing, that was obvious, but if I'd been standing outside a similar block of flats in a rough part of London, I would have been much more nervous, particularly for Locket. Maybe it was ignorance that made us feel safe, but I don't think so. The fact that we were carrying with us more money than many Romanian people can earn in a lifetime should have terrified us. But it didn't.

Adrian returned, triumphant. 'The great detective,' he said, throwing out his chest and swaggering about. He was back to his old self, fully recovered from his trip to the orphanage.

'You have her address?'

'Yes,' he said. 'It's very near here, only five minutes in the car.'

We climbed back into the car and some of the children waved to us as we left. Fleetingly, a strange sort of calm came over me. I knew, suddenly, that Michael was going to be ours, that his mother would give consent, that everything would be all right. It was a ridiculous notion but for a moment the feeling was very strong.

The district where Michael's mother lived was slightly better than her former home. School had just finished for the day and the children were going home. I wondered briefly how Michael's mother could bear to watch these children when her own were living in filthy rags in orphanages. Despite the poverty, I noticed the pride everyone seemed to take in their appearance. The children's shirts were clean and ironed, their white socks gleaming. There is a very obvious difference in poverty between East and West Europe, if Romania is typical. Personal cleanliness and tidiness are all important, whatever the circumstances. I have been to several Romanian homes since then and they are always the same – nothing out of place, the furniture polished until it shines.

'I think it best if you let me go first and talk to her,' said Adrian. 'If we all arrive at once she may send us away.' It made sense and so we sat in the car while he went up to the apartment. It was a long wait, or so it seemed. None of us talked and tension was high. I kept glancing towards the entrance to the building but by the time Adrian did eventually run down the steps, I no longer wanted to hear what he had to say – the moment of confidence was gone. 'She says, no,' he said and then he threw back his head and roared with laughter at the sight of my crestfallen face. Some joke. 'It's all right, it's all right,' he said, 'Adrian the great detective has spoken with her and she is happy to talk about you adopting Michael. Come upstairs.'

'Just like that?' Alan said.

'Yes, but she needs to meet you. It would be good if you could show some photographs of your home and your son. The man is with her. I don't like him, he will ask for money, but remember that they are her children, not his.'

You could see immediately that she was Michael's mother – the same round brown eyes and, when she smiled, the same hint of humour. She had dark curly hair, slightly olive skin and looked about thirty- five, though I suspect that she was probably quite a lot younger. She wore an old cotton dress, well washed but neat and pressed. She was plump, and just for a moment I hated her. It was clear she was not going without food, just as surely as it was clear that on the other side of the city her son was slowly starving to death.

With a gesture, she introduced us to her man. He looked a pitiful creature, incredibly thin, pigeon-chested and stooped, but his eyes were sharp and hard, his face like a little weasel. Adrian was right, this was not a man to trust, or like.

We sat down on a banquette. In front of us was a table, highly polished, upon which there was a faded mat. I looked around the flat which was clearly just one room, plus kitchen. It was tiny and spotless, you would have imagined that she had been expecting us all day. Her name was Lenuta – Helen in English, Adrian told us.

Adrian began to talk. He introduced each of us in turn. 'We must not hurry this,' he said in English, under his breath, in between floods of Romanian. 'Show them now the photographs.'

Alan drew out pictures of our home, of Charlie, of the animals. They were all passed round and studied. I kept watching Lenuta's face. There was a kind of deadness of expression I couldn't quite identify. Was she being incredibly brave in what had to be the most appalling circumstances – every mother's nightmare – or did she simply not care?

Adrian talked some more and then she began to talk, at first slowly, haltingly and then with growing confidence. 'What is she saying?' Alan asked.

'She is telling us about the family, about the two sisters and Michael. She asks whether you would like to adopt the sisters as well. I've said no, is that right?' We nodded. 'She has told me that her husband is dead and she cannot support the children. This new man of hers is ill, she must work, the flat has no running water and they must wash and bathe on the ground floor. There is just this one room, it is not possible to raise three children here.'

I glanced at Alan, he shifted uncomfortably in his seat. It would have been better if there had been a chance to talk but there wasn't time. I knew I had to speak now for me, for Alan, and for Michael. Suddenly it all seemed wrong, everything was wrong. We had come to this impoverished country to take a child away from its family and to bring it up in the comparative luxury of our home in Oxfordshire. It was madness – what we should be doing was supporting the family so that they could stay together. 'Adrian,' I said, 'tell her we will give her all the money that we were going to spend on the lawyer and flying backwards and forwards to Romania. It would be a great deal of money, perhaps ten, fifteen years' salary. Would she have the children back if we helped her like this?'

I saw the look of relief on Alan's face. As with most things, we clearly felt exactly the same.

Adrian spoke rapidly to her. She shook her head and looked at me. 'No,' she said, in English.

'Why, Adrian?' I asked.

'She cannot give them a good life here in Romania,' Adrian said. 'However much money you give her, there is nothing here for children. She wants them to have a new start in life, she wants them to be adopted. She has made her decision and there's nothing you can do to change her mind.'

It was then that I started to cry again. The boyfriend, for want of a better description, started to speak and soon a lengthy conversation began, if conversation is the right word. Everyone spoke at once; no one listened. Alan, Locket and I sat mute round the table. I felt utterly exhausted and suspected they did, too.

'The man wants money,' Adrian said under his breath, 'we must be very careful.'

'What does the mother think?' I asked.

'All she wants is for the children to be adopted. She has asked whether you could try and find someone else to adopt the girls.'

'There's Russell,' I said to Alan.

'Tell her,' said Alan, 'that my eldest son and his wife are planning to adopt a Romanian child. It is possible that they may consider adopting her younger daughter.' Adrian relayed the message and she smiled for the first time.

'Adrian,' I said, 'could you ask her if she knows which orphanages her daughters are in?'

Adrian asked the question. She nodded, picking up the pen which Alan had laid on the table and indicating that she wished to write. Alan gave her a piece of paper and she wrote down the names of her three children: Mirella Trifan, Christina-Daniella Trifan, Marian Aurel Trifan. Against Mirella's name she wrote down an orphanage and the name of a town which Adrian recognised and said was some sixty kilometres from Bucharest. Against Christina-Daniella's and Marian's, she wrote Orphanage No. 6.

'So she doesn't realise the younger children have been split up,' I said quietly to Alan.

'Obviously not. We mustn't tell her though, it might upset her.'

Adrian overheard us and understood. 'Don't worry,' he said, 'if you wish to find Michael's sisters I will do it.' He grinned. 'It's not a problem, I am the great detective.'

'I would like to find them,' I said, 'it's not just a question of helping them to be adopted but also it's vital that Michael should keep in touch with them.'

'Don't worry.'

While we had been talking Lenuta and her man had been in earnest discussion. 'What are they saying?' I said to Adrian.

'The man, he wants money, she does not. Leave it to me.'

'So is she going to give us her consent?' I asked.

'I don't know, wait,' said Adrian.

There was more talk. The man was angry. Lenuta turned away and put her hands over her face. I wanted to go to her and comfort her but when she looked up she was not crying. It was impossible to tell how she felt, one moment she was shouting, the next oddly silent. Suddenly, with a gesture of finality, Adrian turned away. My heart lurched, I glanced at Alan, he had gone very pale. So . . . it was over, we had lost him.

'Have you some wine in your bag?' Adrian asked, suddenly.

'No,' I said, 'only whisky.'

He sighed. 'It is too much, still . . .' He almost snatched the whisky from me and gestured at the woman. She left the room, returning moments later with five tiny glasses on a little wooden tray. She laid them reverently on the table before us. Adrian broke the seal on the whisky bottle and filled the glasses. He passed one to each of us. Then he raised his glass and spoke rapidly in Romanian – it seemed to be some kind of toast. We all drank. Our hearts were leaden but it would have been rude to refuse. Then, extraordinarily, Adrian's face broke into an enormous grin. 'It is done,' he said, 'the boy is yours.'

I stared at him like a mad woman. 'What do you mean?'

He gave an exaggerated sigh of impatience. 'It's OK, she wants you to have Michael. I told you, it is not a problem. This is what you want – yes?'

All doubts were gone. Of course it was what we wanted. 'Yes, oh yes,' I said.

More whisky was poured. Locket asked permission to take some photographs of Lenuta, so that we could show them to Michael when he was older. It seemed unreal. On the wall behind where we had been sitting there hung, in terrible irony, an icon depicting Mary and Joseph, devoted parents, watching over their son. I stared at it for a few moments. Lenuta followed my gaze, and then turned away. Why? Out of sorrow, anger, humiliation? It was impossible to tell. Still no emotion crossed her face.

'Could you tell her, Adrian,' I said, 'that we will always love and care for her son. He will be just as important as our other children. He will be very, very precious to us – always.'

'There is no need.' Adrian's voice was dismissive, almost bored. The business of the day was done, negotiations were completed, he had lost interest.

'Tell her, Adrian.' My voice shook.

'OK,' he said, and began speaking rapidly. She nodded, glanced at me and then began clearing the glasses.

There was no sense of joy or relief, just a kind of numb shock. The whisky bottle on the table seemed to loom unnaturally large, but then so it should, for it was the price of a child.

6
PROMISES

I woke before Alan the following morning and was glad of the time alone to think over the events of the past few days. Our finding Michael seemed then to me extraordinary. It still does. If we had visited Orphanage No. 4 a day earlier, he would not have been there; a day later he might not have been so fresh in Dr Unescu's mind; ten minutes later and she would have gone home. Already I could not bear the thought of having missed him – yesterday, he'd had nothing, today he had a future. It seemed to me to be fatalistic, our meeting him pre-ordained. Fanciful stuff, maybe, but I knew then as I know now that Michael was meant to be our son, and the relief that we could now proceed with the adoption was enormous.

Adrian collected us from the Hotel Bucuresti at six forty-five that morning. He looked tired, which was hardly surprising for, after the gruelling day he'd spent with us, he had gone straight to the airport and worked all night, managing just a couple of hours' sleep at his desk while his boss covered for him. It said a lot for Adrian's stamina, but did not increase our confidence in the control of air traffic over Bucharest Airport. He took us straight to his flat, where Marianna was helping Irena prepare for school. We gave them all the baby equipment we had, all our local currency and all of our gifts – the remaining whisky, cigarettes and soap. In addition, we paid Adrian for his help in locating Lenuta, and gave Marianna payment in advance for looking after Michael.

We had hatched a plot with Adrian the previous evening. We knew adopting Michael was not going to be straightforward. The biggest stumbling block, of course, was the lack of a Romanian adoption law, but in addition we knew we had to face unsympathetic local Social Services whose report, Ivan confirmed, we must have in order to proceed with the adoption. Our faith in the British Embassy, based on our own experience, was fairly non-existent, and there were plenty of horror stories around about their general ineptitude and lack of concern. All this meant that we did not know, and could not guess, how long it was going to take to get Michael out of the orphanage and so we had to make contingency plans to keep him alive and as healthy and as happy as was possible in the circumstances. We agreed with Adrian that Marianna would visit him twice a day, at around eleven o'clock in the morning and again at six, to clean him up, to give him comfort and companionship and, above all, a good meal and plenty to drink. It was clear that in this stifling weather many of the babies were dehydrated and this was something that worried us considerably. We decided that it would be preferable to attend to Michael in the orphanage garden, to give him some much needed fresh air but also for the sake of the other children in his room. To feed him in front of them would have been a terrible thing to do.

Adrian was confident that by bribing the orphanage helpers each day, he and Marianna would be allowed to take Michael out into the garden and eventually, perhaps, back to their flat. I was not too sure about this latter idea. It seemed to me unbearably cruel that Michael should be expected to adapt, on a regular basis, between the awful conditions in the orphanage and the comparative comfort of Adrian's home. However, we did not pursue this particular aspect at the time, not wishing to upset them – we were very dependent upon Adrian and Marianna for Michael's survival.

My opinion, of course, was only that of a layman but instinctively I felt that Michael could slide downhill very fast unless we were very careful. Clearly he was suffering from severe undernourishment, and what little food he was given was not doing him a great deal of good because of his chronic diarrhoea. In addition, his high temperature and creaking chest were very real worries in themselves. Somehow, we had to build up his strength and his spirit to survive for however long it was going to take us to free him.

We were all very anxious that morning as we sat in Adrian's flat talking to Marianna and, with Adrian's help, explaining the situation. Would she be able to take sufficient time off work to look after Michael? Yes, she would. Had we given her enough money to cover her loss of earnings? More than enough money, she insisted.

'Marianna was very upset when I told her about the children,' Adrian said. 'She cried very much when I spoke of Michael. She will do everything she can to feed him and make him well again.'

As I looked into her eyes – big, brown, kind eyes – I so wanted to trust her, but Kerry had told us some horrific stories. Apparently several couples had entrusted newborn babies from maternity homes to Romanian foster parents while they returned to England to sort out the paperwork. The moment their backs were turned, the babies had been put in orphanages and the foster parents had simply pocketed the money they had been given for the babies' care. By Romanian standards, Adrian and Marianna had done very well for themselves. That particular morning Marianna was stylishly dressed in denim dungarees, a white T-shirt and trainers – nothing like the drab clothes worn by most of her fellow countrymen. How had they come by this obvious wealth? By deceit? By sheer hard work? How could we know, how could we trust them? We had to trust them because we had no alternative.

At half-past seven, we left their apartment, waved Irena off to school and set off for the orphanage. Now that we knew he was to be ours, I was longing to see Michael again, but I also felt a desperate sort of guilt at having to leave him. Even if we had not had to return home for Charlie and Locket's sakes, we still needed to go back to England for the home study. But despite the logic of the situation, I had this overwhelming feeling of letting Michael down.

Once more, we walked up the broken concrete path, past the playground, past the hens, past the rows of cots – a walk that was to become so familiar to us, yet always difficult and painful, a walk I will never forget. Inside the orphanage we asked to see Dr Unescu and were told she was not yet on duty. We had only an hour to spare before we had to check in to the airport; we could not wait for her to arrive. Adrian made a fuss and we were shown into a little office just off the main reception area and, for the first time, met the principal. She was a large woman, about my age, with dyed, brassy-blonde hair, long red fingernails and bright blue eye-shadow. Her eyes were hard, her mouth greedy – I hated her on sight.

Adrian quickly explained that we had found Michael's mother, that she had given her consent and that we would like to adopt him. He told the principal the name of our lawyer and explained we were returning to England to finalise the paperwork. She appeared completely unmoved by all this information until Adrian, with a flourish, produced a large carrier bag full of whisky and cigarettes. Then, like the switching on of a light, she instantly became obsequious and ingratiating, telling us what a lovely child Michael was and how like me he looked. It was a nauseating performance.

'Tell her that we wish Marianna to feed Michael twice a day,' I said to Adrian.

'No,' Adrian said.

'Why,' I asked, 'surely it is important to ask her permission?'

He shook his head. 'She is a fat, greedy woman, it will cost too much. We will bribe her staff, it is better that way.' Alan and I exchanged worried glances. Law-abiding citizens by nature, it seemed obvious to us that we should seek permission from the woman in charge of the orphanage. After all, our request was such a reasonable one in the circumstances. I started to protest but Adrian waved a finger at me reprovingly.

There was a sudden commotion outside in the reception area, a cry from Marianna, and there was Michael. We had told Dr Unescu that we would let her know the outcome of our meeting with Michael's parents and clearly they had been expecting us for Michael had been dressed up for the occasion, which we found deeply repugnant. He wore a faded velour top, a pair of dungarees similar in style to the ones he had been wearing before but clean and dry, and on his head the nurses had placed a little bonnet, which was tied excrutiatingly tightly under his chin. He was more alert than he had been on the previous occasion but his breathing was still terribly laboured – I could hear it right across the room. We left the principal avidly sorting through the gifts we had given her, and went to join Marianna and Locket, who were sitting with Michael. I picked him up and hugged him. He smiled and clung. He felt right in my arms, as though he belonged – he did then, he always has done since. Any parent who has more than one child knows that you love your children differently, and so it is with mine, but the basic grit in the guts, the overwhelming need to protect, is the same for all of them, however big and independent they become. The feeling that I could cheerfully murder anyone who hurt Michael was there from the very beginning, and standing that morning in the orphanage, holding him to me while he fought for breath, I knew I loved him just as much as any mother loves their child. It was an instinctive thing, just like the love one has for a newborn baby, for I did not know him yet . . . Yet . . . Please God, one day soon, we would have all the time in the world to get to know one another.

We took some photographs and then I sat Michael on my lap and undid the bonnet. There were red weals under his chin where it had been tied and, as I began to ease it off, it stuck to the back of his head where the dried blood from his sores had welded it to his hair. Gently I prised it away. He did not cry but it must have been painful. I had some Sudocrem with me, which I put on the sores and then turned to give the cream to Marianna for future use. As I did so I saw that she was crying – great tears were pouring down her face, though she made no sound. In that moment I knew that Michael was in safe hands during our absence. I put my free arm round her and she, Michael and I clung together for a moment. We said nothing, words were not necessary, but between us we had made a pact – to keep this child alive.

Kerry had given me a pack of twenty-four bottles of vitamins. I asked Adrian to explain to the nurses how many drops to give. Before our eyes the pack disappeared, leaving us with just one bottle. 'Marianna had better keep that one,' said Adrian. 'We will not see the other bottles again.' He was right. Kerry had also given us some sachets of Dioralyte. Learning my lesson from the vitamins, I explained to

Marianna how to use the sachets and gave them to her.

The business done, we sat in the reception area with Michael while we talked and played together. He made no attempt to move from our laps and showed little interest in a fluffy toy we had brought with us; it was Adrian's car keys he liked best. Contact was what he clearly wanted most – to be talked to, rocked and touched and held. His hands and feet, I noticed, were very delicate, his long, slender fingers in stark contrast to my rough, tough, chunky boy at home, with his square feet and hands and sturdy boy's knees. I tried to judge Michael's size so that I could send Marianna some clothes for him. It seemed to me that he was equivalent to an eight- or nine-month-old baby – it was a terrible thought when one realised that he was only ten days away from his second birthday.

At last Alan said that we must be going. There was some query over our flight time and we were already running late, he said. It was the moment I had dreaded. A nurse appeared from nowhere and went to take Michael from me. I hugged him one last time. He whimpered, seeming to realise that we were leaving him. Everyone was talking at once. The principal had come out from her office and was smiling and waving at us. Adrian and Marianna were arguing over the flight time, and the nurses were chattering away at us as they clustered round Michael. I could only sit there, numb with misery – it felt as though they were taking away a part of me. My final sight of Michael, as they carried him back to that dreadful basement, was of one nurse holding him while the other jammed the bloodstained bonnet back on to his head and tied it tightly under his chin.

'We had better go,' Adrian said. I was crying, Marianna was crying, Locket was dry-eyed but the colour of parchment, and Alan was making a brave but futile attempt at maintaining a stiff upper lip. Adrian suddenly threw back his head and laughed. We stared at him as if he was a mad man. 'The little devil!' he said. 'Your son has gone off with my car keys. He will do well in life, that boy.' We all laughed. It was such an enormous relief from the tension and pain. 'I won't be a moment,' said Adrian, and he ran down the corridor after the nurses. None of us went with him; none of us could bear to see again the place which Michael was forced to recognise as home.

We did not speak on the way to the airport, and at the check-in, when Marianna and Adrian offered to wait with us, we were anxious to say goodbye to them. We needed to be alone. We promised that on the weekend flight we would send out clothes and nappies for Michael, and above all food – milk, juice, rusks, everything we could think of to help build him up. We hugged them and watched them as they walked out of the airport building. It was extraordinary – three days previously we had not even met Adrian and Marianna Gligor. Now they felt like our oldest and best friends. 'Dare we trust them?' Locket asked, voicing all our thoughts.

'Adrian is a rogue, so who knows,' said Alan with a slight smile, 'but Marianna . . . Marianna will look after Michael, I'm sure of it.' I was sure, too.

The plane, of course, was delayed but by now we were used to delays, and in a strange way, although almost everything about Romania had horrified us, we were not in a hurry to leave. I think we all had the feeling that we were deserting Michael.

We found a bar on a cool balcony above the airport lounge and drank surprisingly good beer while we waited. We were then taken into the bowels of the building and herded together in a hot and airless hall while we waited for the airport buses. It was while we stood around in these uncomfortable conditions that a couple approached us and asked if we were the Fowlers. They introduced themselves as Paul and Stacey Vassis. They were friends of the Martins and Caroline Martin had told them that we would be on their flight. Paul was Greek, Stacey Australian, and they were obviously a very devoted couple. Stacey could not have children, they explained, and Paul was too old to be eligible for adoption of a child in the UK, which was why they were here. As it was, said Paul, he was still very worried about their home study, because of his age. We steeled ourselves and asked how old he was: fifty-one – five years younger than Alan. It did not bode well.

Paul and Stacey had found a baby, a little boy who was eight months old and still living with his mother. They had learnt of him through the Romanian equivalent of the Social Services. The child's mother had approached them with a view to putting him in an orphanage. Paul and Stacey had persuaded her to keep the child until they could adopt him, and were helping to support the family. They had already been to Romania twice and still could not get their papers signed. The mother was becoming very restive; she no longer wanted to keep the baby but she was becoming increasingly fond of him as he grew older. It was a nightmare situation for everyone concerned and as they told their story, we were all snivelling.

It seems ridiculous now, a group of strangers standing around in an airport terminal, wiping their eyes. It is hard to explain the enormous emotional strain we were all under, and the incredible feeling of camaraderie we had with other adoptive parents. This network of self-help and support was something we were to become very reliant upon in the weeks ahead. Everyone's story is different, but the nightmare situation is the same. It is terrible to give one's heart to a child and then be powerless to relieve his or her suffering, yet this was the situation we all had to face as we battled against seemingly impenetrable red tape.

We became separated from Paul and Stacey as we struggled on to the dilapidated Tarom plane. As we took off, the plane circled once over Bucharest before heading west, towards home. The three of us strained to look out of the window. Michael was down there somewhere, alone, and fighting to survive. I took Locket's hand and squeezed it; she still looked very pale and strained. We were leaving a part of ourselves behind. We would not be free now to get on with our lives until Michael was with us. Our commitment to him was total. The plane nosed its way into the clouds and the ground was suddenly obscured from view.

7

FORMALITIES

T HE trouble with Romania is its location – no country can expect a peaceful history so placed, for it is vulnerable from east, west, north and south. Just about everyone has invaded Romania. The Romans were there for two hundred years. For a while it was part of the Ottoman Empire and later the Romanians were forced to pay homage to the Hapsburgs. Indeed, it was only at the end of the First World War that one of the results of the Treaty of Versailles was final independence for Romania, which up until that time had spent all its history paying lip service to one country or another.

The period between the wars was really Romania's only time of prosperity and stability since the Roman occupation two thousand years before. The Second World War put an end to it. Romania, although strictly speaking neutral, was dragged into the conflict by the Germans, who by 1940 had more or less taken over the country. In 1944, however, Romania rose up against Germany and joined with the Russian Army in the final campaign of the war. The loss of life was terrible, indeed the losses of the Romanian armed forces were only exceeded by those of the USA, Great Britain and the USSR. What was the reward for their suffering? In 1947, King Mihal abdicated, Romania became a republic and within a few years was completely dominated by the Soviet Union. Since then, Russia has drained the country dry and has all but destroyed the people's national pride and hope for the future.

When we had flown out to Romania we had, up to a point, been prepared for the suffering in the orphanages – not fully prepared, for it was far worse than we had expected, but at least we were braced for the horror we found. What we had not appreciated was that the orphanages are only a symptom of the suffering of the people as a whole. No one in Romania has anything. Everyone is too cold in winter, too hot in summer, undernourished, overworked and desperate for a better life. The grey, drab squalor in Bucharest is particularly depressing because it underlines the hopelessness of Romania's situation. You cannot help being aware that they are very splendid people. Without doubt they are enormously gifted, extremely clever, and rich in culture. Theirs has always been a very civilised nation. When the Romans invaded Britain, they stumbled across savages still painting themselves in wode. When they invaded Romania, they found a people very like themselves, educated and articulate. Indeed, so at home did the Romans feel that they were very reluctant to leave Romania, and many never did.

Romania's resources do not end with her people. The country is beautiful, and rich in minerals and agricultural land, but the nation never sees its own produce. After the death of Ceauşescu they were promised that the harvest of 1990 would be kept in Romania, instead of being shipped off to Russia. It never happened. Indeed the price of food continues to spiral. Under Ceauşescu a melon cost five lei; now it costs thirty. The people are in despair, and there seems to be no solution. They thought they had rid themselves of the man who was destroying their nation – now they find they have simply destroyed the figurehead. On that first visit to Bucharest, we were only dimly aware of the country's plight. I do remember, however, arriving back at Heathrow and Locket and I going to the barely adequate ladies' loo while we waited for our bags to reach the carousels. We walked around the cloakroom, touching the clean white surfaces, fingering the towels, exclaiming over the soap. We had only been out of the country for four days, yet Romania's deprivation and squalor had made such an impact on us that the ladies' loo at Heathrow seemed like a palace. Indeed, looking back on it, all three of us were terribly disorientated. A combination, I suppose, of the enormous cultural shock, and, particularly, the emotional upheaval we had all been through in finding and committing ourselves to Michael.

Russell was at Terminal 2 to meet us. We were desperately pleased to see him but I do not think any of us made much sense. He was patient with us and on the journey home we told him of Michael and showed him the Polaroid photographs we had taken that morning. That morning . . . had it really been so recently that we had left him?

Our reunion with Charlie was lovely. He was clearly very, very pleased to see us, although he had obviously been happy without us. He had even started to call Margaret 'Mummy' which did not upset me at all – it simply meant that she had been doing the good job I knew she would. We had a late lunch but none of us was hungry. I kept looking at Charlie, at his sturdy limbs, his skin already golden brown from the glorious weather, his clear blue eyes, his bright cheeks. The contrast with Michael was terrible. There in Romania, surrounded by other sick children, far from home and what we would consider normal, I had not really acknowledged quite how ill he was. Now, set against Charlie, incredibly seven months younger, Michael's pitiful condition seemed even harder to bear.

After lunch, Alan and I made a plan. We wanted to trust Adrian and Marianna, and we did up to a point, but we knew Michael was in considerable danger – he was ill, he was weak, he was undernourished – and we had to get him out and get him out fast. For the next few weeks it was going to mean pooling all our efforts. Before leaving Bucharest we had made one more telephone call to Ivan to tell him of our decision to adopt Michael. He made no comment other than to say he would need an adoption declaration from us, signed by a notary public in this country. He also wanted another full set of documents notarised and an AIDS testing kit. Neither Alan nor I had worked for a week and Locket had done none of the school work set for her while she was away. Tensions were running high. Above all, we were worried sick about the Social Services. We had to have a Social Services home study completed, and fast, if we were to bring Michael into the country legally, and we knew Jane Allan was hostile to the whole concept of Romanian adoption. Other couples, like the Martins, had brought their children into the country without Home Office approval, but we wanted to do things properly, for Michael's sake as much as our own – at least we did, if it were possible.

After a short, troubled sleep, we set to work on Thursday morning. Alan had the necessary declaration typed up and taken for notarisation, along with the extra file copy that Ivan needed. Mr Beasley of Linnells shook his head sagely. 'How many pages are there to this?' he asked Alan.

'Somewhere between thirty and forty,' said Alan.

'I'm supposed to charge you £15 per page, that's the statutory fee,' said Mr Beasley, 'but in the very special circumstances, shall we call it £40?'

It was the first of many such incidents we experienced in the weeks that lay ahead. People were so kind. As soon as they knew what we were doing and why, they would do everything they could to help. Indeed, while Alan was sorting out the documentation, I had contacted the John Radcliffe Hospital and from them had found a firm who supplied AIDS testing kits. The managing director could only let me have a box of twenty, at a price of £150. I groaned. He asked me why I needed the kit and when I told him, he said the actual manufacturing cost for twenty kits was £58, which was what he would ask me, and he would send a courier over to us immediately at no extra charge.

We caught our breath over a quick lunch. Alan had been in touch with Harry McCormick because we needed to send out both the AIDS testing kit and the documents to Ivan as quickly as possible. Harry had given us the name of a woman called Miranda Cavill, who was travelling out to Bucharest on Sunday. She was Romanian, apparently, but married to an Englishman, and he was sure she could be relied upon to take a parcel out for us. Alan contacted her. She was very co-operative and agreed immediately to help us.

After lunch, we telephoned Jane Allan of Social Services and said we needed to see her urgently. Much to our surprise she agreed to see us at half-past three the same afternoon. Reluctant to leave Charlie again so soon after our return, the three of us drove into Oxford and presented ourselves at her office, together with photographs of Michael and a copy of our private home study. We collapsed into her office chairs. I stuck a bottle of juice in Charlie's mouth and we started to talk. It was the first time since our return from Bucharest that we had really had a chance to relive the whole experience. The words just poured out. Jane listened, asking the odd question here and there. I produced the photographs and tried not to cry when I explained to her Michael's state of health. Charlie sat on my lap, sucking quietly on his bottle, as if recognising that this was serious business.

'So you see,' Alan concluded, 'we have to get him out quickly or he may die before we can save him. We have a private home study, we have all the documentation. Please, please help us.'

There was a lengthy pause and then she smiled. 'I'll help you,' she said, 'I must admit I hadn't realised just how awful things were. You've opened my eyes. As you know I haven't been in favour of these Romanian adoptions while there are still British children needing a home, but I can see in your case . . .' She looked again at Michael's photograph. 'In any event we have to do what we can to help this little chap.' I could have hugged her. 'I'll need two sessions with you,' she said, 'and I'll have to interview two of your referees.' We all consulted diaries and Jane agreed on two dates: Friday 6 July and the following Wednesday, the 11th. If all went well and she approved us for the adoption of Michael, she reckoned it would only take until Monday the 16th to complete the home study.

It was better than we had dared hope. We left her office euphoric, drunk with relief, and drove straight to Locket's school to collect her. She looked tired and pale. She admitted to having had a rough day. 'I was so bad-tempered with everyone,' she said, 'and really I was so pleased to see them and get back to normal.'

'I expect it's because you're tired,' I suggested.

'No,' Locket said, 'I keep getting irritated with everyone – they make such a fuss about trivial things. It makes me angry and I know it shouldn't.' I knew exactly what she meant; Michael and his suffering changed one's perspective on just about everything.

That night, for the first time since going to Bucharest, we relaxed a little. Our neighbours, the Reeves, came round after supper and we showed the photographs of Michael and told them all about him. We telephoned Murray and Claire and my mother. Perhaps it was not going to be so difficult after all. There was still the stumbling block of no Romanian adoption law, but Ivan had been confident that the new law was just a few weeks away – two, maybe three at the most – and with luck would coincide with the completion of the home study. We began to believe that we might have Michael with us by the beginning of August.

Armed with this very real sense of optimism, we told Charlie all about Michael for the first time. We put one of our precious photographs in his room and within a few hours, he was pointing at it with shrieks of excitement. To demonstrate our faith we bought a double buggy in which Charlie took his pre-lunch nap, with the promise that Michael would soon be sharing it with him. How he would react when presented with Michael in person was anyone's guess, but, in principle, Charlie seemed quite taken with the idea of a new brother.

On Friday, Alan felt sufficiently confident to go back to work. He had an appointment in Bristol but he went via London and the Romanian Embassy, to have the papers stamped first. I concentrated on Charlie and we spent a happy morning together, mooching around in the sunshine. Just before lunch I rang Caroline Martin, just to thank her for all the help she had given and to tell her about Michael and where we had got to.

She listened to the story. 'So, who is conducting the medicals?' she asked.

'We've arranged that our lawyer will take a doctor to the orphanage next week,' I said. 'He's going to do blood tests for both AIDS and hepatitis B.'

'Which of you is going to be there?' Caroline asked.

'Neither of us,' I said, surprised.

'You must be there,' she insisted, 'you really must.'

'Why?' I asked.

'For two reasons. Firstly, you must be sure that they use a sterilised needle. In testing Michael for AIDS they could well give it to him. Secondly, you can't trust anyone. You must bring a sample back here to the John Radcliffe for testing.'

'I'm sure our lawyer is honest,' I said.

'You can't be sure,' Caroline insisted. 'In a country like Romania you cannot trust anyone. For two dollars, for a dollar even, a lab technician would be perfectly prepared to say that Michael's test was negative, when in fact he was HIV positive. Let's face it, if Michael has AIDS and therefore you don't proceed with the adoption, then your lawyer will lose his fee. Ideally, you should commission an

independent medical as well, but at the very least you must bring a
sample back here for testing.'

What she said made sense and her words carried more weight
knowing that she was married to a doctor. I telephoned Alan at work.
He listened to what I had to say. 'She's right, of course,' he said,
without any preamble. 'The question is, which of us should go? We
can't both leave Charlie again, can we, not so soon? I think it had
better be me. At least if I go I can take a good supply of food for
Michael and make sure it gets to him, check up on Adrian and
Marianna, and make sure that Ivan has the documentation. I'll go, I'll
ring Harry right away.' There was just one seat left on Sunday's Tarom
flight, and Alan took it.

It worried me, Alan going back to Bucharest so soon. He looked so
tired – the sense of urgency we both felt of needing to bring Michael
home was starting to take its toll. But one of us had to go and I knew
Alan was right, it should be him. Charlie needed me. He had not slept
well since we returned and was eating poorly. Although he had us
home again, he was starting to react to the stress of us being away,
and no doubt the general tension in the air.

That same afternoon, Charlie and I went shopping. We bought
crates of milk and juice, rusks and dried baby food, creams for
Michael's sores and mosquito bites, shampoo and bath care. Bearing
in mind the heat in Bucharest, we also bought a dozen little body-suit
vests which I thought would be cool and comfortable for him to wear
during the day instead of the orphanage rags. We staggered home with
our booty to find that Alan had come back from work early and was
trying desperately to get through to Romania to tell both Ivan and
Adrian that he was coming out again on Sunday.

Ask anyone who has adopted a baby from Romania and they will
be able to tell you in their sleep the key telephone numbers during the
period they were trying to bring their children home: 010 400 . . .
Some nights you would have to dial a hundred, two hundred times to
get through. Other nights it might only take ten minutes but after a
few minutes you would be cut off. It was time-consuming, frustrating
and it all added to the tension. That night we started dialling Romania
at five o'clock. We took it in turns, Locket, Alan and I, and we finally
got through just after ten. It was all fixed up – Adrian would meet
Alan at the airport and Ivan had arranged for a doctor to be at the
orphanage on Tuesday, at ten o'clock.

'Now all we have to do,' said Alan, 'is to find out how to bring the
blood back here without it going off.'

The following morning, in between packing supplies for Michael, I
telephoned our doctor, Adrian Young, very aware of how hard he
works and the fact that it was a Saturday. 'Come round to the surgery,'

he said, 'and we'll talk about it.' I told him the problem, slightly anxious as to how he would react but the solution was easy. It was perfectly all right, he said, to take a sample of Michael's blood on Tuesday, as long as Alan kept it cool, and he suggested a cool bag. However, while the blood must be kept cool, it was also vital that it did not freeze.

'The flights from Bucharest are notoriously unreliable,' I said, 'I don't know what time he will be back on Wednesday.'

'Not to worry,' said Dr Young, 'let's give you an appointment for first thing on Thursday morning. You can bring the sample in to me then. Bearing in mind that it's so vital, I'd rather handle this sample myself. Just imagine if one of the receptionists dropped it!' I tried very hard not to imagine any such thing. I showed him the AIDS kit we had been given, with which he was happy, but he gave me some sample bottles he preferred we used.

On Saturday we also rang Kerry to see if she would like us to bring anything out for her. She needed more milk for Alexander and some antibiotics from the doctor, which she had arranged via her mother-in-law. Alexander's diarrhoea was worse and he had a slight fever. Poenaru was as elusive as ever and she and Karen were at breaking point. 'I'm sorry you have to come out again,' she told Alan, 'but I'll be terribly glad to see you. I'm going mad here and I'm sure my family have forgotten I exist.'

Mrs Male came over the same evening with Alexander's milk and medicine. No, they had not forgotten that Kerry and Alexander existed. They felt as frustrated and as helpless as she herself did.

The next day we had been due to have a family party. Alan's brother and his wife had been away on holiday for some time and were due to come and see us, together with one of their daughters-in-law and grandchild. Murray and Claire were coming over, as were Russell and Mitch. I wanted to cancel it and drive Alan to the airport but he would not hear of it. 'Life must go on,' he said. 'It will do you good anyway.'

I felt awful watching him drive off – and more than a little envious, too. I wanted to see Michael again, to reassure myself that Marianna was looking after him. Still, it would not be long now.

'But what if the AIDS test is positive?' somebody rather tactlessly asked me during that Sunday. I remember muttering some platitude and taking Charlie into the garden and walking down to the river with him. I put on his life-jacket and we rowed up the river a little. Water always has a calming effect on me. I tried to answer the question in my own mind and failed.

When I had been expecting Charlie, the gynaecologist had recommended that I had an amniocentesis because of the high possibility of my having a Down's syndrome baby at my age. I had agreed to the test, and in doing so it was naturally assumed that if the test had proved positive, I would have had a termination. We were very lucky and no decisions were necessary because the test was negative, but I have often wondered since how I would have reacted if Charlie had been a Down's baby. To kill a baby already moving inside you, to end its life simply because it does not conform . . . my mind cannot easily accept such an idea. But I had gone along with the test . . . The analogy between Michael with his AIDS test and Charlie with the amniocentesis was all too apparent. Yes, of course it was important and sensible to have Michael tested for AIDS and hepatitis B, indeed, it was a requirement of the Home Office. But what if he proved to be positive in one or both diseases? What did we do then – simply return him to the scrap heap and look for another child? The idea was as alien to me as killing my child because he was not perfect.

I tried to close my mind to the possibility of a positive test. There were so many conflicting stories about the likelihood of AIDS. At one extreme end of the scale, we had been told not even to look for a baby in Bucharest, since AIDS was so prevalent. At the other end, we had been told that there had been some cases in Orphanages Nos. 1 and 2, but the problem was now identified and all the babies in Bucharest had already been screened. I paused in my rowing and looked at my watch. If the flight had been anything like on time, Alan would be halfway there by now.

Charlie was sitting between my knees, watching the water intently. He already shared my love of boats and boating. 'It'll be all right, old chap,' I said, hugging him to me. *It had to be.*

8

BACK TO BUCHAREST

AFTER Locket and Charlie had both gone to bed, I sat staring at the telephone for some time. It was Tuesday night. Alan was due back from Bucharest the following afternoon. Only one more day to go, but what worried me was that I had not heard from him. We had not made any commitment to ring one another because such things are not possible with the Romanian telephone system. However, I knew he had intended to get in touch with me as soon as he had seen Michael, to let me know how he fared. It was after midnight in Bucharest now. Remembering how exhausted we had been on our last trip, I was loath to try and contact him so late but I had a very strong feeling that something was wrong. I began dialling 010 400 . . . again and again. Finally, down the end of what seemed like a long tunnel, I heard someone say 'Hotel Bucuresti'. I had no idea of his room number. I shouted 'Alan Fowler, English,' down the telephone, not really expecting to have any positive response.

And then, miraculously, there was Alan's voice. 'Thank God you telephoned,' he said, 'I've been trying to ring you for two days. Kerry and Karen are in big trouble and I need you to pass messages through to their families.'

'OK,' I said, 'but tell me about Michael first.'

'Darling, this is important, we might be cut off at any moment.'

'Please,' I pleaded, close to tears.

'He's well, at least he looks a lot better, plumper. I'll tell you all about him tomorrow but you must get this message through to the Males immediately.'

It transpired that Kerry had finally snapped the day before. In desperation, she and Adrian had gone to the Ministry Building in Bucharest, where they believed their files were being kept, and had bribed one of the clerks there to look up the records. She had found Kerry and Karen's files quite quickly and, astonishingly, they had both been signed by President Iliescu a fortnight previously. Whether it was due to inefficiency or because, for whatever reason, Poenaru had deliberately withheld the release of their files, Kerry was unclear. Either way, it was an outrage – Alexander and Emily's adoptions had been approved for two whole weeks, while the girls had festered and fumed and thought themselves unable to leave the country. On the face of it, the news was wonderful, but Alan was worried. The following day Kerry and Karen were due to travel to Gaesti, where the maternity home was situated, in order to obtain the final signature of the mayor there, which was needed in order to obtain passports for the children. They had just heard, however, that Daniella, Poenaru's hard woman assistant, had learnt of the hijacking of the files and was after their blood. 'I don't like it,' said Alan. 'Anything could happen. They could be arrested for taking those files, and God knows what would happen to the babies then.'

'So, what do you want me to tell the Males?' I asked.

'Just have them on stand-by,' said Alan. 'It's unfortunate that I have to fly out tomorrow, but I would suggest to Steven Male that he rings his wife tomorrow afternoon and to keep trying until he reaches her. If he has no luck then he should assume things have gone badly wrong and should telephone the Embassy immediately.' I promised to ring the Males first thing in the morning and was just about to ask for more news of Michael when we were cut off. I tried telephoning again but there were no lines so I gave up and went to bed, miserable for Michael and frightened for Kerry and Karen.

By the time Alan arrived home the following day he was thoroughly depressed. He had the blood sample with him but he did not think it was any good. He had managed to keep it cool right enough, but too cool he thought. Certainly it did not look very good – it had gone brown and had formed into great globules. He seemed to feel that his whole trip had been a failure and yet when we began to discuss it, clearly he had done magnificently. He had spent most of Monday with Michael, at Adrian and Marianna's home. Marianna was sweet with Michael apparently and he was clearly becoming very fond of her. They had bathed and fed him and, although he was still very passive, he seemed quite relaxed and friendly.

'Has he tried to walk at all?' I asked.

'No, he just sits and plays, like I suppose Charlie did at about eight months.'

On the plane going out to Bucharest, Alan had met Miranda Cavill, who had volunteered to be a courier for us. Although Miranda was by birth Romanian, she had been married to an Englishman for some years and appeared very Westernised. An extremely vivacious, attractive woman, Alan felt she was the sort of person who got things done and had been very grateful when she had volunteered to help us in any way she could, should we hit any snags while in Bucharest. After leaving her at the airport, it had occurred to Alan that she might well know a reliable doctor who could give Michael an independent medical. He had telephoned her the same evening and luck was with us – she had a family friend who was a leading paediatrician in one of the major Bucharest hospitals. With permission from the orphanage, Marianna and Alan had taken Michael to Miranda Cavill's house on the evening of Monday the 2nd, where they had met Dr Magdalena Dragon, a woman in her mid-fifties who clearly knew her business. She had examined Michael thoroughly and although she had confirmed that he was far from well and desperately undernourished, in her view there was nothing major wrong with him. All his organs functioned properly, as did his muscle control. His legs were only wasted from lack of use, his chest, although badly infected, would soon clear up with fresh air and a good diet. And, the best news of all – she had confirmed that AIDS was not as widespread as the media had led everyone to expect, and there had been no cases of AIDS at Orphanages Nos. 6 and 4.

It was during that Monday, also, that Alan and Adrian went in search of Christina-Daniella, Michael's little sister, who had been taken from the cot which she had shared with her brother – was it weeks or days before? Alan and I had discussed Michael's two sisters at length on our return from Bucharest. The temptation to say 'to hell with it, we'll manage somehow, we'll adopt the whole family' was enormous, but it was also impractical. There was the very real problem of space and resources and there was also the question of Locket and Charlie. Adopting one child was something we felt we could handle, but three would dilute our parental attention so far as Locket and Charlie were concerned to the point where they would suffer considerably. Then, there was the danger of Charlie being left out. He would still be the baby of the family, with, presumably, Mirella, Christina-Daniella and Michael enjoying a closer relationship with one another than with him. Nevertheless, we felt we had a responsibility to Michael's sisters. Michael was our son now, emotionally and morally, since Lenuta had given her consent to his adoption, and therefore it was our responsibility to ensure that we did whatever we could to help his sisters and, of course, keep in touch with them.

So far as Mirella was concerned, we considered at the time it was very ulikely that she would be adopted, not only because she was seven but also because she was in an orphanage outside Bucharest. Christina-Daniella presented a different problem. We had discussed with Russell and Mitch, at some length, the possibility that they might adopt her and they were cautiously enthusiastic about it. At the same time all of us had doubts. Certainly we were a complicated family but we could not help wondering whether we would be pushing our luck to introduce the bizarre circumstance of Michael's brother being his sister's father. It was bound to be confusing for the children and seeing each other every week to ten days would be unsettling for them. They had been used to living together, sharing a cot. They had been cruelly parted and presumably suffered greatly as a result. In a way, we all felt it was better that they did not meet again until the scars had healed, or that they were brought together quickly and permanently in a new home. This brought us back full circle: could we in fact adopt Christina-Daniella as well as Michael, but not Mirella? Three children under three and a half was a tall order, and again there was the question of Charlie being the odd one out. In the end we had come to the conclusion that there was no point in agonising about it. The best thing to do was to find Christina-Daniella if we could and then decide.

It took Adrian and Alan four abortive visits before they finally tracked her down to an orphanage only two or three miles away from her brother. I never saw the orphanage myself but Alan reported it to be a more pleasant place than No. 4. The children were slightly older and more able to take care of themselves, which made the staffing levels more acceptable and the children's care altogether better. Neither the principal nor any of the doctors were at the orphanage when Alan and Adrian arrived, but there was a senior nursing sister in charge who took them straight to see Christina-Daniella. She was playing with other children in a sunny nursery. Like Michael she was deathly pale, with dark circles under her eyes, her hair cut in the traditional orphanage crew cut. She wore a faded pink dress and little white boots, but she was altogether sturdier and healthier than either Adrian or Alan had expected, bearing in mind the condition of her brother. Her suffering had clearly taken a different form. The moment she saw Adrian and Alan approach she started to scream. She clung to the nurse, crying, hiding her face and, although they were very gentle with her and patient, neither of them could get anywhere near her. They managed to take a few photographs, which I still have. They show a very sad, lost, disturbed little girl with a face so hauntingly like her brother's that they never fail to bring tears to my eyes. For whatever the spark Michael has, that grit in the guts, that raw courage, that optimism, that humour, it has deserted Christina-Daniella. The terrible experiences the family have suffered show on her face, and her scars will take far longer to heal than Michael's. The nursing sister was enthusiastic about the possibility of ourselves or Russell and Mitch adopting the little girl. Yes, she was available, they had every reason to believe that she was free from AIDS and hepatitis B, and her medical records were good. She was also sure that with love, time and attention spent on her, Christina-Daniella could learn to relax and be a happy child.

Alan left the orphanage with a heavy heart. Right at the very end of their visit, Christina-Daniella had begun to unwind a little. She had even waved to them from the balcony. It left him in a complete quandary as to what to do – loyalties were divided in so many directions as they drove away. Clearly our instincts were right and it was not sensible for Russell and Mitch to adopt the child. She was already disturbed and the confusion of belonging to a family where her brother was only in her life part-time was not something she was going to be able to handle. Either we adopted her or she stayed where she was until, hopefully, somebody else decided to take her into their family.

Alan had agreed that the following day he would return in the morning to see the principal and this he did, arriving with Adrian just after 8.30 a.m. The principal, an unpleasant woman – reminiscent, Alan said, of the principal of Orphanage No. 4 – was in fine temper. The nursing sister should not have shown Christina-Daniella to Adrian and Alan for she was not available for adoption. An Italian family had already decided to adopt her.

'Are you absolutely sure?' said Adrian.

'Quite sure,' she replied.

Alan and Adrian consulted. 'This woman is bad,' Adrian told her. 'If you wish it I can stop the Italian adoption. She can be bribed – money, presents – it's not a problem. If you would like the little girl I can arrange it.'

Alan had to think quickly. He put himself in the place of the Italian couple who presumably had met Christina-Daniella and loved her. Supposing somebody did the same thing to us and Michael? It was an appalling thought. 'No,' Alan said firmly, 'we mustn't do that, it would not be right. Tell her we are glad that Christina-Daniella is to have a new home.'

The principal looked disappointed and it made Alan suspicious that she had been hoping to become involved in some horse trading for the little girl. Outside the orphanage, he voiced his opinion and Adrian agreed. 'I think we should keep a careful watch on Christina-Daniella,' said Alan, 'in case that woman was making up the whole story about the Italian couple in the hope of extracting money from us. The child needs help.'

'It's not a problem,' said Adrian, 'leave it to me. I will visit the orphanage regularly and make sure the little girl is adopted. If not, who knows, maybe you will reconsider.'

At ten o'clock the same morning, as agreed, Alan had met Ivan at the orphanage and blood samples had been taken. Michael had screamed a great deal, which Alan found very distressing. In the afternoon he had taken Michael for his passport photograph and then returned him to the orphanage. Having spent most of the day away from the orphanage, Michael had been very distressed at being returned there. When Marianna came back from having put him in his cot, she was crying too. It was a very difficult situation. It appeared there was no possibility of Adrian and Marianna being allowed to have Michael living with them until the adoption could be finalised. Alan had pleaded with Ivan to try and make this possible, but it was not to be. Indeed, Ivan was adamant that they must not even take Michael out of the orphanage at all. Alan's view, and instinctively it was mine, too, was that Michael would actually suffer more being taken out every day and returned every night. He had therefore told Adrian and Marianna to visit Michael twice a day, but not actually take him home any more because Ivan had forbidden it. They in turn had asked Alan to reconsider his decision so far as Sundays were concerned. To his horror, he then learnt that on Sundays the orphanage only employed two members of staff, who were left in charge of one hundred and fifty children which, of course, meant that many of them were neither fed nor changed in the whole twenty-four hours. It was too awful to contemplate, yet Alan was sure it was true – both Adrian and Marianna had been very distressed when they told him about it, having seen the suffering for themselves. It was therefore agreed that they could take Michael out on Sundays, but not during the week. Before he left Alan had restocked them with lei and more gifts to keep the orphanage staff happy.

Once I'd heard about it, I kept thinking about Sundays at the orphanage. How could the principal allow such a thing to happen? How could she enjoy Sunday with her family knowing that the children in her charge were so neglected? It didn't bear thinking about.

The following morning, I presented myself at Dr Young's surgery with a heavy heart. 'I don't think the sample's any good,' I said, handing it to him, carefully.

He held it up to the light. 'It looks fine to me. What do you think is wrong with it?'

'Alan believes he may have let it become too cold. Look, it's gone all lumpy and brown.'

Dr Young grinned at me good-naturedly. 'That's the blood clotting,' he said, with commendable patience. 'Your boy would be in dead trouble if his blood didn't do that. I've arranged for the sample to be picked up at midday today. I'd like to think you'd have the results before the weekend but I doubt it. Try ringing Monday morning.'

Alan was ecstatic. He had felt sure that the whole purpose of his visit had been destroyed. The relief was enormous.

That same afternoon I went with Charlie to collect Locket from school. She was still very pale and quiet, certainly not her normal ebullient self, and oddly unenthusiastic about the forthcoming summer holidays. Over tea in Oxford I asked her whether she was happy about our adopting Michael or whether something was worrying her. She was happy about it, she assured me, very happy, though she was worried about the effect it would have on Charlie. In recent months she and Charlie had become very close. He adores his big sister, and I asked her if she was worried about the impact Michael would have on her relationship with her baby brother. She admitted she was. 'You see, everybody else has someone,' she said. 'There's Lorne and Innes, Russell and Murray, and now Michael and Charlie. Not only am I the only girl but I am also the only one who hasn't got another half.'

'It makes you special,' I said. It was not a platitude, it was how I felt. Locket is my Achilles' heel, she always has been, and always will be. We spent many difficult years on our own together – it has made us very close and formed a bond which sets us apart a little from the rest of the family.

'I'm not jealous,' she said, hastily, 'don't think that, it's just that I wish I had brothers and sisters of my own age.'

We talked it through from every angle while Charlie stoically battled his way through a plate of spaghetti. Our lack of attention to his table manners necessitated a very large tip at the end of the meal, but Locket seemed more cheerful and relaxed. At least she had the problem off her chest.

When we arrived home at Hampton Gay, there were several messages to ring the Males in Abingdon. 'I think there's some sort of panic going on,' said Margaret, 'I don't know what, I didn't dare ask.'

I telephoned immediately. Margaret was right. On Wednesday, the day that Alan had left Romania, Adrian, as arranged, had taken Kerry, Karen and the two babies to Gaesti for the mayor's signature. Although they had been kept waiting for several hours, they had succeeded in obtaining the signatures and the last hurdle had been to obtain the children's birth certificates. After a further delay, Alexander's was produced but, before Emily's was issued, Daniella had arrived and instigated an incredible scene. She had told the mayor that both Kerry and Karen were unsuitable parents to adopt the children, that they would abuse them and there was no way he should have signed the documents. A terrible row had followed, with everyone shouting and no solution reached. In the end, they had been forced to return to Bucharest without Emily's birth certificate and Daniella had told them that she would telephone the Passport Office in Bucharest to ensure that neither Emily nor Alexander could leave the country.

Daniella's vindictiveness was incredible. All Kerry could think was that she and Poenaru were excrutiatingly embarrassed at being caught out, and that Daniella had gone into the attack as a means of defence.

Whatever the reasons for her actions, the Males were frantic with worry. What if the girls were arrested for taking their files, what if the babies were taken from them? 'Have you heard from them today?' I asked.

'No, we haven't been able to contact them,' Mrs Male said. 'I was just hoping your husband was still out there and could help them.' I explained that Alan had returned home. Steven, of course, was flying out and so was Karen's Alan from New York, but neither could get a flight until Sunday, by which time anything could have happened.

When Alan returned home from work that evening, we were all very subdued. It was so awful – after all the girls had been through, to be so near and yet so far. We wanted to telephone the Males to find out how things were going but felt they would probably want to keep their line free.

At ten o'clock the telephone rang. It was Kerry, sounding slightly the worse for wear. Adrian had taken Karen back to Gaesti during the day and had managed to obtain Emily's birth certificate with a great deal of bribery and corruption and Adrian-type bluff. Kerry had just telephoned Daniella and they had agreed to meet the following morning to discuss what should happen next. She had them over a barrel, of course – they had now officially adopted their children under Romanian law but unless Daniella gave the Passport Office the go-ahead, they could not leave the country. Kerry and Karen had decided the solution that night was to hit the Romanian plonk fairly hard; it seemed the only sensible thing to do. We had to agree with them.

On a lighter note, Karen had some news. On the way back to Gaesti, they had called in on Orphanage No. 4 to see Michael. He had been in the garden with Marianna, having his supper, and had seemed in good spirits. Karen was obviously very taken with him and it was cheering to have such an up-to-date report. Nevertheless, their experience was unsettling, to say the least. Kerry and Karen were on the spot and, as such, could control their destiny a great deal more efficiently than we could hope to do. Moreover, by far the most important factor was that they had custody of their children. They could care for them, protect them, learn to love them. However long it was going to take to free Alexander and Emily from Bucharest, at least the children were not in danger. If Ivan proved to be another Poenaru and we were subjected to a waiting game, the delay could cost Michael his life. We just had to put our faith in Ivan, and, please God, hope we were right to do so.

The following day Jane Allen came for the first of her two home study sessions. She arrived at one thirty and stayed until quite late in the afternoon. We discussed every aspect of our family, warts and all, and in a strange way Alan and I found it quite therapeutic. Suddenly we could understand why the psychiatrist's couch works. By the end of the meeting, although it was clear she could make no decision until she had interviewed our referees, it was obvious that she approved of the idea of us adopting Michael. She also talked to Locket who, rather nobly, we thought, gave us a good reference so far as being parents were concerned. Indeed, we found the whole meeting much less traumatic than we had imagined.

The following day was Saturday. Alan, Charlie and I went to Heathrow to make a delivery to yet another of Harry McCormick's contacts, Marian Gaylor. We now had the final documents required by Ivan, plus a present and cards for Michael, as the following day was his second birthday. Harry introduced us to Marian, herself a mother of young children, who like us had added to her family by adopting a Romanian orphan, and who also like us was finding it increasingly difficult to simply forget what she had seen in Romania. As a result she was making frequent trips to Bucharest to organise aid for the orphanages, as well as caring for her family back home. We learnt that she was staying with Ivan, who had helped her with her adoption, which was comforting, and she promised to see that Michael received his birthday present and cards. We felt oddly flat when we said goodbye to her, feeling that we should be going to Bucharest too, although in truth at that moment there was nothing we could do to move things forward. We took Charlie to the top floor of the park to see the hustle and bustle of the airport – 'brmm-brmms', whether in the air or on the ground, are his main passion in life. Forget the country idyll; Charles Fowler would like to live permanently at Terminal 2, Heathrow Airport.

On Sunday, 8 July, I woke early with an immediate sense of unease and discomfort. It was a beautiful morning and I remember standing at the open window and gazing out across the fields to the ruined manor. Today was Michael's second birthday and I thanked God for Adrian and Marianna, for otherwise, it being a Sunday, he would have spent it neglected and alone. Even so, he would wake up in the morning and go to sleep at night in that terrible cot, breathing that rancid air . . . I thought of children's birthdays as they should be, of doting, proud parents, presents, a party, cake, jelly, chocolate biscuits, balloons, crackers . . . I squeezed my eyes tight shut and put a hand over my mouth to stop myself shouting aloud. No child should have to live as Michael does, no child should suffer as he does. I wanted to rage and scream and beat my head against the wall. From the next room Charlie began calling out. The anger left me. 'Three will be different, Michael, I promise. You'll have a birthday to remember, darling, we all will,' I whispered into the morning air, before going to fetch my son.

Once a month during the summer we have evensong at our little church in the middle of the fields at Hampton Gay. With a population of only eleven more regular services are not justified. David Wilcox, our vicar, had already agreed to be a referee for our home study, so he knew all about Michael. He came to lunch that day and afterwards, at the service, he asked the congregation to pray for Michael. I tried to tell myself that perhaps by this time next month he would be here with us. It seemed unlikely, but in theory it was possible.

There were two main stumbling blocks still ahead of us. Firstly, there was the completion of the home study, although this now seemed to be almost solved, thanks to Jane Allan. Once it was completed, it was required by the Home Office in London, who would put it with our file once it reached them from Bucharest. In order to obtain entry clearance, i.e. a visa to bring Michael into this country, Ivan was required to lodge our file with the British Embassy in Bucharest. The file than travelled in the diplomatic bag to the Home Office, for consideration, and if they decided that Michael was a suitable case for adoption, then they would grant a twelve-month visa. The diplomatic bag only travels from Bucharest to London on Thursdays and Ivan assured us that the following Tuesday he would take our file to the Embassy to make sure it was there in good time. This part of the procedure we could at least influence; the second stumbling block we could not. Since 10 June there had been no law for adoption in Romania. It had been decided, rightly, that it was crazy for President Iliescu to be personally signing each adoption paper, and adoption was instead to become a judicial process in line with most other nations. So far so good, but although a new law kept being promised nothing was happening.

Kneeling there in our little church, I prayed and prayed that some solution would be found, quickly. You could have heard a pin drop when David asked that we pray for Michael. If you believe in the power of prayer, then Michael had his full share that day.

The next day we had a wonderful piece of news. Charlie was still in his high chair at breakfast when the telephone rang. It was Adrian Young, our doctor. 'I thought I'd let you know right away,' he said, 'the test results are in and Michael is clear – no AIDS, no hepatitis B. Good luck with the adoption.' Suddenly optimism returned. Michael did not have AIDS, he was not HIV positive. He was still very ill, still in danger, but there was no terrible decision to be made about his future. Our job was to bring him home, and as for Michael himself – he had to stay alive long enough to be free.

9
ON THE RACK

BY Wednesday, 18 July, we had enjoyed such a run of good luck we should have known it had to end. Good as her word, Jane Allen had completed our home study report and considered us suitable to adopt Michael. She had sent us extracts from it (some of the report is confidential) and the full report she had sent directly to the Home Office. So far as the British end of the whole adoption process was concerned, all we needed now was confirmation that our file was in the diplomatic bag and on its way from the British Embassy in Bucharest. God willing, once the Home Office had our file they would grant Michael entry clearance. We knew that on the previous day, Ivan had been intending to meet the Consul, Bob House, in order to hand over our documentation. So, on Wednesday, having already learnt that it was foolish to leave anything to chance, Alan spent some hours trying to telephone Bucharest in order to check the hand-over had gone smoothly. It had not. Bob House at the Embassy had received no file from Ivan because, apparently, Ivan had only been prepared to wait ten minutes and then had left, before Bob could see him. More tortuous telephoning followed and at last we managed to contact Ivan. Ivan had not waited ten minutes, he had waited two hours and still no one had been prepared to see him. He promised he would try again that afternoon. Back to Bob House again, who still denied that Ivan had been kept waiting, but agreed to see him that afternoon. He also confirmed there would still be time for our file to be included in the diplomatic bag on Thursday, provided there were no mishaps, unexpected events or missing pieces of paper.

He is a very pleasant man, Bob House. Alan liked him immediately for at last it seemed that we had found someone at the Embassy who was genuinely concerned and anxious to help. Alan asked him if he had any news on the progress of the Romanian law and it transpired that Bob had seen Ion Mazilu that same morning, who had said that a draft proposal was to be discussed by Parliament the following week. We had not realised that Mazilu was still on the scene. Since the days when the Martins had dealt with him, we had been told that he was no longer in charge of adoption. It was good to know he was and better still that things seemed to be moving in the right direction. Our papers would make the diplomatic bag on Thursday and the law was at least drafted.

On Thursday morning, still leaving nothing to chance, Alan telephoned Bob House again. He was not in his office. There had been a burglary at the Embassy overnight and he was with the police. Was this the unexpected event that would stop our papers being put in the diplomatic bag? The girl at the Embassy switchboard did not know, but we began to panic badly. If our papers did not make the diplomatic bag, we would have to wait another whole week and, more importantly, it meant another week for Michael incarcerated in the orphanage, as well as another week of building tension for us. Alan telephoned again half an hour later. 'You're a very nice man, Mr Fowler,' Bob House began, 'but there is no need to keep pestering me. I am doing the best I can.'

'What about our papers, have you received them?'

'Yes, yes,' said Bob, 'I saw Ivan yesterday afternoon. I have to do some work on them but there should be enough time, the bag doesn't go until midday. There would have been no problem at all but for this burglary. I hope I'll find the time, though.'

We sat around in the kitchen staring at one another. 'It's a little boy's life,' I said, 'surely he must realise how important it is.'

We waited until ten-past twelve, Bucharest time. Alan rung again. Mr House was unavailable; he was with the police once more. 'Did our file make the diplomatic bag?' Alan asked, desperately. All the receptionist could tell us was that if Mr House said it would, then it would have done, and with that we had to be satisfied.

On Friday morning, bearing in mind that we still had Ion Mazilu's home telephone number, we decided it might be an idea to hear from the horse's mouth just how advanced the new law really was. Assuming our papers had made the diplomatic bag, and by exerting a great deal of pressure, we reckoned it would be only a week or ten days before we could have entry clearance, which, of course, would be useless to us without an adoption law. We telephoned Ion Mazilu at 5 a.m. British time, 7 a.m. Romanian time. As always he was charming, courteous and very helpful. What he had to tell us, though, threw us into complete and utter panic. Yes, he confirmed, Bob House was right, Parliament would consider the new legislation the following week, but although he hoped the law would be passed, Parliament was due to recess in nine days' time and there might not be time for the matter to be considered when there were so many other important issues to debate. Alan put down the telephone and one look at his face told me things were very wrong. Still reeling from the possibility of missing the diplomatic bag, we were now faced with a far more serious delay. If the law was not passed in this session then it would not be considerd again until September at the very earliest. Shocked and desperate, we sat on the floor in Charlie's room and tried to discuss the problem rationally. Somehow we had to bring pressure to bear on the Romanian Parliament to make sure the adoption bill was included. If we failed then it could well be October before our case was even heard. By October Michael could be dead.

We had a very subdued breakfast with Charlie and when Margaret arrived, we gave him over to her care and sat down and talked the whole thing through again. We needed to create a stink in high places, and we needed to do it fast. We decided it was probably best to start with the press and telephoned Bob Graham of the *Daily Mail*, whose reporting from Romania and involvement in the orphanage problem was well known. We told him what we had heard from Mazilu and, like us, he instinctively trusted the man. 'I tell you what I'll do,' said Bob, 'I'll ring Petra Roman, the Prime Minister, on Monday and see if I can't twist his arm a little. I'm sorry but it's the best I can do.' His best was certainly good enough for us – ringing the Prime Minister of Romania direct had to be a brilliant start.

However, we felt we could not let the matter rest there – it was too important. We needed a diplomatic contact. We telephoned the one or two people we knew who were likely to have some knowledge of diplomatic sources, but without success. Abandoning the diplomatic approach, we tried the political one. We telephoned Suzy Gale. Suzy Gale is married to the MP Roger Gale, and since the story of the Romanian orphanages first broke, she has made it her special task to use her own and her husband's influence in any way she can to help the orphans. She listened to what Alan had to say and confirmed that, as far as she was aware, the possible delay in the new law was news to everyone. Although it was obvious that Parliament had to recess sometime during the summer months, no one had considered the possibility of the adoption law not being passed before it did so. 'Willie Waldegrave is our man on Romania,' she said. 'I think the best thing to do is to write to him, I'll give you his fax number. Send me a copy and I'll see what Roger can do.'

We sat up most of Friday night, composing a letter to William Waldegrave, and faxed it on Saturday morning. 'So,' said Alan, 'we've made a fuss via the press, made a fuss via the politicians – we still have to crack the diplomats in some way.'

Neither of us had any ideas and then, by chance, my mother telephoned during the day to see how things were going. 'Do you remember Kesta George?' she said.

'Yes, I do,' I said, vaguely, 'isn't he a cousin of the Rathcreedans?'
'That's right,' said my mother.

The Rathcreedans are very old friends of ours. I remembered Kesta as being older than me, a teenager when I was a child, a young married man when I was a teenager. It appeared that my mother had discovered he was a civil servant and a high-ranking one at that. He had in fact been Geoffrey Howe's number-one man at the Foreign Office. 'He'll be very busy at the moment, I should think,' said my mother, 'with Geoffrey Howe having just resigned. However, he sounds worth trying. I was talking to Ann Rathcreedan at lunch yesterday and she said that he's had a lot of dealings with Romania, on trade missions, that sort of thing. Why don't you give him a ring?'

We were clutching at straws but this did seem a fairly substantial one. On Saturday evening I telephoned Kesta. He was out but I was told to ring back later and I did. Kesta was not inspired by my story. 'I always have trouble with the Romanians,' he said. 'I know them quite well, I've visited Romania over a number of years. They can be very difficult people to deal with.'

'What can I do?' I wailed. 'We need to bring pressure to bear on the Romanian Parliament. We have the press hassling the Prime Minister, we hope to have William Waldegrave taking some action – .'

'The problem is really a diplomatic one,' Kesta interrupted. 'The Romanians are unlikely to take notice of anyone's entreaties unless they come via the Embassy. The British Ambassador is a man called Michael Atkinson. If I were you I'd write to him and ask him to intervene on your behalf.'

Again, Alan and I sat up late into the night and composed a letter to Michael Atkinson. We looked him up in *Who's Who* to make sure we were spelling his name correctly and giving him the right number of letters after his name. Then we faxed the letter to Bucharest, sending copies to Robin Hoggard, who runs the Romanian desk at the Foreign Office, and, of course, to trusty Bob House. It was only forty-eight hours since we had spoken to Ion Mazilu and when finally we slumped into bed on Sunday night we felt we had at least made a little progress.

On Monday morning we telephoned the Foreign Office and spoke to Robin Hoggard. The news was not good. Michael Atkinson was in England. He had come over for some sort of diplomatic conference and Robin had bumped into him in the corridor a few days earlier. Now, however, he had retired to his home for a few days' leave.

'Can't you arrange for us to meet him?' Alan persisted.

Robin Hoggard was not impressed. 'I'm sorry about the situation in which you find yourself, but there's nothing I can do.'

'Who's in charge while Michael Atkinson's away?' Alan asked.

'Tony Godson,' was the reply. We faxed Tony Godson.

In the midst of all our own struggles, we had thought very little of Kerry and Karen, not because we did not care, but there simply had not been the time. Now we learnt their troubles had come to an abrupt and happy end. After much haggling, Kerry had finally sweet-talked Daniella into relaxing her attitude and both Alexander and Emily had been given passports. For Karen and Alan it was the end of their saga, for they did not need any other documentation to take their new little daughter into the States. They had flown out immediately, but not before making Adrian an offer he could hardly refuse. Alan ran his own business and was so grateful to Adrian for being instrumental in finally releasing them all from the deadlock that he had offered him a job in his company. He suggested that as soon as visas were available Adrian, Marianna and Irena should visit America, and that he would pay for them to do so.

Kerry, Steven and Alexander's route home was not quite so simple. They arrived at Heathrow without entry clearance, for their Social Services home study was not yet completed. They had a very uncomfortable half-hour at Heathrow before being let in, were told that they would be reported to the Home Office and that Alexander would only be granted a three-month visa. Still, they were home. On Monday afternoon Locket and I went to visit them. The tired, strained look had left Kerry and Alexander was clearly thriving – a big, bouncing, bonny boy already.

'Oh, I've had some nice news, today,' Kerry said cheerfully, unaware of the bombshell she was about to deliver. 'Karen rang – Alan's managed to rush through a visa for Adrian and Marianna. They are due to fly out to the States for a holiday on 4 August.'

I stared at her, horrified. 'Adrian and Marianna are going to the States in a fortnight! What about Michael?'

'Oh God,' said Kerry, 'I hadn't thought of that. Hasn't Adrian told you?'

'No.'

'He should have done,' said Kerry, 'or at least he should have told me to tell you about it. I spoke to him last night because he's supposed to be finding Alex's birth certificate for me. He told me all about it then. Oh, incidentally, there is a message for you – he says Michael has very bad diarrhoea again and he needs some more Dioralyte.'

I drove home in a daze. What would happen to Michael on 4 August? How bad was his diarrhoea? And what on earth would we do if the new law was not passed in time? Michael was accustomed, now, to two square meals a day – he could not suddenly be deprived of them. I would have to go out there. Maybe Ivan could fix it so that Michael could live in a hotel with me. Perhaps we should simply kidnap him. I arrived home tense, miserable and desperate.

That night we telephoned Adrian and he confirmed that yes, he and his family were going to go to America but the date was not yet fixed. He also confirmed that Michael was not too well but that Marianna was looking after him and we should not worry. We worried.

The following day, Tuesday, 24 July, we tried to put the new law out of our minds for the moment and concentrate on entry clearance. We had made an appointment at the Home Office in Croydon to see Mike Line, the man in charge of foreign adoption. He had a number of queries to go through with us regarding our file, which he had indeed received from Bucharest. Once these were resolved, he said, the file could be passed on to the Department of Health, who would consider it along with the home study report. If they were satisfied, entry clearance would be granted.

Mike Line proved to be much younger than we had expected. The questions he had to ask were straightforward, until it came to the question of Michael's history. While the orphanage had told us that Michael had been in No. 6 from soon after his birth, his mother had told us that he had only been in an orphanage for eight months. When I started to tell Mike Line this he became very grave. 'If the documentation is wrong,' he said, 'we'll have to send it back to Bucharest for verification. We must know his precise background.'

Alan and I stared at one another in horror. 'I think we may have misunderstood the mother's translation,' Alan said, hurriedly. 'Everyone at the orphanage was very sure that Michael had been there since birth. I am sure the documentation is right.'

'Well that's all right then,' said Mike Line.

We breathed a sigh of relief, the catastrophe averted. 'So what happens now?' we asked. The papers were to be passed to a woman called Donna Sidonio at the Department of Health. She would require at least a week to study our papers and if she was satisfied she would advise Mike Line accordingly. 'How?' Alan asked.

'By telephone,' Mike said.

'And then what happens?' we persisted.

'And then I advise the British Embassy to grant you entry clearance.'

'How?' Alan raised his eyes to heaven. 'By diplomatic bag?'

'No, I can telex it,' said Mike.

Things were definitely looking up. 'So would it be reasonable to say that by the end of next week we should have entry clearance?'

'Assuming your papers are in order,' said Mike Line, 'I don't see why not.'

We had done everything we could so far as entry clearance was concerned, but there was no let-up. The following day, Wednesday, was a Tarom flight day, so we went back to Heathrow and, thanks to Radu Grigoriou, general manager of Tarom, we delivered yet another

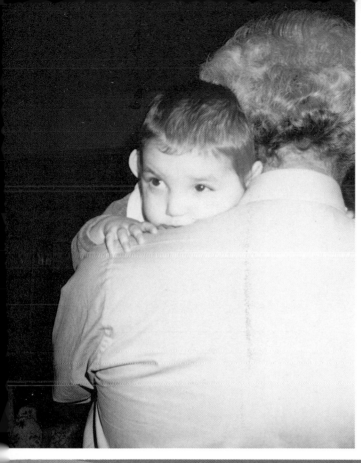

*Alan with Michael
shortly after finding
him* (left)

*In Lenuta's flat – the
bottle of whisky was
the price of a child*
(below)

Michael and Marianna (right)

'Granny', myself and Michael at the orphanage after the accident to his eye (below)

Locket and I introduce Michael and Charlie for the first time (far right)

'Granny', 'Grandpa' and Christie with Charlie and Michael at our farewell party (below right)

Michael's christening
(above)

Michael with Alan –
four months after we
first found him (right)

suitcase full of juice, milk, Dioralyte and dried food for Michael. On our return, Alan made the usual telephone calls – to Robin Hoggard at the Foreign Office, to Bob Graham at the *Daily Mail*, to Suzy Gale and, that night, to Nicolae Ivan. No one had any news; all we could do was to wait. There were just two days left before Parliament was due to recess.

The strain on us as a family was beginning to tell. Alan and I were snapping at each other and were very overtired. Locket, who had enjoyed a brief stay in Cornwall with some close friends of ours, was cheerful enough but she said she found the tension in the house almost unbearable. Charlie was definitely off colour, eating badly and running the occasional temperature. He also was having a pretty lean time of it. Every available minute Alan and I had, we were talking, talking, talking of ways to try and beat the system.

By Friday morning we could stand the suspense no longer and at 5.45 a.m. we telephoned Ion Mazilu again. *The new law had been passed by the Upper House*, we were told. Parliament had delayed recessing for twenty-four hours and as a result the bill should be passed by the Lower House the following day, Saturday, the 28th. Whether our efforts had helped we would never know, but it could not matter less. The new law was all but passed and the relief was enormous. We shed a few tears over our morning tea.

However, we still did not know what the new law meant. Later in the morning we rang Robin Hoggard at the Foreign Office, where he had just received a résumé of the new law via the British Embassy in Bucharest. In the résumé it stated that it was necessary for us to attend the court hearing personally, but if we could not do so, then we would need to give our lawyer power of attorney. We rang Suzy Gale to bring her up to date with the news we had heard from Mazilu, bearing in mind that she was in touch with the many other parents in similar positions to our own. During the afternoon we had a power of attorney typed up and sworn, and that night we rang Ivan to see what news he had. He confirmed that the new law was through, but the news was not good. The timetable for the court process was at least six weeks: fifteen days to obtain a hearing, another ten days for a second hearing and at least another fifteen days after the hearing before judgement could be finalised. He felt that in our case it might be possible to reduce the time to four weeks for two reasons. Firstly, our original papers had been prepared under the requirements of the old law and therefore it would appear to the authorities that we had been waiting for some considerable time for the new law to be published. Secondly, Michael was ill and in danger of not living long enough to be adopted. This short cut was good news but the problem was that Ivan did not know when the four weeks could begin because at the moment the law had yet to be published. He also said he did not need power of attorney, maintaining that the British Embassy had things wrong, again.

Our elation of earlier in the day evaporated. Six weeks is not a long time in ordinary circumstances, but in our case such a delay could prove fatal for Michael. The threat of Adrian and Marianna leaving the country and the prospect of Michael without care for weeks on end did not bear thinking of – we could not allow that to happen. We spent Saturday and Sunday faxing everyone again – Tony Godson, with a copy to Bob House, begging him to do something; William Waldegrave; Bob Graham; Suzy Gale. By Sunday night we were exhausted and we appeared to have got nowhere. We telephoned Adrian and, somewhat reluctantly, when cross-examined by a tired, tetchy Alan, he confirmed that he, Marianna and Irena would be going to New York on 4 August, but that we were not to worry for Marianna's mother would look after Michael. We could not understand why it was so difficult to drag this information out of Adrian. Did it mean he had not really made any plans for Michael?

By the time Alan had finished speaking to Adrian I was climbing the walls. I had never met Marianna's mother, although Alan had. He assured me that she was a dear old girl. She spoke no English so he had not been able to speak to her directly, but he felt sure she was the sort of person who would take her responsibilities towards Michael seriously. Still, of course, he could not be sure and neither could I. All I knew was that Michael was becoming used to a level of care which must continue. 'Law or no law,' I said to Alan, 'I shall have to go out there and meet Marianna's mother for myself and make sure that everything's all right. Damn Adrian – why did he have to go now?'

'Let's talk to Margaret in the morning,' said Alan. 'I think we should probably both go.'

The usual telephone calls on Monday, 30 July, confirmed that there had been no movement over the weekend, though everyone was saying that the court procedure was going to be a lengthy one and that there was no telling when the courts would be ready to start dealing with adoption cases. In any event, everyone was talking in terms of weeks and possibly months, certainly not days. We started trying to think of alternatives. Could Ivan fix it so that we could take Michael out of the orphanage? Could we take the whole family, including Michael, to the Carparthian Mountains for an indefinite holiday? Could we take Michael out of the country without his being legally adopted? Our ideas became more and more drastic as we talked. In most European countries, taking Locket and Charlie on an extended holiday would have presented no problem at all, in fact quite the contrary, it would have been fun. Fun is in short supply in Romania, like everything else. With Charlie eighteen months old and Michael two, it was hard to see how we would cope. The drinking water was downright dangerous and bottled water often not available. The food was out of the question, and nappies, washing powder, creams, medications – none of the normal baby paraphernalia was available in the shops. We would have to take everything with us, including all their food. Still, on one point we were sure: somehow we had to find a way of shortening the time Michael had to spend in the orphanage. We had to do *something*.

On Monday afternoon we had some very cheering light relief, in the form of the arrival of the Rigbys. We have known Sally and Steve Rigby for many years. He is headmaster of a boys' prep school in Sussex, and they have four small children. They are very warm people and having them to stay was like suddenly being enveloped in a great big hug. We realised, suddenly, that we had become very isolated. Our social life had ground to a halt and neither of us had been working properly for weeks. Freeing Michael from the orphanage had become all-consuming. To have the diversion of the children during the day and Sally and Steve's very real interest and concern at night was a wonderful relief.

Charlie, though, was still far from well. He ran a very high fever all during Monday and in the afternoon I took him to the doctor. He could find nothing obviously wrong with him and allayed my worry that the unexplained fever could be meningitis. Although I was reassured up to a point, I could not help feeling that there was something really wrong with him, not just one of the normal childhood complaints. But, by the following morning he seemed a little perkier and my fears appeared groundless. I put my feelings down to the general nervous, neurotic state we were now in.

On Tuesday, while breakfasting with the Rigbys, we made our decision. Having consulted Margaret, we had decided we would go out to Bucharest the following weekend, the same way as we had before. Alan would go on Saturday, 4 August, in order to see Marianna before she and Adrian left for the States, and I would leave on Sunday, so that we could spend a couple of days seeing how Michael fared and making sure that 'Granny', as we now called her, was giving Michael the right level of care. There was also another train of thought in our minds. Perhaps if we were in Bucharest we could find some way of speeding up the adoption process. By the time we got out there, it looked almost certain that we could have entry clearance, so that the British end of the initial adoption process would be complete. Maybe we could get our papers signed in the old way, or maybe we could find a way of circumventing the legal system.

We were beginning to feel desperate. Another call to Adrian had revealed that Michael'a diarrhoea was now acute, and he was on penicillin following a bout of fever. This time even Adrian sounded worried. Hour after hour, Alan and I agonised over what to do for the best and over the telephone we tried out our various theories on Ivan. He was not too helpful. He understood us wanting to come to Bucharest to check up on Michael's wellbeing as Adrian and Marianna were going to America, but he maintained that it was pointless to imagine we could make any progress with the Romanian law – we simply had to wait for it to take its course. As for taking Michael out of the orphanage, it was impossible.

We spent Tuesday fretting and fuming with the poor Rigbys, but we did have a call from the Department of Health to say that they had passed our file. As far as they were concerned, they were happy for us to adopt Michael and it was now up to Mike Line to authorise Michael's entry clearance.

That afternoon, Alan managed to get through to the British Embassy in Bucharest once more and this time spoke to Tony Godson, the chargé d'affaires. He confirmed that there had been very high-level discussions the previous week with the Ministry of Justice about all the couples like ourselves who had originally prepared files for the old system of adoption and were now faced with long delays while the new law was brought into effect. What Tony Godson had been hoping to achieve was special dispensation for what he believed to be about eleven British couples who either had, or were about to have, entry clearance, and whose adoptions were being delayed because of the lack of any law. It was a frustrating conversation because while it was obvious that the British Embassy was aware of the problem and had discussed it, no solution had been found. The so-called high-level discussions appeared fruitless.

On Wednesday we said goodbye to the Rigbys, and Alan was preparing for another day of telephoning everyone, when something nice happened. My stepson, Lorne, telephoned to say that he and his wife Geraldine's first child had been born – Leo Mackillop, weighing just over eight pounds and hale and hearty. Lorne sounded very tearful but over the moon and we arranged for Locket and I to go up to London the following day to see the baby.

Having allowed ourselves a small celebration, we started telephoning again that afternoon. We decided that we would try to see Tony Godson himself on Monday, our first day together in Bucharest, and Alan managed to arrange an appointment with his secretary and faxed confirmation of our arrival. Since, according to Ivan, the British Embassy was very unfriendly to Romanian lawyers, we also arranged that we would pick up our entry clearance from the Embassy on the same day, and deliver it to Ivan in person so that there would be no room for error. We also decided that while in Bucharest we would check on the progress of Christina-Daniella's adoption, and if there was time, check on Mirella, too.

Bob Graham telephoned us rather belatedly, but understandably so. He had been out of the office covering the IRA assassination of the MP, Ian Gow. He told us that he had made contact with Petra Roman and there appeared to be nothing that could be done to speed up the law. He felt it was important that we should apply no more media pressure as it might prove counter-productive.

In the evening, Alan telephoned the Cavills in Bucharest. Miranda, her two sons and English husband, Brian, were all still out there, staying with Miranda's mother. When they heard we were both coming out, they invited us to dinner on the Monday evening, and in the meantime Miranda said she would find out what she could about the law and its likely publication date. The family was very much part of the original aristocracy of Romania, and she assured us that both she and, in particular, her mother had friends in high places and it was still possible that they might be able to help. This seemed to be the first piece of cheering news we had had in a long time and we were very grateful.

On Thursday, 2 August, a blisteringly hot day, Locket and I made the trek to South London to see Leo, now twenty-four hours old. We found Leo and Geraldine after a lengthy tramp through seemingly endless hospital corridors. Leo looked exactly like his father, a true Mackillop, with a large nose and a wide mouth, and was very alert, hungry and looking more like thirty-five than one day old. We left the hospital in good spirits. Lorne and Geraldine had been desperate for a child. Geraldine was in her forties and had suffered two miscarriages so things had not been easy for them. It was lovely that their story had a happy ending. When we reached home, however, Alan met us at the front door looking very glum. Shortly after we had left, Leo had started to have breathing difficulties and he had been rushed to intensive care. At the moment they did not know what was wrong with him, but assumed it was some kind of infection. Lorne would keep us informed. On top of our own dramas, this seemed to be the final straw, but worse was to follow.

The following morning I had a frantic telephone call from Jo Leeman. Jo and I had never met – indeed, we still have not, but I feel I know her as well as I know anyone. Suzy Gale had put us in touch some weeks previously, because she and her husband were adopting a baby boy from an orphanage some sixty miles from Bucharest and were at exactly the same stage as we were. They had entry clearance and their file prepared, but were in the same hopeless state of flux because there was no law. Night after night she and I had talked on the telephone, often for half an hour or more, and our conversations had been enormously therapeutic for both of us. We were all starting to think that we were going mad – we could not sleep, we could not eat, we could not concentrate on our work. It was oddly comforting to find that Jo and her husband, Brian, were going through exactly the same feelings as we ourselves were. On that particular morning of 3 August, Jo broke her normal pattern of ringing us at night to say that she had received a fax from the Foreign Office in response to one that she and her husband had sent. According to the Foreign Office, no law had yet been passed and if this was so, with Parliament recessed, there was of course no hope of it being passed.

Alan and I panicked badly. 'It can't be right,' he said.

'But if the Foreign Office says so, it must be right,' I said. 'Let's phone Ivan.'

Again we broke our normal habit and telephoned Ivan during the day; luckily we caught him at home. 'As I told you, the law has been passed,' he assured us, 'it just has not yet been published.' It was difficult to know who to believe. We wanted to trust Ivan but we knew so little about him. Surely it was not possible that he was right and the Foreign Office wrong? The only way we were going to find out was to go to Romania ourselves, and that we were doing.

It was only six weeks since we had made our first trip to Romania together, but it seemed like a lifetime. We seemed such innocents the last time we had gone, so unprepared, not only for the enormous bureaucratic difficulties but also for the emotional strain of having made a commitment to a child and then not being able to do anything about it. On a purely personal level I felt I was letting down Michael's mother as well as Michael. Forget for a moment the Romanian or British laws for adoption – in simple terms Michael's mother had said that she could no longer care for her son and wished me to do so. She had handed over the responsibility of his well-being to me. It might sound crazy now, given that it was Lenuta who had put Michael in an orphanage in the first place, but that was how I felt. Michael was sick, slowly dying by degrees, and I seemed powerless to help. Yes, we were doing what we could in sending out regular supplies of food, clothes and nappies, but the fact was that six weeks after Lenuta handed over moral responsibility to us, her son was still living in the horrendous conditions of the orphanage, still the likely prey of a long catalogue of diseases, still the possible victim of a dirty needle. There was a heatwave in Bucharest and a water shortage. It was impossible to keep him cool and even slightly comfortable, Marianna had told us. The children in the orphanage as a whole were chronically dehydrated. It was crazy, inhuman, that Michael should be suffering so much while we were forced to stand by and watch, and with a few rare exceptions, such as Jane Allan, the bureaucrats simply did not seem to care. I remember during this period talking to a spokesman at the Foreign

Office one day and being given the usual platitudes. At one point I was told that, really, the Fowlers were becoming a nuisance. 'What kind of childhood did you have?' I remember screaming down the phone. The official had been amazed at my lack of control and had said so. Talking to these sort of people was worse than useless, and still Michael was incarcerated in the orphanage.

Meanwhile, Leo was very ill. He had been christened at the Brompton Hospital before undergoing major surgery. He had a blocked aorta and it was touch and go. Two little boys, in very different circumstances, yet both fighting for their lives. The night Leo lay in intensive care, wired up to every possible machine following his operation, Alan and I mistakenly watched a television programme on the orphanage problem in Romania. They showed Orphanage No. 4 briefly, and too much of the now familiar conditions. After it was over Alan and I lay in the dark holding hands and wept for Michael, for Leo . . . 'Suffer the little children' had a new interpretation for us that night.

While we were away, we had arranged that Locket should stay with a school friend, Jemma Cooke. The family live near Chinnor and I knew she would be well looked after by them. We had promised her that, as and when we were able to bring Michael home, she could come out to Bucharest again to collect him. Apart from the question of expense, we also felt that another trip to the orphanage which did not result in Michael being allowed out would be very harrowing for her. Yet it worried me leaving her, with Leo so ill and us so far away. I was still worried, too, about Charlie. He was not right. His temperature had gone but he was still not eating properly and he had a pale, wistful look about him. I blamed myself, of course, as mothers do. There had not been a good atmosphere in the house for weeks, maybe that was what was wrong with him, that and the fact that this time he clearly knew we were going away and was very clingy.

As before, Alan left on Saturday. This time we agreed that he would not telephone me. When he arrived in Bucharest he was going to spend all the available time with Marianna, Adrian, and, hopefully, Marianna's mother. Adrian and Marianna were flying out to America at five o'clock the following morning. On Sunday, I followed exactly the same procedure as I had done six weeks before, only this time I did not have Locket with me. Margaret and her family arrived early in the morning, as did Russell to take me to the airport. This time I carried only hand luggage. It was as well because when I arrived, there were terrible delays. Three days previously Saddam Hussein had invaded Kuwait and terrorist attacks on the airport were now feared. It took me an hour and a half to get through passport control and the plane was delayed by four hours. Still, when finally we did take off, with my worries about Charlie and Locket temporarily set aside, I tried to think constructively. We had an appointment with the chargé d'affaires at the Embassy, we had entry clearance and we had three days in Bucharest to make sure that Michael was being properly looked after and to do whatever we possibly could to try and push through our adoption papers.

As the plane began its descent to Bucharest Airport, we were handed our immigration cards. There was a box on the form to be ticked if the passenger was accompanied by a child. I ticked it, believing it was unlikely that anybody would check the form on the way in. It was a mad impulse, but if I had come into the country with a child then it was reasonable I should take one out. It was an idiotic idea, but not impossible to imagine – me bringing Michael out on my passport, masquerading as Charlie. Crazy but worth trying just in case. Everything was worth trying when time was running out.

10
DESPERATE DAYS

AT seven-thirty the following morning Ivan was his usual energetic self, dressed informally in a short-sleeved, open-neck shirt, rather lurid check trousers and the inevitable sailing shoes. We had arranged to meet him in the lobby of the Inter-Continental Hotel, to discuss tactics. He had with him a copy of the law, as yet unpublished, and he read through each clause with us, explaining it carefully and well. It was clear that the whole process took at least six weeks from start to finish, although Ivan did seem genuinely confident that he could reduce this to four or five weeks. There was one aspect which worried him, though. Under the new law the case would be heard in a different sector of the city. Our medical report had been prepared under Sector 2, the sector in which Orphanage No. 4 is situated, as had the checking, stamping and approval of our home study report. Ivan was in some doubt as to whether the court would accept this and felt they might ask for the new sector to recheck it.

'Shouldn't we get the new sector to recheck it in any event,' Alan asked. 'while we're waiting for the law?'

Ivan shook his head. 'We don't want to look for trouble.'

We told him about our appointment that afternoon with Tony Godson and he was clearly impressed. 'We're hoping we might be able to speed our case through in some way,' I said, 'and we wondered whether we could borrow our file.'

'Of course, of course,' said Ivan, and handed it to us. 'You won't be able to hurry things any more though.' He smiled at Alan. 'You're a very nice man, Mr Fowler, but you're too impatient.' It was becoming a family slogan: 'You're a very nice man, Mr Fowler, but...' Ivan must have wondered at our laughter, but he laughed, too. 'I wish you luck,' he said. 'You will not be able to do anything, but why not try?' He shrugged. 'Who knows, maybe you will be successful, let us hope so.' We blinked and he had gone.

With Adrian on his way to America we had lost our transport, but he had not forgotten us and had arranged for his cousin, Christie, an

out-of-work engineer and part-time driver, to look after us. Christie
was a short, plump man with fair hair and a growth on his face
somewhere between a beard and designer stubble. He did not have
Adrian's charisma, nor his command of English, but he was a pleasant
man and anxious to help. Alan had found him as punctual and as
reliable as Adrian had been the previous day, when he had been alone
in Bucharest. After Ivan had left, Christie arrived and took us to
Marianna and Adrian's flat, where Granny was waiting for us. We
hugged each other spontaneously – she had the same outgoing warmth
as her daughter – and Alan unloaded a suitcase full of presents and
food for her and more equipment for Michael. In one of our previous
cases of supplies we had sent a cool bag and this she now stacked with
food and drink for Michael. Her husband appeared, a delightful man
– indeed, they were a delightful couple – kind, caring and with a lovely
sense of humour. With Christie interpreting and with many gestures,
we communicated well.

After half an hour or so, I could stand it no more and begged to go
to the orphanage. Christie drove us there and once more we made the
trek down the concrete path, past the hens and the cots, and up the
gloomy stairs to reception. It was bedlam. Next door to reception, a
great many little children were sitting on pots, screaming, and another
gang was outside on one of the balconies. The principal greeted us, her
eye on the bag we were carrying. She immediately became vivacious
once Alan handed it over, full as it was with cigarettes, whisky,
perfume and soap. She disappeared into her office and shut the door,
obviously to examine her spoils.

As we were waiting, I had a fleeting glimpse of a child being carried
past with blood all over its face. 'That looks like Michael,' I said,
nervously.

Alan shook his head. 'Calm down – I'm sure it wasn't.'

We waited. Granny had handed over a packet of cigarettes to one
of the nurses to go and fetch Michael but nothing happened. 'Where
is he?' I said, increasingly anxious.

Christie knocked on the principal's door and asked if she could
speed things up for us. There was a lot of discussion going on amongst
the nurses. I knew something was wrong. Christie came back looking
grim-faced. 'He's had an accident.'

'What's happened?' Alan and I chorused.

'I don't know. They say they're bringing him to us now, they just
had to clean him first.'

Alan and I looked at each other in horror. 'That was him with all
the blood,' I whispered, 'I knew it was.' I felt a sense of protection
towards Michael rise in me with such intensity that it was almost
frightening. I wanted to knock these people aside to get to him, to get

to my child. Yes, my child. He was mine now, at a moment like this there was no doubt.

There was a commotion at the door and Michael was brought in. He was deathly pale, his skin slightly greenish, and blood was pouring from an enormous gash above his right eyelid. The cut had missed his eye by literally a hair's breadth. He was screaming. The principal bustled forward, snatched him from the nurse and carried him into her office. With one hand she fumbled in a drawer and pulled out a brown bottle. Someone produced some cotton wool. With horror I saw it was iodine. She began dabbing the neat iodine on to the open wound, some of it spilling into his eye. I screamed at them: 'Leave him alone, let me hold him.'

'No, no.' They continued the process and then somebody produced a piece of plaster and jammed it over the cut, half covering his eye and catching his eyelashes in the sticky tape.

I snatched him from them. 'It's all right, Michael,' I whispered in his ear as he clung to me, his sobs shaking his whole, tiny body. I rushed out of the office and into the reception room. Granny was sitting there, her eyes wide and tearful. There was a couple, who, I learnt later, were French, sitting on the sofa cradling two tiny children. The woman jumped to her feet and held out a rusk. I gave it to Michael – he was clearly ravenously hungry. He took several quick bites, choking over them. His eyes were streaming, his nose was streaming, he could not catch his breath. 'Let's get outside,' I said, shakily.

In the garden, his sobs slowly began to subside. Granny prepared a drink for him and we sat him in one of the rusty old swing seats where apparently Marianna always used to feed him. I held his hand and we offered him a drink. He had three mugfuls, whimpering pitifully between each one as we refilled it.

This was the lowest point at which I have ever seen him, and, please, God, ever will. I believe at that moment he was close to giving up. When Granny began to offer him food, although he wanted and needed it, he was at first reluctant to eat. In the end I sat him on my lap, and stroking and coaxing him he began to relax until eventually he enjoyed quite a good meal. I managed to readjust the bandage to release his eyelashes. The blood was thickly clogged under the plaster. It was a deep cut and the scar is there still. It always will be.

Christie came bustling up. He had stayed behind to find out what had happened. Apparently Michael, in an effort to walk, had stumbled into an old iron cot which had a sharp edge. There had been several accidents in the last week, he said, because they were so short-staffed. A little girl was feared brain-damaged after falling over backwards and cracking open her head. She had nearly died. Another child had broken his leg. I clutched Michael to me, we *had* to get him out.

Once he had eaten his fill and had begun to cheer up a little, I had a chance to look at him properly for the first time. Certainly he had put on a considerable amount of weight since I had seen him last. It gave him a rather comical appearance, for while the top half of his body was now quite sturdy, his legs were still tiny and wasted – little more than a newborn baby's. His face was covered in mosquito bites, some of which had gone septic, and the sores on the back of his head were, if anything, worse. There was also a deep, agonising sore on his back, just below his nappy line, and the whole of the nappy area was red raw. I found to my surprise, when talking to Granny via Christie, that Marianna had used none of the Sudacrem that I had given her. I explained to Granny the importance of it and so together we plastered it all over Michael's face, the back of his head and his bottom. He did not cry at all, seeming to recognise that we were trying to help him. He was wearing no nappy, just a pair of stained pants. We put on a disposable nappy and one of the little cotton vests. Granny explained that every time she put any clothes on Michael they disappeared. 'When we come back this afternoon to give Michael his tea,' Christie said, 'the vest will have gone and he will be back in his orphanage clothes.' This proved to be the case and, unbelievably shocking though this may seem, stealing from an abandoned child did not feel out of place here.

I had guessed at Michael's shoe size and brought out a little pair of canvas shoes. Amazingly they fitted. We popped them on his feet, for the garden was littered with broken glass – Alan had even found an old syringe under one of the swings – and Alan and I crouched down a few feet apart while Michael took a few faltering steps between us, laughing as he did so, his spirits restored. We did this for a little while, not wishing to tire him, and then carried him about the garden, singing to him, cuddling him, bringing him as much comfort as we could. He was obviously very fond of Alan and clearly remembered him from the previous visits. With me he was a little more wary, but friendly nonetheless.

It was because Michael and I had some catching up to do that Alan suggested he helped Granny clear up while we spent a little time on our own. I carried him down the garden and we sat under an old bush in the shade. I pulled some leaves from the bush and he began to play with them. I started singing nursery rhymes to him and he turned and smiled. I kissed him and he snuggled closer to me. It felt right, good, like it was supposed to be.

Alan and Granny were in sight across the other side of the garden and, as they put the last things back in the bag, four pitifully skinny little boys came running out from behind one of the bushes. It is always difficult with Romanian children in these circumstances to tell their age, but they looked about three or four. They ran up to Alan and Granny, hands outstretched. I knew there were just two rusks left in the bag. I saw Alan take them out and divide them carefully in half, giving a piece to each child. They received them with squeals of delight and crammed them into their mouths. One of the little boys began running in our direction and, as he did so, a fifth child appeared from nowhere. My heart sank because I knew we had nothing for him. He ran up to the child approaching us, obviously his friend. The two stopped, eyed one another, and the boy without the rusk stretched out a hand. The tension between them was tangible. The little boy with the rusk suddenly took one quick bite, then took the rusk from his mouth and handed it to his friend, who demolished it in one go. Then together they ambled off in broken shoes, kicking aside the pieces of broken glass and rubbish as they went. If God was anywhere in Orphanage No. 4 that day, he was holding the hand of the starving child who shared his rusk with his friend.

Leaving Michael that morning was not too painful, despite the awful start to the day, for we knew we would be seeing him again later. Granny said she would stay with him in the garden for another hour while we returned to the hotel with Christie, and we arranged that we would pick her up again at five to six, so that we could spend between six and seven with Michael, which was when she gave him tea.

Christie drove us back to our hotel, which was now the Inter-Continental. The trip Alan had made on his own to Bucharest had confirmed that the Hotel Bucuresti was just too gruesome and although the Inter-Continental was of a somewhat different standard to other Inter-Continentals around the world, it was a big step up from the Bucuresti – there was real food for a start. For lunch that day we went to a restaurant on the twenty-first floor, and had as near a normal meal as we ever had in Bucharest, washed down with a bottle of decent wine. During lunch we talked exclusively about Michael and Charlie. Bearing in mind that the Inter-Continental was almost civilised, we began to wonder whether it would be possible to bring Charlie with us when we came to collect Michael. It had to be better for the boys to meet on neutral ground. We were feeling fairly optimistic – we had the file, we were due to be at the Embassy at two thirty, and although we were upset by Michael's fall in the morning, at least we now both felt happy about Granny and her ability to offer Michael the same sort of care which Marianna had given him.

We presented ourselves at the front entrance of the British Embassy on time, and were shown into the main reception area, which is very different from the back door we had used before. This is what a British Embassy should look like: deep-pile carpet, expensive sofas, glass tables, marble ashtrays, several good paintings of English landscapes, and a number of plants which were quite definitely alive and flourishing. After a wait of about ten minutes, we were shown upstairs into the holy of holies, the British Ambassador's office. Tony Godson proved to be a pleasant enough man and willing to help, but it was immediately apparent that there was nothing he could do. Again, he told us there had been high-level talks with the Ministry of Justice and that a number of names of couples had been put forward for priority treatment. When we asked to see the list of the names, it transpired that ours was not included because although entry clearance had been recommended, the British Embassy in Bucharest had not been notified in time to include us on the list. This in itself was not too worrying, since clearly no progress had been made with the Ministry of Justice – whether we were on the list or not was hardly relevant. Tony Godson was very courteous, gave us the usual twenty-minute audience and then told us that he would pass us on to Bob House, who would give us our entry clearance. As we were leaving, we asked him whether he would mind if we approached the Ministry of Justice directly. We explained about Michael's accident and said we felt it was imperative to do something quickly. He said that this would be perfectly acceptable and Bob House would give us the name of the contact there.

Although we had an appointment with him, Bob House was out and so we sat on and on in reception, growing increasingly depressed by the fact that the meeting with Tony Godson had not lived up to our expectations. At last we overheard the receptionist telling someone on the telephone that Bob House had gone out for the rest of the afternoon. When we queried this with her, she confirmed that this was the case. With time so precious, this was desperate news and we had just arranged with the receptionist that she should ring us first thing in the morning when Bob suddenly walked through the front door. He was exactly how we had imagined him, breezy, energetic and obviously anxious to help. He led us into his office and we explained that our main purpose for seeing him was to obtain our entry clearance and give it to our lawyer. He said he would go and fetch it, having checked first that it was not on his desk. He came back fifteen minutes later, looking worried. He said everybody had checked but the entry clearance had not been received. Alan freaked, we both did. 'Can we telephone Mike Line at the Home Office then?' Alan asked. 'He promised us it would be here.'

Bob House looked doubtful. 'It means booking an international call. It will take at least two or three hours to come through.' Something about our sheer desperation must have got through to him. 'Look,' he said, 'I'll go back upstairs and have a thorough check – maybe somebody missed it.' An agonising twenty minutes later he returned with a triumphant smile. 'It came in over the weekend,' he said, 'and was filed by mistake. It's being typed up for my signature now. Don't worry, everything's all right.'

The relief was enormous. Having thought we had completely buttoned up the British end, this final trauma would have been just too much. While we waited for the letter to be typed Alan told Bob about our meeting with Tony Godson. Bob grinned. 'I understand your frustration,' he said. 'You're a very nice man, Mr Fowler, but do me a favour, don't send any more faxes to Tony Godson with a copy for me. The name of Fowler is becoming too well known in this embassy.'

'Good,' said Alan, unrepentant.

We asked him then about their contact at the Ministry of Justice, and checking his file he gave us the name of Dinu Ianculescu. 'He's head of the Ministry of Justice for Foreign Affairs – a pleasant chap. I can't honestly see you getting anywhere with him, though – we didn't. Still, there's no harm in you trying. After all, you've worn us down with your persistence.' I suspect he was sorely tempted to substitute the words nuisance value.

With the various delays, we had spent three and a half hours at the embassy by the time we left and had to race across town in order to pick up Granny. At the orphanage Michael looked a lot better – they had removed his plaster and although the wound was deep it did not, at any rate as yet, look infected. As Granny had predicted, the clothes we had dressed him in that morning had disappeared, even down to the nappy. We fed him, changed him and applied more cream to his sores. Already it seemed to us they were looking better.

As we sat in the garden, a group of small children came out on to one of the balconies above us. It was the same group we had seen earlier in the day sitting on their potties. Although they had been pitifully thin and covered in sores, they had all seemed quite jolly then. Not so now. It was evening, bedtime. They were all stark naked, presumably waiting to be dressed. They were tired, probably hungry and thirsty, and there was no one to comfort them, no one to read to them, no mother's goodnight kiss for them. They wandered about aimlessly, some crying, some not even seeming to have the strength to protest. Several attached themselves to the balcony railings and rocked to and fro, or repeatedly banged their heads against the metalwork. It was agony to watch. I glanced at Granny, who was hurriedly mopping her eyes. After a few minutes one of the nurses shouted at them to come inside. Most ambled off; a few stragglers were pulled roughly through the doors. It was a sight which will haunt me always. Every time I put my own children to bed in their cosy rooms, I find it difficult not to think of the misery of those little children.

We were due at the Cavills at eight o'clock and needed to go back to the hotel first for a bath and change, so again we left Michael with

Granny. I felt closer to him that evening – he recognised me and seemed pleased to see me – and with the entry clearance reverently placed in Alan's briefcase, he felt even more like ours.

The smart residential area of Bucharest takes its street names from the capital cities of the world. The Cavills live in Madrid Street, a pleasant, quiet, leafy street with houses well spaced. The architecture was sufficiently strange to us that it was impossible to tell how old the buildings were, but in the Cavill's case a huge vine with a great, thick trunk clinging to the front of the building, suggested that the house was at least a hundred years old.

The door was opened by Miranda, who Alan now knew well but who I had never met before – a dark, vividly pretty woman who seemed more Italian than Romanian, very excitable, the words tumbling out one over the other. She explained, as she led us upstairs, that this in fact was her mother's house but she and Brian were living there with their two boys during the summer holidays because they were starting a computer business in Romania. They had just returned from the coast that day, having completed some very successful business negotiations, and were in high spirits. We were introduced to the assembled crowd: Brian Cavill, tall, fair, very English, their two boys (obviously very close in age but unrecognisable as brothers since one favoured his mother and the other his father), a man named Barry who was in business with them, and what appeared to be his fifteen-year-old daughter. Drinks had been poured and we had just sat down when Miranda's mother entered. She was known to everyone as Mutti and introduced herself as such. Alan had told me what a charming, warm person she was and I instantly liked her. It was strange to meet in Eastern Europe what I can only describe as an aristocrat. She was a tall woman who held herself beautifully and her voice would have been cultured in any language. She was a part of old Romania, the Romania of between the wars, when for the one period in her history, the country had been allowed to be itself. The house suited Mutti, or at least one day it will – they had only just begun decorating and renovating, there was a great deal still to do, and everything had to be imported.

In describing Mutti as aristocratic, it would be wrong to think of her as being rich. Here, as in every home in Romania, it was clear that both money and the simplest of household goods were in very short supply. Everything was a struggle for the Cavills, though undoubtedly the English connection helped. As a family I instantly admired them for their tenacity and loyalty to their country. Mutti was a widow. It would have been so easy for her to have simply abandoned Romania in favour of a very comfortable old age in the Home Counties with Brian and Miranda. But no, they were trying to do something, start a business, rescue a beautiful old house. They were demonstrating their faith in the freedom being granted to their people under the new regime. Whether that faith was justified is another matter, but their industry was both inspiring and touching.

While Mutti prepared supper, refusing all help, we talked. The Cavills told us about their business, Barry and his daughter talked of their first impressions of Romania, and inevitably the conversation swung to Michael. I was finding the evening difficult, my mind was full of Michael. His accident in the morning had shaken me more than I realised, though it was not so much because he could so easily have lost his sight, which was in itself serious enough. It was his attitude to his injury which I could not bear. I wondered what on earth would have happened if we had not arrived at that moment, how he would have coped. I realised that what I had glimpsed for the first time beneath his brave façade was his vulnerability, how close he was to giving up. We had to help him *now* – there had to be a way.

Alan skilfully directed the conversation towards the problem of the new law and Miranda swiftly delivered a body-blow. She had spoken to a friend in the Government, someone very high up, a colleague of her late father's, and he had told her that no law could be published at the moment because there was no paper in Romania to print it on. We stared at her incredulously. 'I know, I know,' she said, 'it seems crazy but those are the facts. The law has to be printed and circulated to all the judges and law courts around the country. Without paper they can't do it and until it's published, there simply is no law.' This, of course, was more or less what Ivan had told us.

'Oh, for Christ's sake,' said Alan, 'we'll just have to ship out some paper then.'

Miranda stared at him. 'You're serious?'

'Yes, of course I'm serious,' said Alan. 'Michael is in great danger and we're totally committed to him now. I dread to think how much this whole thing has cost us but, frankly, what's the odd ton of paper when we're talking about Michael's life.' The room went very silent.

'It is awful,' Mutti said, into the silence.

Taking the opportunity of having everyone's attention, Alan launched into the story of our visit to the embassy. 'We've been given the name of this man, Ianculescu, he's with the Ministry of Justice. You don't by any chance know him?' He looked at Miranda and Mutti. Both shook their heads.

'I can make some telephone calls,' Mutti said. She disappeared into the corner of the room and began telephoning while we continued to discuss the problem. Mutti suddenly interrupted us. 'I've just remembered, your father's best friend' – she mentioned a name – 'he knew everyone at the Ministry of Justice. You could mention him, Miranda.'

'I'll do that.'

'You mean you'll come with us to see Ianculescu?' Alan asked.

'Of course,' she said.

There was much discussion then about the programme for the following day and it was decided that the best thing we could do was to pick up Miranda at eight o'clock, aiming to be at the Ministry of Justice by about eight fifteen. Miranda had a very important business meeting at noon but we all felt this would give us sufficient time to try and find Dinu Ianculescu and talk to him.

Over dinner, which was delicious, we talked through all the possible arguments we could put forward to Ianculescu if we were lucky enough to be able to see him. Michael's accident would certainly help, as would his general state of health. We decided this was probably our strongest card and we would play it for all it was worth. It suddenly occurred to me that it might help if we could persuade the doctor who had examined Michael – the Cavills' friend, Magdalena Dragon – to say he was very unwell and needed the urgent attention of doctors in England. We telephoned her and, although she was very friendly, she was not prepared to make any such statement, not without examining his eye, and certainly there was no time before the trip to the Ministry of Justice to organise such an examination.

After dinner, during which I suppose we drank a fair amount of wine, we sat down in easy chairs and were offered coffee and brandy. It was then, while we drifted off the subject of Michael and were talking generally about the sad state of Romania, that Miranda and I suddenly found ourselves at loggerheads. She asked us why, since we obviously had come to care about Romania's children, we felt justified in saving just one child. Shouldn't we do more, she asked – why weren't we adopting several children, why didn't we open a home for Romanian children in England, why this, why that? I suppose in my defence I was very tense, but suddenly I could feel myself losing my temper. What was she doing for the orphans of Romania? I asked. She, after all, was Romanian, she had more of a responsibility than we did and, unlike Adrian, she could not make the excuse of not knowing about the children's suffering. She, after all, had access to the world's free press. She was helping in a different way, Miranda insisted in reply. She was starting a business to provide work for people to enable them to keep their children in their homes.

We were bristling with rage at one another. Somewhere in the recesses of my mind I knew I had to be careful, that this woman was the best passport we had for getting Michael out of Romania. Yet I felt her criticisms were so unfair, and I was annoyed with Alan for staying silent and not backing me. He was being sensible – logic should have told me that, but logic played no part here. The subject was too emotive. We continued to argue and just when it looked like things might be about to become seriously out of hand, Mutti suddenly stepped in, reprimanding Miranda sternly, as if she was a small child, and asking her with an amused smile why she herself was not adopting a child – after all she only had two.

The heat went out of the argument. Miranda explained that with her business commitments, two children was the most she felt she could handle. She apologised for her outburst. The danger passed but I was left with a feeling of unease and the realisation I would never understand her – she was so unpredictable, I even wondered whether she would really attend our appointment with the Ministry of Justice by the morning.

My fears were groundless. The following morning Christie picked us up at half-past seven from the hotel and we arrived in Madrid Street at five to eight. Miranda was already waiting for us, dressed in a lovely cream silk suit. She looked good – just right. Her good humour was apparently quite restored and she was clearly spoiling for a fight, but not with me. 'We'll get Michael out,' she said, 'just watch me.'

We drove to the Ministry of Justice, a huge, imposing building, very reminiscent of our own Law Courts. We had a struggle to find the right room but eventually were shown into a large waiting room, furnished with nothing but a huge refectory table, around which were a number of chairs. There were about twenty people from all walks of life waiting to be seen, which was surprising for so early in the morning. There was a board on the wall which indicated that a different Minister of Justice was on duty each day, and on Tuesday it was Ianculescu. We could not believe our luck. On the table there was a piece of paper and as each new person arrived, he or she signed the paper, thus forming a queue. We added our names to the list and sat down to wait.

It soon became clear that the Ministry of Justice dealt with its queries quickly. People were going in and out of the office within five minutes. It also became clear that they were seeing not Ianculescu but a woman, who presumably was his assistant. 'We have to get past her,' Miranda whispered.

Miranda began talking to the other people who were waiting. Next to us sat a man who, it transpired, had just been acquitted of murdering his nephew. He was a wild-looking man with staring eyes and a great bush of hair. He certainly looked like a murderer, but the jury had decided he was innocent. Not so his brother, though, whose son he had been accused of murdering. His brother was harassing him, which was why the man was here to try to take out a court order to stop him.

An old man shuffled up to Miranda, sat down and began a long discussion with her. 'What's the trouble?' I asked.

'It is a boundary dispute,' she said. 'His neighbour has pulled up this old man's vine. The old man says that the vine was on his land, not the neighbour's and that he had no right. The vine produced many grapes and the old man seeks compensation, but he cannot write out his deposition for he does not read or write.'

'Will you do it for him?' I asked.

'Yes, of course, if we have time.'

The old man began dictating to her, and with a stubby pencil, Miranda began writing out the deposition for him. I admired this side of Miranda very much. She looked so out of place in her expensive suit, surrounded by the ordinary working people of Romania, but she did not talk down nor indicate in any way that she considered herself better than them. Quite the contrary, she was one of them and I liked that in her very much.

At last it was our turn. We left the old man, wished him good luck, and went in to see Dinu Ianculescu's assistant. Miranda explained who we were and why we had come. Initially the woman seemed reluctant but Miranda began dropping names and it worked. The old-boy network is alive and well in Romania, as it is everywhere else in the world. In seconds, it seemed, we were shown into Ianculescu's office.

There were three people in the room, including Dinu Ianculescu himself, a kindly, elderly man who incongruously looked not unlike Arthur Askey, with his semi-bald head and large glasses. He shook our hands warmly and seemed pleased to see us, though he could speak no English. With him were another assistant – a tall, thin man, who was equally friendly and spoke quite excellent English – and a secretary, a pretty woman in her mid-thirties. We sat down and began to talk, or rather Miranda talked and we all listened. It was impossible to follow exactly what she said but clearly she began by reminiscing about her father and her father's friends. Ianculescu lit a cigarette and appeared to relax. He was smiling and very affable. Gradually Miranda worked her way round to us and began explaining our problem. The atmosphere in the room changed, and everyone listened to her intently. 'I have told Mr Ianculescu,' she said suddenly to me, 'that Michael is dying, that he requires urgent medical attention, that you must get him out.'

They began to ask questions – when we had first found Michael, why we wanted to adopt him, about our family. We showed them pictures of our house, of Locket, of Charlie and finally, of Michael. The photographs were passed round to everyone, including the secretary, and there was much discussion. What seemed to impress them most was that we had arranged for Michael to be fed and looked after during the adoption process. 'You must care very much for the little boy,' Ianculescu's assistant said to me solemnly.

'We do,' I replied.

They began to talk amongst themselves – the waiting was agony. Alan and I kept looking desperately at Miranda for a translation. She indicated to us to be patient. At last Dinu Ianculescu straightened up and lit another cigarette. He shrugged his shoulders. 'So many children,' he said in English, looking at me. 'French, Italian, American, Canadian, Irish . . .'

I understood his drift. He was saying that there were many families like us, caught up in a system with no law. 'I know you can't help them all however much you might wish to,' I burst out, suddenly, 'but couldn't you help just one little boy?' I raised one finger and then despite my efforts not to make a fool of myself, I burst into tears. 'Sorry,' I muttered.

He stared at me for a very long time, then murmured something under his breath and picked up a clean sheet of paper. He began writing on it, speaking out loud as he did so. 'What's he doing?' Alan asked Miranda.

Miranda repeated the question to Ianculescu. He stopped writing for a moment and spoke to her rapidly, looking at me while he did so. 'What's he saying, Miranda?' I asked, desperately. There was hope in her face, and in Alan's. I was too afraid to hope.

Miranda, too, was close to tears now. 'He says he's preparing the necessary declaration, according to the new law. He says when he has prepared this, he will telephone his friend, who is the head judge of all the judges in Romania. He will try and arrange a court hearing for this afternoon. He asks when you are going home?'

'We were going home tomorrow,' I said.

'He says if you could wait until the weekend, you can take Michael with you.'

I burst into tears afresh. It was incredible, unbelievable . . . to take Michael home by the weekend! 'Tell him, thank you,' I said. 'I don't know how to tell him how grateful we are.'

'He knows,' said Miranda.

'I'm sorry about the tears,' I said.

'It's OK, we all feel the same.'

I looked around and saw that the secretary, too, was crying, as was the assistant. Even Dinu Ianculescu himself had become rather pink and was obviously moved. I looked at Alan, he was shaking his head in disbelief and smiling, but, I suspect, like me afraid to believe it.

It took two and a half hours for the statement to be written out and typed up, during which time we sat on in the tiny office, our minds whirling. After the initial excitement I began to wonder about Locket and Charlie. Would Margaret stay on until the weekend, could Locket stay with the Cookes until then? Could we even get a flight out of Romania on Saturday? Would the paperwork really go through? Long ago, we had realised that nothing in Romania was as straightforward as it seemed. Yet everything did seem to be going according to plan. Halfway through the statement, Ianculescu telephoned his friend. Yes, he would be delighted to handle the case and an appointment was made for two o'clock at the Supreme Court.

As we began to relax a little, I looked around the room, a lawyer's office typical the world over, full of great books and piled high with files. Suddenly, I caught sight of the view from the window: there, in theatrical splendour, filling the entire window, was Ceauşescu's palace. The sun was still rising from behind the palace and, thus backlit, the building looked more like the set of some lavish opera than real life. It was an extraordinary feeling to be sitting in the office of this little man who had given Michael his chance for freedom, watching him as he laboriously wrote out the deposition, and staring out at the palace of the man who had begun it all, who had created the misery, who had put Michael in his stinking cot.

At last the document was completed and signed, and Ianculescu then had a number of instructions for us. We had to find Michael's mother and bring her to the court for two o'clock. On the face of it this did not present a big problem, provided of course that she was in and not at work, but we agreed that this was something we could do.

He then informed us that the moment Michael was adopted he would cease to be a Romanian citizen and that he would have to be put on our passports in order to leave the country. This seemed strange because we knew that he would not be accepted as a British citizen until he had been adopted by us, under UK law, which could not take place until he had been in the country a year. Still, we did not argue with him, the important thing was to find Michael's mother and to be on time for that court hearing.

At last we left Dinu Ianculescu. It is difficult to find the words to thank a man who in all probability has saved the life of your son. We did our best, and I think he knew how much we cared, how grateful we were. I hope so, for we will never forget him – never. Once outside, Miranda began panicking. She had to keep her business appointment, but first we had to go to the Secretariate of the Supreme Court and confirm our appointment for two o'clock. This we did, and then Christie drove back with terrifying speed to Madrid Street. Once there, we had a cup of coffee with Mutti while Christie delivered Miranda to her appointment. She and Brian were seeing round a factory and then going to someone else's offices, but we agreed that we would meet her back at her mother's house at one forty-five sharp. Mutti was kindness itself and told us to bring Michael's mother into the house as soon as we had found her, for coffee or drinks.

It is difficult to explain how we felt at that moment. We were elated, yes, but also in a severe state of shock. Our primary reason for coming out to Romania on this particular trip had been to safeguard Michael's care. We were also determined to try and do something to unlock the apparently hopeless situation of a law that was passed but unpublished. Miraculously, we seemed to have beaten the system, but it just felt too good to be true.

When Christie returned, we drove swiftly to our hotel and asked him to wait in the lobby while we dashed upstairs. We tried to ring Ivan to tell him what had happened and ask whether he would be prepared to attend court with us at two o'clock, but we could get no reply from his home. We telephoned Bob House at the Embassy and asked him about the passport problem. 'It's impossible,' he said firmly, 'for Michael to go on your passport. If you do get a court hearing this afternoon and the adoption of Michael goes through, you will be adopting a Romanian citizen, whatever Ianculescu says, and the Romanians will have to issue a passport.'

Alan and I sat on his bed and talked it through. There was nothing we could do at this stage. If Michael did become stateless, we would have to deal with that as and when it happened. The important thing was to concentrate on the court case. We tried Ivan once more but with no luck, so we went downstairs again and with Christie drove to Lenuta's flat.

We had a great deal of money with us, over one thousand pounds, most of which was for Ivan's fees and expenses, so I stayed in the car with the briefcase while Alan and Christie went upstairs to find Lenuta. I remembered the last time I had sat in the car outside this flat, too frightened to hope that she would give her consent for Michael to be adopted. I felt the same now. What if she was out, would we be able to find her? We had promised Christie $50 if he could find Lenuta in time for the court case and he was determined to do so. He was no Adrian, he was not as clever, as quick-thinking or as authoritative, but he cared about what we were doing, about Michael, I was sure of it. They were back in just a few moments. All was well. Lenuta and her man had been just about to go out – we had caught them with seconds to spare. She had agreed to attend the court case and was on her way downstairs.

On the journey back to Madrid Street, Lenuta and I sat in the back of the car. We exchanged a smile but said nothing to one another – we couldn't, we knew not a single word of each other's language. I studied her surreptitiously as we drove. The tragedy of the circumstances had blinded my powers of observation the first time we met. I saw now that she was a good-looking woman, if a little overweight.

Her dark, curly hair was thick and shiny, she had good skin and huge, brown eyes. I wanted to like her and had wrestled with my feelings a great deal in the weeks since we had found Michael. This woman had given him life, and then she had given him to me. I wanted to be able to say to Michael, 'Your mother is a good woman, a brave woman,' I wanted to put conviction behind those words. It was her good health that upset me. Yes, she was poor and yes, she was living with a sick man whom she probably had to support, but still she was well fed and what I couldn't come to terms with was that, while she ate more than adequately, her children starved. Not once had she asked how Michael was, if he was well, if he was being well cared for. Was she afraid of our answer? Did she really not care one way or the other? Or maybe, to stay sane, she had been forced to put him out of her mind as soon as she had taken the decision to abandon him.

We arrived at Madrid Street in good time, at twenty-five to two. Mutti ushered us in and, as promised, made some coffee. She offered Michael's mother a cigarette, which she accepted, and we sat round the table, making polite conversation. Lenuta was obviously impressed with Madrid Street. She kept looking around her in apparent wonder. She asked if she could go to the loo, which I suspect was so she could have a look at the rest of the house. We sat on. It was a quarter to two and Alan and I began to be anxious.

'Do not worry,' said Mutti, 'Miranda knows how important this is, she'll be here in a moment.' She wasn't. It was ten to two.

'It will take us ten minutes to get to the court. I think we should go without her,' said Christie.

'But how can we, we don't know where to go?' I said.

'We know it's the Supreme Court,' said Alan, 'but we don't know the name of the judge.' Although the judge's name had been mentioned at the meeting, it had been Miranda who had written it down, Miranda who had the name of the court, indeed all the details.

We began urgently discussing every possibility. Christie could drive round to where he had dropped Miranda but as we already knew, she and Brian were moving on from there to another meeting place so there seemed little point. Mutti made a few phone calls, to people she thought they might be seeing but nobody knew where they were. Five to, still nothing. We all trooped downstairs, out of the cool of the old house and into the heat. Alan ran to one end of the street, I to the other, hoping to see Miranda along our way. Nothing ... Two o'clock. 'What do we do?' we asked each other desperately.

'We should go,' said Christie. 'We'll go to the court, we can manage without this Miranda. You have the papers, your file?'

'Yes,' said Alan, 'but we don't know where to go, Christie.'

'Don't worry, I will find it.'

It was twenty-past two by the time we reached the Supreme Court. Alan and I were numb, we just could not believe this was happening. How could Miranda have let us down? We had left a very worried Mutti – she could not understand how her daughter could have been deliberately late for something so important and was sure she must have had an accident. Christie made inquiries at the information desk at the Supreme Court. He queued like everyone else, as the minutes ticked by. Adrian would have simply walked to the front of the queue and we would have been on our way in seconds. 'I know where to go,' Christie said at last, in triumph.

We followed Christie at a run up the stairs, myself, Alan and Lenuta. She had smiled sympathetically at us. She seemed calm, relaxed and apparently happy about what we were trying to do. Leaving Lenuta and me outside, Alan and Christie went through a door into the reception area for the various courts. It was an enormous building, with people milling about, and Lenuta and I stationed ourselves at the top of the stairs so we could see Miranda if she arrived. It was our one hope that, having realised how late she was, Miranda would have gone directly to the court.

Alan emerged five minutes later. He was nearly in tears with frustration. 'They've never heard of us,' he choked.

'But if this is the Supreme Court they must have done,' I raged.

'It is the Supreme Court,' said Christie, 'definitely.'

'Yes, Christie's right,' said Alan, 'he's definitely brought us to the Supreme Court. I just don't understand it, and where the hell is that bloody woman?'

It was now ten to three. 'The courts close at three o'clock,' Christie said quietly, recognising our desperation, our misery. We stood around not knowing what to do.

'Why don't we try ringing Madrid Street and/or Ivan,' I said, 'at least we'd be doing something?'

Alan went back to reception and asked if we could use the telephone. The answer was no. We did not know what to do, whether to dare risk leaving the lobby and therefore miss Miranda, or go in search of a telephone. We split up into two parties: Alan and I went in search of a telephone, Christie stayed with Lenuta. We found a telephone quite quickly. It was out of order. I remember standing beside Alan, staring at the useless receiver. We had failed Michael, we had got so far but not far enough. Would the judge see us again, after we had failed to keep our appointment? And what had happened to Miranda, why had she let us down, *why*? In the end there was nothing we could do but give up.

We arranged with Lenuta that we would pick her up again the following morning at eight thirty, and we asked her if she would be prepared to spend however long it took to try and organise a new hearing. She smiled a great deal, nodded her head and said the day was ours. I suppose the whole experience was a novelty to her, certainly she was not even slightly angry about the waste of time.

Christie dropped us back at the hotel and then took Lenuta home. We agreed that he would return at half-past five to take us to the orphanage to see Michael. It seemed a long time since we had seen him. We were utterly exhausted, drained. We took it in turns to keep telephoning Miranda. Eventually, at about five o'clock, Alan got through to her. She was quite casual. She was sorry that we had missed one another, but she had gone straight to the court. Why hadn't we been there?

'But we were there,' Alan said.

'No, you were not. I was there on time,' Miranda insisted. 'I could do nothing without you and no papers.' It was pointless arguing with her. She was not even slightly apologetic and clearly had no idea of the agony she had caused. I knew we should feel grateful to her for what she had achieved for us, but at that moment I hated her. She gave us the name of the judge, Marian Popa, and said that she would telephone him to say that we had been held up in the traffic and to apologise. She did not offer to say it was her fault.

We telephoned Ivan again, and eventually he answered. We explained to him briefly what had happened and he agreed to come over to the hotel at seven o'clock to discuss the matter. He was clearly surprised – pleased would be too strong a word – by what we had achieved and felt that there was a chance that we could resurrect the case for the following day.

We felt a little better and joined Christie for a beer in the hotel bar before driving round to the orphanage. When we reached the orphanage, Granny was in the garden with Michael, and was in a very angry mood. She had arrived at the orphanage that morning to take Michael out for his lunch but had forgotten to take any gifts to use as bribery. As a result they had not let her see him. Being fairly elderly, it was not possible for her to rush home in the midday heat, fetch the presents and come back again in time to feed Michael before his sleep, so he had missed his meal entirely. She was very angry, not surprisingly. Twice a day for nearly six weeks now, her family had come to the orphanage and brought gifts so that Michael could be fed, and on the one occasion the gifts had been forgotten, they had refused access to him. I could not help wondering how Michael felt; he must have missed her and he must have been very hungry. He was well into his meal by the time we arrived but he, too, seemed tired and tetchy. The mosquito bites on his face were clearing and the scar near his eye seemed to be healing well, but he was very hot and thirsty. He seemed to be developing a bad cold, there were sores all round his nose, and his breathing was more laboured than we had ever heard it before. I thought of the court case we had missed. I wanted to scream and rage against fate. Michael needed to be out of the orphanage today, but the missed appointment could set us back weeks.

Another couple wandered into the garden with a baby. I had long ago ceased trying to age Romanian children. The little girl looked about three months; it turned out she was just over one year old. They were an English couple whom Alan had met once before, and when Michael was fed, Alan and I went and sat with them. Their family situation was not unlike our own, except that they were a lot younger. They already had a son of three and when planning their next baby had suddenly been seized by a fit of conscience – they felt they should be helping a Romanian orphan, rather than bringing another child into the world. The result was Imogen – a tiny, fragile scrap whom they clearly adored – but they were beside themselves with frustration and worry. They were taking Imogen out of the orphanage and back to their hotel every day. When they returned her to the orphanage at night she sobbed and sobbed. The whole situation was proving desperately upsetting for them all. They were at the same stage as us – they had entry clearance and were waiting for a court hearing. They were worried about their little boy at home, whom they had not seen for three and a half weeks.

We told them about our experiences and gave them the telephone number of Ianculescu. Perhaps he would be prepared to work miracles for them, too.

Michael was strangely passive. He sat on my lap, his eyes half closed. 'He's not well, he's not well at all,' I said to Alan.

'I know – I'm sorry but we have to go now.' It was ten to seven and we were due to meet Ivan at our hotel at seven o'clock.

I said a rushed goodbye to Michael. I knew I would see him the following day. We had already agreed that we could not possibly fly home on our Tarom flight in the morning – we were due at the airport at ten and we had to sort out the court case first.

Ivan was prompt, as usual. We met in the lobby and we told him again precisely what had happened. 'Marian Popa is the highest judge in Romania,' Ivan confirmed, 'I doubt that he will see us or hear our case, but we can try. You say you have arranged for the mother to come here in the morning?' We nodded. 'That is good. What time will she be at the hotel?'

'About nine fifteen,' Alan said.

'That is perfect.' This was a favourite Ivan expression. 'I will be here at nine thirty. We will go straight to the court and see what can be done. I suspect nothing, but who knows.' He looked at Alan and smiled slightly. 'Mr Fowler, you have done well to get this far, but why are you always in such a hurry?'

'We have to get Michael out,' said Alan, 'he might die if we don't.'

'No,' said Ivan, 'the boy is strong.' And with that he left.

That evening we had dinner in the downstairs restaurant of the hotel, which is patronised mostly by Romanians and where the meal is paid for in lei rather than dollars. The food was very good, at least it was better than the Bucaresti, and the wine, a Romanian Cabinet Sauvignon, was excellent. Even so, we could work up no enthusiasm for food or drink. We felt such idiots. If only we had made a note of the judge's name, we could have then found the right court. Although Christie was no Adrian, he could have interpreted for us sufficiently at the court hearing. If only we had telephoned Ivan from Ianculescu's office and he could have met us at the court and represented us so that it would not have mattered if Miranda had turned up. If only, if only ... We went round and round it.

'I can't bear leaving him again,' I said. 'Now I know him better, now we've had these few days together, it makes everything so much worse.'

'I know,' said Alan, 'we can't go on being torn in two like this. If this court hearing doesn't happen and we are faced with weeks of delay, we'll just have to bring the whole family out to Romania.'

'But without the case we can't get his release from the orphanage,' I said. 'I'm not sure this spending the day in the hotel and the night in the orphanage is the right thing – the contrast is too great.'

'One step at a time,' Alan said, with a forced smile.

I cried myself to sleep that night, I suspect Alan did, too.

In the hotel lobby at nine o'clock the following morning, both of us were convinced that something would go wrong – that Christie would not be able to bring Lenuta to us in time, or that Ivan would fail to turn up. Christie and Lenuta were five minutes late, by which time we were beside ourselves with anguish. Christie saw our racked expressions and laughed. 'Christie always does what he says he will – not like that Miranda,' he said. 'Did you think I wouldn't come?'

'After yesterday,' said Alan, 'you can't blame us.'

'It was not me who let you down,' said Christie, pointedly.

As we sat in the lobby waiting for Ivan, Christie told us a little about Lenuta, who sat impassively beside us. 'She is a nice woman,' he said, 'we talked yesterday going home, and today again in the car. She is good at making babies, she is not good at looking after them. She knows this. She is funny, she makes me laugh.'

I had noticed the humour in her eyes on the previous day, as we had rushed around in our efforts to find the right court. It was his mother's humour that had helped keep Michael alive, I was sure of that. 'There are many questions I want to ask her,' I said to Christie.

'Later,' said Alan, 'let's try and get this court thing sorted first.'

Ivan arrived on time. If he had not, I think Alan and I would have been biting lumps out of the carpet. He told us to follow his car and we drove at breakneck speed through the streets of Buchurest. Like everything else about Ivan, his driving was incredibly fast and impatient.

When we reached the Supreme Court we instantly realised our mistake – it was the building opposite the one in which we had been. We asked Ivan how we could have made the mistake. 'There are two Supreme Courts,' he said, 'one for Romanians and one for international matters. You were in the court for the Romanians.' So it was that simple. No wonder Miranda had not been able to find us – she had been in the correct court, we in the wrong one. Still, I could not forgive her. She had agreed to be at her mother's home at one forty-five and she had not been there.

Ivan started up the steps to the Supreme Court and it was all we could do to keep up with him, we were literally running behind him. I glanced at Lenuta as we raced along and she grinned, raising her eyebrows to heaven. She was about to sign away her son, yet she was smiling. I shut my mind to the thought.

Ivan went straight to the offices of Marian Popa and spoke to a secretary. We waited and within a few seconds we were shown into his office. Ivan immediately changed. He became extremely deferential – it was an interesting metamorphosis. 'This is Marian Popa, head of all the judges,' he told us, then introduced us.

Marian Popa was a charming man, very warm, very kindly, with lovely twinkling blue eyes. He was kind, not only to us but also to Lenuta, which in my eyes made him very special indeed. He talked to us all, through Ivan, asking us why we were adopting, asking us about Michael and about our other children. He then talked to Lenuta.

'Bring out the photographs,' Ivan whispered.

We brought out the now well-thumbed photographs and showed him pictures of our home, of Charlie and Locket, and finally of Michael, with the bandage across his eye.

'The boy will be all right,' Marian Popa suddenly said, in English, 'he is going to a good home. You are nice people, I like you.'

Tears sprung into my eyes. I think I must have cried more in Romania than I have ever done in my whole life.

'When do you want to take the boy home?' Marian Popa asked via Ivan.

'At the weekend?' we said.

He nodded, it was an affirmative nod – we could not believe it – and it appeared that we were back on course. We shook hands, thanked him and were ushered into the secretary's office again.

'What happens now?' we asked Ivan.

'We will now go and see the judge of Sector 2 of Bucharest, to arrange the hearing.' Marian Popa had followed us out, and he now signed our file with a flourish and handed it to Ivan. We shook hands all over again, me wiping my eyes ineffectually as we did so.

It was steeplechase time again. Ivan roared out of the room and down a long passageway which formed one side of a quadrangle. In the far right-hand corner we knocked on a door and were asked to enter. A nasty little weasel-faced man sat at a desk. One look at him and my heart sunk; I knew we had trouble. He did not rise when we entered, nor attempt to shake our hands, he simply nodded us into seats and then continued with his work as if we did not exist. I glanced nervously at Alan. We waited. At last he looked up and Ivan handed him the file and began to explain our position. The conversation became heated. Alan reached for my hand and squeezed it.

Ivan turned to us theatrically. 'Under the terms of the law, we cannot have a court hearing for fifteen days.' Alan and I began to protest. Ivan held up his hand to silence us. 'I have agreed with the judge to reduce that to five days, so the hearing is being set for next Tuesday, at eleven o'clock.'

'But Marian Popa said we could take Michael home for the weekend.' I turned to the judge. 'Please, please can't you make it earlier – the boy is very sick.'

The judge stared right through me. 'It is not possible,' said Ivan, 'you must agree to five days. I have done the best I can. Do not argue with him.'

I looked at Lenuta. 'What about Michael's mother, will she have to come back yet again?'

'No,' said Ivan, 'I have arranged this with the judge. She may swear in front of him, now, and then she need not do any more. At least it will be all over for her.'

We reeled out of the judge's office. 'Why couldn't we argue with him?' Alan asked.

'Because,' said Ivan, with forced patience, 'he is very powerful. If you upset him, he will not hear your case at all.'

'But Marian Popa – ' I began.

'Marian Popa can only advise these judges what to do, he cannot order them. I have done the best I can. I think Michael will be the first child out of Romania under the new law. You should be satisfied with this.' He looked at Alan. 'You're a very nice man, Mr Fowler but you are too impatient.' For once his words did not bring a smile to our faces. 'Come,' Ivan said to Lenuta. He left us and began dashing around the quadrangle with Lenuta in hot pursuit, into one door, into the next . . .

Ten minutes later it was all over. Lenuta had sworn her declaration. She had given away her son. Ivan led us outside the Supreme Court and Alan handed him an envelope containing his fees to date. 'So,' he said, 'the court case is next Tuesday. There will be no need for you to attend, I have everything I need.' He gave a wave of the hand and was gone.

Christie picked up Alan, Lenuta and me. We told him what had happened and he did not seem to understand our misery. 'So,' he said, 'the news is good, very good. Michael has only to spend a few more days in the orphanage.'

'But it may not be just a few more days,' Alan said, 'we've no idea what happens after the case, whether we can short-circuit the whole procedure or whether it will still drag on for weeks before it's finalised.'

'Still, at least Lenuta's part is finished,' I said, 'I would hate for her to have to do this all again.'

Lenuta looked happy enough, despite what she had just done. We arranged that Christie would drop us off at the hotel and then take her home, and I was aware that we were seeing her for the last time. There was so much we wanted to ask her on Michael's behalf.

'How long have your children been in an orphanage?' I asked, via Christie.

The story unfolded in more detail than before. The children's father had been shot and wounded in the run-up to the Revolution. He had been taken to hospital, but in Romania you are not treated in hospital unless your relatives pay on a regular basis. She had to visit the hospital with money for her husband, she had to earn her own living, and she had to look after the children. It was impossible, so she had put the children in an orphanage. Her husband had subsequently died and now she had a new man. She made it very clear that having decided to part with the children, she would never have them back. They were part of her past, the past she would rather forget.

'But Michael's papers say he has been in an orphanage for two years, his whole life,' I said.

No, this was not true, Lenuta assured us, it was only eight months. It explained a lot, of course, why he had no symptoms of rocking or head-banging, why he could still smile, why he had not given up.

As we neared our drop-off point, I said to Christie, 'Can you ask Lenuta if there is anything she would like, anything we can do for her?' It suddenly seemed so awful. She had given us her son for the price of a bottle of whisky. We had given her nothing.

The reply was swift. A little gift of any sort would be very helpful. Her man, he needed medicine. She was out of work at the moment, so there was no money coming in. They would soon be moving flats.

In the back of the car, Alan emptied his pockets, which did not amount to much. I searched in my bag and found some perfume and a few packets of cigarettes we had been using to give the orphanage staff. We handed over our gifts, so little in the circumstances. She took them with a nod and a smile.

'Christie, ask her if she would like news of Michael in the years ahead? I could, perhaps, send her a photograph of him every year on his birthday, something like that.' Christie asked the question. She seemed to hesitate and then suddenly agreed – yes, this is what she would like but she did not yet know her new address. We agreed that Christie would be a go-between. We hastily wrote down his address and telephone number and also that of Ivan. It occurred to us that if her current man died and she married again, she might not want the new man to know of her children, in which case she might want the photographs to cease.

'We will send photographs every year to your new address, unless you tell us to stop,' we said, 'and please tell Christie if you move again.'

We drew to a halt outside the hotel. I did not know what to say. I squeezed her arm. 'Goodbye, and thank you. We'll take care of him, great care of him.' I began to cry again.

Alan said his goodbyes and pulled me out of the car. Christie joined the stream of traffic once more; Lenuta did not look back. 'It just seems so, so . . . awful,' I said tearfully.

'Yes,' said Alan.

In the hotel lobby we made a concerted effort to pull ourselves together. We had telephoned Margaret the night before, to say we would have to miss the Tarom flight and that we did not know when we would be coming home. Margaret, bless her, had said she would stay for as long as it took us to get Michael out. Now, clearly, there was no point in staying in Romania since the court hearing was not for another six days. I went upstairs to our bedroom and telephoned Margaret, while Alan went across the road to the Lufthansa office, for Tarom only flew three times a week. We met again half an hour later. We were in luck, there was a flight out, but it meant leaving for the airport in forty minutes.

It was a mad panic. We rang Christie and brought him back to the hotel, we checked out and fortified ourselves with two large vodka and tonics in the bar by the swimming pool at the top of the hotel. It was not possible to go and see Michael again, we had realised as soon as we knew the time of the flight. Granny would have given him his lunch and he would now be starting his siesta. To wake him up to say goodbye would be unkind. Christie had spoken to Granny who assured us he was no worse – if anything, his cold was a little better – but still we felt terrible about leaving him. In addition, we were also very conscious that we had not checked on his sisters. While Adrian had been in Bucharest, he had regularly visited Christina-Daniella, but this responsibility he had not passed to Christie. Of Mirella we had heard no news. It had been our intention to instruct Ivan to keep an eye on the girls but in the fluster of the last two days we had forgotten to do so. Aware of how easy it was to lose track of children in Romania, we resolved to telephone Ivan as soon as we arrived home.

It was a very low point for us, climbing into Christie's car and heading out of Bucharest towards the airport. We had achieved something, but still it felt as though we had failed Michael. It was the only way we could see it.

_11_
FREE

O n the face of it, it seems ludicrous that we should have travelled home so despondently, with a court hearing just six days away. We had left for Romania four days previously with no entry clearance, an unpublished adoption law and every likelihood that even when that law was published, there would still be six weeks of waiting while the judicial process ran its course. In the circumstances we had achieved a great deal, but I suppose part of our frustration was the fact that we had come so near to releasing Michael and if only Miranda had been on time we would have been bringing him home with us.

With hindsight, I believe it was not as simple as that. When pictures of starving Third World families are flashed across our television screens, we are all shocked and saddened by what we see. Yet a starving Ethiopian child is almost without exception seen clinging to his starving mother – a deplorable, terrible state of affairs, but at least with some warmth and comfort in all their suffering. I believe the reason the Romanian orphans struck such a chord in people's hearts and consciences is because Ceauşescu's children are alone, abandoned. They have no one to comfort them, no one they can call their friend, no one to protect them or champion their rights. It was this aspect of Michael's suffering which we found the hardest to bear. For most of the day he was in quite considerable pain and this he had to bear alone. Any mother confronted with leaving her child at nursery school for the first time faces a particularly exquisite form of torture for the two or three hours she has to wait until she sees how her child has fared. We were suffering from the same sort of feeling, but on a grand scale. Accidents were commonplace at the orphanage – we knew that. Michael was ill and presumably confused. These funny people kept appearing out of the blue, taking an enormous amount of interest in him and then disappearing again. It had to be unsettling and he had to cope with it . . . alone.

We were also tired of fighting. It seemed as if we were trying to bring Michael home *in spite of everything* – the Romanian authorities had made it difficult, the British authorities had made it difficult, even the orphanage would not let us near him without constant bribery. It was such a struggle and so often we were made to feel as though what we were doing was not quite right. It is difficult to explain, but most of the officialdom we encountered seemed to disapprove, or at any rate not support, adoption. I often think about the many couples we have seen waiting in orphanages, waiting at the British Embassy, waiting at courts, in hotel lobbies . . . and the anxiety and stress is always instantly recognisable. We were lucky, we already had children, but for most of the couples adopting, the situation was different. First, they had had to cope with the heartbreak of probable childlessness, then the harrowing and often painful experience of treatment for infertility, then an unsuccessful application to adopt a baby in this country. After all this, they had witnessed the terrible suffering in the Romanian orphanages – and still they had to fight destructive opposition and endless red tape to have a child of their own. It made me very angry – it still does.

Locket and Fran picked us up from the airport when we finally arrived at Heathrow at eleven o'clock that night. I have known Fran a very long time. She was sixteen and straight out of school when she came to help me with Locket as a baby so that I could start my business to support us all. She has worked for me on and off ever since. We have our ups and downs – I sack her periodically, she tells me what to do with my job on occasions – but underneath it all we are good mates and she has been a marvellous friend to Locket. She has her own gardening business now, but still helps us in moments of crisis. This was a crisis. She had been looking after the animals during our absence and had picked Locket up from the Cookes on the way to the airport. She and Locket were both in good spirits. Locket, we soon discovered on our way home, had a new man in her life called Simon, which accounted for her good humour. We did our best to explain what had been happening in Bucharest, though I am not sure that we made much sense.

Charlie was, of course, in bed when we reached home but Margaret seemed confident that he had been happy enough, though he was still not really well and eating very little, which is so very uncharacteristic of him. We went to bed, exhausted, and there was a very happy little boy to greet us at five o'clock the following morning, though Margaret was right, he did look unusually pale.

It was another day of phone calls. The Foreign Office saw problems with the new law and was also unclear whether the question of passports had been sorted out. We brought Suzy Gale up to date with our exploits so that she could pass on any information on the new law that we had gained to other couples. At the Inter-Continental we had managed to photostat Ivan's copy of the as yet unpublished law, which we now sent to the Foreign Office (apparently the Embassy had not thought to do this). I rang Jo Leeman – they were no further forward with their court-hearing date, but inspired by our story they decided that the only thing they could do was to go out to Romania themselves. Jo was very tired and tearful.

That evening we received a call from a woman called Theresa Broad, who Suzy Gale had told to contact us to find out the latest information. She had been told by her lawyer that it was necessary for at least one parent to be at court for the hearing. Alan told her that we had queried this in front of the weasel-faced judge and that he had said it was only necessary for Ivan to be present. Still, Theresa was not going to take any risks: she was going out to Romania the following weekend. Alan and I talked it through and Alan rang Ivan. As things stood under the terms of the new law, we were supposed to wait fifteen days following the court hearing before the adoption could become official. However, in view of the special circumstances and Michael's ill health, Ivan was relatively confident that he could waive this fifteen days to two or three. If Alan's presence was going to help achieve this, then it had to be sensible for him to attend. We asked Ivan for his view. His answer was characteristically swift and to the point. 'Be my guest,' he said. 'Who knows, it may be useful.'

That evening we devised a plan. Alan would travel out on the Sunday Tarom flight so that he could attend the court hearing at ten o'clock on Tuesday. If things went badly and we were stuck with the fifteen-day wait, then presumably he would come home. The question was, what would happen if things went well? We talked it through from every angle. The whole situation had reduced us to emotional wrecks: we felt guilty about being in Romania, away from Locket and Charlie, and we felt guilty in England away from Michael. Everyone needed us – we were torn in half. There was only one solution: Locket, Charlie and I would fly out to Romania on Wednesday, the day after the court hearing. If things went well, we could then all fly home on Sunday; if they did not, we would stay with Michael until he was free. The moment the decision was made, we felt enormously better. We would be together at last and that was all that mattered. Even if Michael had to sleep in the orphanage, we would spend our days together, whatever it cost in bribery. We would be a family.

Despite her love life, Locket's priorities were very clear. She wanted to be with her new little brother and was quite prepared to stay in Romania for as long as it took. Meanwhile, I paraded Charlie before the doctors once more. Nobody could find anything drastically wrong and though they thought we were mad taking a baby out to Romania, they did not feel that he would be in any danger, as long as we took our own food and drink for him.

Now we were in a frenzy of activity. Shortly after our first trip to Romania, we had moved Charlie out of his little bedroom opposite our own and into a larger room opposite Locket. He loved his new room and up to now we had simply shut the door on his old room. We had made the move because we assumed that Michael might well be disturbed at night, and if he was close to us and away from the other two children he would be less disturbing to them. Now, suddenly, there was a baby's room to equip: a new cot, new curtains, some pictures, toys of his own, clothes. Fran set about redecorating it. I chose quiet, subdued colours, aware that there was very little colour in Michael's life at the moment and anything too gaudy might alarm him. The sensations were exactly the same as equipping a room for any newborn baby. However much fun a woman in late pregnancy may have preparing for her baby, there is always nervousness. Will the baby be all right? Was one flying in the face of providence by making so many preparations? So I felt with Michael's room – suppose the law was never published, suppose the court hearing went against us, suppose, suppose ... Still, the preparations went on relentlessly: enough food, clothes, nappies and drinks to last two babies for at least a fortnight and most of it to travel by hand, bearing in mind Tarom's unique ability to lose luggage.

We faxed Bob House at the British Embassy – could it be for the last time? – to say that we were all coming out and please could he sort out the passport problem. We telephoned Christie and told him our plans. Our own phone never stopped with friends ringing up to find out what was happening, desperate couples referred to us by Suzy Gale seeking advice. Even the Foreign Office had started to refer telephone calls to Alan, since he knew more about the new law than they did. It was a ludicrous situation.

In all the confusion surrounding our hasty departure, I did at least remember to telephone Lorne and Geraldine to check on Leo. He was doing well and due out of hospital within a week or two. It was hard for them. After all the time they had spent yearning for a baby, Geraldine was now home – without one. She spent most of every day at the hospital caring for Leo, but there were no facilities for her to stay overnight on a regular basis. 'I feel he belongs more to the hospital than to me,' she said. 'He can't possibly realise I'm his mother.'

'I'm sure he does,' I said, with more confidence than I felt, thinking of another confused little boy. Firstly Marianna had cared for Michael and then had gone, then Granny – what would he think when I took over? Would he ever learn to trust anyone again, set as these events were against the background of first his father, then his mother and then each of his two sisters disappearing from his life? So preoccupied had we been with freeing Michael from the orphanage, there had been little time as yet to consider how yet another change would affect him, even if it was a change for the better.

When Alan left on Sunday morning Charlie, understandably, was very tense. We saw him off from the airport together and it was a poignant parting for, if all went well, it could mean that this was our last moment together with just one little child. There were no regrets, just a recognition that things would never be the same again.

Back home, my mother was staying for the weekend and Locket, after a party the night before, returned to the fold. It was our monthly church service again. Once more David said prayers for Michael. I remembered thinking last month that Michael might be with us. He was not, but surely by next month . . .

Later that night Alan telephoned to say that, predictably, the flight had been three and a half hours late and that Christie had not been at the airport to meet him. He was very tired and said he did not feel terribly well. We agreed that we would not speak again until after the court hearing on Tuesday, when he would ring me with the results at the very first opportunity. In fact he telephoned again late the following evening. At Orphanage No. 4 he had met a chap called Steve Kelly, who had just been told by the Embassy that the courts were prepared to wrap up the formalities within four days of the hearing. If Saturday could be counted as a day then we would just make it in time for our provisional flight home on Sunday. Still, like all the rumours, we took the news with a pinch of salt.

Alan also had news of Miranda. The people with whom she and Brian had been doing business had been involved in a car crash and two of them had been killed. The Cavills were in a terrible state because the men had been friends as well as colleagues. It was dreadful news and I felt sorry for them, naturally, but there was still a reluctance on my part to forgive her. I was not proud of myself, but it was how I felt.

On Tuesday morning I woke with a sick feeling in the pit of my stomach and realised it was because it was the day of the court hearing. All morning I kept looking at the clock, aware that Romania was two hours ahead of us. I did not move from the telephone from eight thirty onwards. At ten o'clock English time Alan rang.

'We've done it,' he said.

'Do you mean it?' I asked, still terrified to believe it.

'Yes,' he said. 'It only took about ten minutes. The judge was a woman, about fiftyish, very pleasant, very kind. They adjourned for a minute or two to make their decision and then there was a lot of laughter and jollity and of course the photographs were passed round.'

'And the fifteen days?'

'It's been waived,' he said. 'Ivan is fairly confident that we can collect the passport tomorrow, and then all I have to do is get it stamped with a visa at the British Embassy.' He groaned. 'Wait for it – the Embassy is closed on Wednesday, Thursday and Friday this week, so I'm going to have to persuade Bob House to open up especially for us.'

'You're a very nice man, Mr Fowler but –' I suggested. Despite the excitement of the news I remembered to ask Alan how he felt.

'Not good,' he said, 'feverish and I have an upset tummy. When I have things sorted out with Bob House, I think I'll go to bed.' Alan is one of those men who never goes to bed unless he feels really dreadful. It did not bode well.

After I had hung up, I went in search of Locket, Margaret and Charlie and told them the news. We sat around in the garden drinking coffee. We had done it, Michael was ours and it was now a question of obtaining his passport and then having it stamped by the British Embassy. We needed a birth certificate, too, but that was not required to enter England. He was ours, he was ours . . . Nevertheless, I was reluctant to believe it, afraid to give in to the happiness and relief I knew waited around the corner, *if only nothing else went wrong.*

On Wednesday, 15 August Fran drove us to the airport. Charlie slept a little in the car, which was good, and when we arrived he was in an instant fever-pitch of excitement. We checked in at the British Airways desk with hand luggage only, then joined the long queue for the departure lounge. Security had become very tight, due to the Gulf crisis, and it took us an hour to get through passport control, by which time Locket and I were exhausted from carrying the baggage and Charlie. Once in the departure lounge things improved. We bought some food and drink, although Charlie refused to eat anything. We made friends with an American family who had small children and were travelling on to Washington after a holiday in Europe. Things did not go well. First the plane was delayed an hour, then there was a bomb scare and we all had to be evacuated from the departure lounge, and then there was another hour's delay. Finally the three of us, very weary indeed, boarded the plane, just about four hours late.

Sitting opposite us this time was a group of people I could not quite pinpoint. There were two women and a man, clearly not adoptive parents. We began talking and it transpired that we were sitting opposite Carol Sarler of the *Sunday Times Magazine*, a photographer and a specialist from Great Ormond Street Hospital, who had come out to assess the possibilities of introducing occupational therapy in the orphanages. Once the children had more to eat and something better than rags to wear, the next hurdle had to be to provide activities for them. We got along very well, we shared each other's bottles of wine and Charlie was in his element, running up and down the aisle of the plane and making friends with everyone. He was the only child on board and took full advantage of it. Charlie always has had a great sense of occasion. I am absolutely certain that he realised this was no ordinary holiday. He was on his way to find his new brother – that is what we had told him. He was, of course, far too young to express himself with any lucidity, but his excitement literally fizzed in the air and he could hardly contain himself. By the time we arrived at Bucharest, Locket and I were on our knees but Charlie was in terrific form. As we climbed the now familiar steps into the departure lounge at Bucharest Airport, I could see Alan and Christie standing by the diplomatic desk, which thanks to Adrian we now used as a matter of course. Alan was waving something in his hand.

'What's he waving, Locket?' I asked.

'I think . . .' she turned to me with a great grin, 'it's a passport, and I'm not going to give you more than one guess as to whose it is.'

It was an emotional reunion. Charlie was astounded to meet Daddy in this extraordinary place and took instantly to Christie, with whom he became firm friends. On a cloud of euphoria we swept through the diplomatic exit, waved our hand luggage at Customs, and moments later were in the taxi on the way to the hotel. Things were going well, very well. We had yet to have Michael's passport stamped, but at least we had it, and although the Embassy was closed, Bob House had agreed to open up for us the following afternoon. 'You're a very nice man, Mr Fowler, but . . .' we all chorused.

While Alan cuddled Charlie in the back of the car, I studied Michael's passport. It really was a most extraordinary document. As if still under Communist rule, it was named 'Passport for the Socialist Republic of Romania'. Michael's name was given as Marian Aurel Fowler, a glorious combination of his two names, and his place of birth was given as England. Still, it was a precious, precious document and with it Alan had the stamped and certified adoption certificate. He really was ours, he really was.

At the Inter-Continental, we had been given the same room that Alan and I had shared a few days before. Now, though, there were two cots in it. It was starting to feel real, as if it really was going to happen. Locket had the room immediately opposite us. We ordered room service. Charlie would still not eat anything but he accepted a bottle of milk, and with the aid of his lambskin rug, his precious bear, Farquharson, and his usual bedtime story, he went to sleep in the rickety little wooden cot without any trouble. Alan and I adjourned to Locket's room where we sat over a bottle of wine, talking through our plans for the following day.

In the morning we were going to the orphanage to collect Michael. We had to say it to ourselves several times to believe it. This was his last night in that dreadful place, tomorrow he would be free. In practical terms, Alan had arranged that Granny should bring lunch for both Michael and Charlie to the hotel, so that with everything else so strange and possibly frightening, Michael would have the reassurance of seeing Granny, whom he knew well, and the same food he was used to being given. She had said that, provided Christie drove her, she would do this every day until we went home. Going home – that seemed to be the priority for us all now. Michael was still fairly poorly, Alan was better, but feeling a little shaky, and Charlie was still not eating. Getting the children out of Bucharest was vital.

'Romania frightens me.' Karen's words came back to me. There had been demonstrations at the airport when we arrived, and demonstrations in University Square as we had driven through it. It was an angry city, and with the heat still terrible, tempers were frayed. We were not allowed to go to the orphanage until ten o'clock the following morning, so Alan said that he would drop in at the Tarom office first thing and see if we could change our flight from Sunday to Saturday so that at least it would mean we only had two more days in Romania.

We slept eventually, though uneasily. Charlie woke us at five o'clock as usual the following morning but mercifully this was seven o'clock Romanian time and therefore almost acceptable. We took him down to breakfast in the hotel restaurant, the only time we fed the children in public. It was not a success. There were obviously no high chairs and the only food we dared to give him was that which we had prepared upstairs, plus a little bread. Soon he was down from the table and walking up to complete strangers to introduce himself. They turned stony gazes on him which threw him completely, he was not used to this at all. It was interesting, though, for it helped to clarify in our minds the growing impression that Romanians did not seem to like their children very much, and certainly made absolutely no concessions for them. Christie, an essentially kind man, had admitted to beating his four-year-old regularly and was absolutely astounded that we did not beat Charlie. It was strange in a way. The Romanians are very emotional people and so it would not seem unreasonable to expect them to be very warm towards their children. Instead, they are incredibly harsh, perhaps because life is so hard for them. Certainly Charlie was not being bad, he was not shouting, crying or throwing his food about. He was simply being sociable, which is his way, but such were the hostile looks from our fellow diners that we made a fairly swift exit.

Tarom was not enthusiastic about our chances of getting on the Saturday flight but promised to try, and at nine forty-five on the dot, Christie arrived to take us to the orphanage. We took drinks and rusks, as well as the buggy which Marianna and Granny had been using for

Michael to ferry him backwards and forwards from Granny's flat. It was filthy, I noticed, except for the patch where Michael had been sitting. The whole canvas was stained yellow and it made one realise just how polluted the atmosphere in Bucharest must be.

The moment we stepped out of the car at the orphanage everything began to feel unreal. When we discussed it afterwards, Alan and Locket admitted that they felt the same. We walked down the concrete path for the last time, but instead of going up the stairs Charlie and I went to wait in the garden while Locket, Alan and Christie went off with the precious piece of paper which confirmed the adoption. It is difficult to explain the reluctance that Alan and I both felt about taking Charlie into the orphanage. It was something to do with the way he looked – so brown, blond and healthy. Somehow it seemed to us that we would be vulgarly parading our good fortune in the face of so much misery. So, instead, Charlie and I sat on the rusty old swing where I had so often sat with Michael. We were quite alone and I found that I could not equate the two worlds. Here I was with Charlie in the orphanage, which was Michael's place. It was what we had dreamed of, bringing the family together, but at that moment it held no reality.

Alan came to join us. 'I've left Locket and Christie upstairs with Michael,' he said. 'Luckily Dr Unescu was there. She was delighted when I showed her the adoption paper. We're free to take him and go, just like that.'

'I wanted to ask her what jabs he has had,' I said, 'and also about his routine. Life here may be ghastly but it's what he's used to – I don't want to change things too quickly and upset him.'

'She's up there now,' said Alan. 'Go upstairs and talk to her and you can change Michael while you're there.'

The previous evening we had decided that it should be Locket who took Michael out of the orphanage. For some reason it seemed right that his big sister should be the one to free him, and in practical terms it also felt right that Alan and I should be with Charlie.

Michael was very jolly when I found him with Christie and Locket in reception, almost as if he knew this was his big day. His sores were still awful but the cut above his eye had healed nicely. Granny must have been stuffing the food into him because he had a huge pot-belly which looked very out of place with his spindly little legs. He recognised me and put his arms out to be picked up. I hugged and hugged him.

Dr Unescu arrived and Christie explained what I wanted to know. The doctor was all smiles and said that she would prepare a piece of paper for us, giving the dates of Michael's immunisation and also details of his daily routine. I asked if she would come out into the garden to be photographed. After all, she had played a very important part in Michael's life and one day we would want to tell him all about her. She agreed, if reluctantly.

Locket and I took off Michael's orphanage clothes for the last time. They were a filthy old pair of cotton dungarees and a dirty grey shirt. He had no nappy underneath and the dungarees were soaking wet. The clothes were only fit for the fire but I left them reverently on the sofa, assuming they would be used again. We dressed him in a T-shirt and shorts. The T-shirt, for a six-month-old, was a little tight for him, thanks to Granny's good food. The shorts, labelled 0–3 months, fitted him perfectly. He was two years and five weeks old. I could have cried at the sight of his tiny white legs had it not been such a wonderfully happy moment. He seemed to adore the attention of both of us and when he was dressed, I left Locket with him and went downstairs to Charlie.

Alan and Charlie were involved in a very complicated game of hide-and-seek around the swings. I scooped up Charlie. 'You're going to meet Michael at last,' I said. The laughter died. Suddenly he was very serious, years and years older than his mere eighteen months. On cue, around the corner of the building came Locket, carrying Michael. I walked towards her with Charlie. We stopped beside one another, each with a child in our arms. 'Charlie,' I said, 'this is Michael.'

Without hesitation, Charlie threw his arms round his brother and kissed him, a great big, smacking kiss on the cheek. Michael was very startled. He stared solemnly at Charlie, then at me, and then grinned – that same huge grin which had enslaved us the first time we met him.

We sat them side by side on the old rusty swing and gave them rusks and drinks. Michael ate his own and then Charlie's rusk, drank his own drink and then Charlie's. Charlie was in a state of enormous excitement, Michael more cautious but friendly. The sight of them together, one so strong and well, the other so weak and pale, was unbearably touching.

Dr Unescu arrived and allowed herself to be photographed once or twice. She seemed anxious to get away and almost embarrassed. 'See if you can speed up the immunisation details,' I said to Christie. 'I'm longing to get away from this place.'

While Alan and I waited for Michael's paperwork and played with the two boys, Locket had a mission of her own to accomplish. A few days before we had left for Bucharest, she had taken a telephone call from a woman who was desperately trying to adopt a little boy named Thomas Dinca, who, like Michael, was at Orphanage No. 4. Again, the woman was a Suzy Gale contact. Locket had taken all the details and had promised to talk to the orphanage staff about Thomas, and to take some photographs of him. The woman had been sponsoring him since January but every time she tried to start the adoption procedure, the orphanage told her that he was not available for adoption. Armed with her camera and Christie as interpreter, Locket said she would go in search of him. 'Do you want me to come, too?' I asked, remembering her pale little face when we had visited the bowels of the orphanage before.

'No, no, I'll be fine,' she said cheerfully.

I watched her go off with Christie. She had grown up, changed a lot in the last few months. It was more than simply the passage of time, the move from child to adult. Romania had changed her, as it had changed all of us. There was a new confidence about her, a new maturity, the teenage self-centredness had gone.

She was back ten minutes later. 'Did you see him?'

'Yes,' she said, 'he's absolutely sweet. He's about three, very thin but otherwise in quite good nick. I've discovered what the problem is.'

'What?' I asked.

'He's a gypsy.' She glanced at Christie who had become absorbed with Michael. 'Christie says – "the English lady must not adopt him because Thomas is no good." It's ridiculous, of course, but I think that's why the orphanage staff are being so unhelpful. I'll ring her when I get home. He's a sweetheart, it would be lovely if she could help him.'

At the sight of his sister's return, Charlie began running round the garden with excitement, which, with its broken glass and syringes, terrified me. Michael tried desperately to follow him, taking two or three steps and then collapsing. It was a relief when Christie reappeared, waving the records we required. I took the paper from him. On one side was a list of immunisations and their dates. Although it was written in Romanian it was fairly easy to decipher. It appeared that Michael had been covered for everything except measles and rubella. On the back written in English, were brief details of his day: rise at eight, wash and dress, breakfast – bread, fruit, cereal, yoghurt. Midmorning – biscuits. Lunch – cheese, bread, meat, fruit. Rest . . .

I could not read any more, tears blocked my vision, angry tears, frustrated tears. How could they write such lies, how could they imagine for one moment we would believe them? When we had found Michael he was starving to death and we had seen enough of the other children in the orphanage to know that they, too, were being given barely enough food to stay alive. I found this ridiculous document obscene beyond belief. I knew I should try to see the other side of it, try to recognise that perhaps the orphanage authorities were saying what they wanted to give the children, rather than what in fact they did give them. Presumably this was the principal's doing; no wonder Dr Unescu had looked so embarrassed. 'Please let's get out of here,' I begged Alan.

'Yes, let's go,' said Alan, quietly. He picked up Charlie, I carried

Michael, and with Locket and Christie we walked for the very last time out of the garden, down the broken concrete path and past the hens. At the gateway, we all stopped and looked back for a moment, so very conscious of what we were leaving behind. We were carrying one child into freedom with us, but there still remained over one hundred and fifty children for whom tomorrow held no promise. No one came to say goodbye, no one waved, no one even noticed our going. But the lonely, friendless days were over for him. Now he had us, now he had a family.

It was the end of the beginning.

12

A NEW FAMILY

THE end of the beginning . . . It could be said that walking out of the orphanage for the last time was the right place to end Michael's story. Not so – for truly to understand the suffering of Ceauşescu's children, it is important to appreciate not just what Michael was when we found him, but what he should have been, and what he became.

On their third birthday, all orphans and abandoned children in Romania are assessed. If they cannot walk and are not potty-trained, then they are considered to be 'irrecuperable' and placed in asylums. If he had lived, this would have been Michael's fate, despite the fact that he was so obviously sane, and it is with this knowledge of what the future would have held for him that I feel I need to tell you what happened to Michael during his first few months as our son.

When we meet people for the first time these days, the origins of our various children are not even slightly relevant to us. Yet very often Michael is introduced by well-meaning enthusiasts as the little boy we rescued from Romania. The equally well-meaning, kind-hearted people who are the recipients of this information then tell us how wonderful we are, how privileged Michael is, how Christian our attitude, how caring . . . I am afraid to admit that invariably this has me bristling with barely concealed indignation. It is not that I wish to conceal Michael's origins – far from it, I want him to be proud of them. It is the idea that he is our charity case, that we have done him a favour, which I cannot bear, for it is not Michael who is lucky to have us, it is us who are lucky to have Michael. Particularly so when set against the dramatic backdrop of the Gulf War, which inevitably showed human nature at its worst, Michael has shown us human nature at its best. Of course, like everyone else, he has his faults, but his immense courage, his humour and his quite extraordinary kindness, have been an inspiration to us all. We are better people for knowing him.

On that swelteringly hot day in Bucharest, when we drove Michael from one world into another, we could not know this, although looking back on it we were strangely confident. We had been told plenty of horror stories. Orphanage children were said to be desperately aggressive – they had to be to survive. Charlie would be bitten, punched, pinched, would never be allowed to play with anything, eat anything without having to fight for it. Being so close in age, there would not be a chance of their relationship working. We were told that orphanage children cling for the first few days and then refuse all physical contact. That they do not eat properly – they binge until they are sick and then starve themselves again, because this is what they are used to doing; that some can take no solid food and can only be fed by bottle, even at the age of four or five. Then there was the language problem. Michael appeared to speak not at all: he responded neither to us nor to Granny when she prattled away to him in Romanian. For all we knew, he could have a severe hearing problem, yet none of this worried us, we gave it not a thought. For some idiotic reason we had complete confidence – in ourselves, yes, but above all, in Michael. Nothing seemed to upset him that day. The bustling hotel lobby, the lift with its strange sensations and finally the long, dark corridor to our bedrooms – he took it all in his stride. Once inside our bedroom, he took tottering steps behind Charlie, examining everything, looking around him, accepting graciously the toys that Charlie brought him. We had said goodbye to Christie in the hotel lobby and it felt good to be just the five of us for the first time.

Michael, it has to be said, smelt terrible. The orphanage smell clings to your clothes long after you have left. We did not want to rush him, but he badly needed bathing. We played together for an hour or more, the boys running between our room and Locket's. Michael was becoming increasingly confident with his walking, as falling on the soft hotel carpeting did not hurt him. He fell often but never cried, just said a little 'Oh,' under his breath before getting up and continuing on his way. It was six weeks before he cried to be comforted when he hurt himself. In the orphanage there was no point in crying. It is a waste of energy when there is no one to pick you up and make a fuss of you.

At last, steeling ourselves, we recognised that we must bath him or Granny would arrive for lunch and then it would be time for his rest. We settled Charlie in his cot for his midmorning nap and so as not to disturb him we decided to bath Michael in Locket's room. We ran the water, not too deep, and filled it with bubbles. As I began gently to take off his clothes, there was suddenly an enormous explosion, followed by a jet of very horrid diarrhoea which seemed to go just about everywhere. Granny had told us only the day before that Michael had recovered from his diarrhoea, but apparently he had not. At least it made us feel less beastly about the bath – it really was essential now.

He screamed with terror while I washed him all over, including his hair – I felt terrible, as if I was already betraying his trust. There was nothing I could do about the matted hair at the back of his head, which was stuck fast to the dreadful sores. It was weeks before gentle cleaning and treatment of the sores were to solve this problem. By the end of the bath, though, he was clean, smelled fresh and, miraculously, he was apparently prepared to forgive me completely. As I dried him by the window in the bedroom, I realised that it was not just the skin on his face that was chalk white and strange – the skin on his whole body was odd. It had a kind of dead, grey look, not dirty exactly, though I suppose the effect was created by never having been properly washed. There was none of that shiny, wonderful elasticity normally associated with baby skin. It could have been the skin of a very old man – indeed, in parts it was a little wrinkled where, one felt, rather like the hippopotamus in the *Just So Stories*, he was not properly filling it. I noticed again his delicate hands – his feet were the same. Extraordinarily, the nails on his fingers and toes appeared as well groomed as if he had just walked out of a manicurist. At the time I could not understand it. The staff at the orphanage were too stretched to feed and clothe the children properly. How on earth could they cope with one hundred and fifty sets of nails, particularly those belonging to squirming toddlers? The next few months provided the answer. The hair and nails of severely malnourished children simply do not grow. Michael was home for five months before I needed to cut his nails.

We dressed him in clean clothes, including waterproof knickers for future accidents, and dried his hair in the sunshine, on the balcony outside Locket's bedroom. By the time we had finished, Granny and Christie had arrived with the most enormous meal for the children: a whole chicken, rice, bread, soup, noodles, rice pudding and grapes. Charlie would eat nothing. He woke up happy enough but apart from juice, he would touch no food at all. Michael, too, was not very hungry but Granny virtually force-fed him, stuffing the food down him, shouting at him if he refused a mouthful. I realised suddenly that in a single morning, my feelings towards Michael and our relationship had changed. I was enormously grateful to Granny for what she had done, but I wanted her to leave my child alone. I greatly disliked the way she was bullying him to eat and I was appalled by her rough handling of him. In the orphanage her behaviour had seemed perfectly acceptable, I suppose because what she had to offer him was so much better than what he would otherwise have had. Here, now, in our world, however, her treatment of him seemed brutal. Glancing at Alan, I could tell he felt the same and Locket had removed herself to the far end of the bedroom, as if she could not bear to watch. We had ordered lunch for the rest of us from room service. Granny drank a little wine, Christie had beer and a burger and chips. When he had finished his own, he ate everyone else's, for none of us was hungry. It was a great relief when they left, although we felt enormously guilty when they were being so kind.

For some reason I felt incredibly tired and Alan suggested that while Michael had his afternoon sleep I should stay with him, and he, Lucy and Charlie would go to the Embassy to have Michael's passport stamped. I put up a token protest and then agreed. I was desperate to spend some time alone with him. When they had left, I gave him a drink and settled him in his cot. I held his hand and sang to him and, despite my terrible voice, he was asleep in seconds. I wondered whether it would always be this easy. I stood watching over him while he slept for some long time – this child, my son. In repose, he looked very old, far beyond his years, but then he had seen more of the rough end of life than most of us would expect to experience in a lifetime. His stomach rumbled painfully. Outside in the street below, there was a demonstration going on with a great deal of shouting and abuse, but none of this disturbed him. I stroked his head. Instantly he jumped and stirred – while he was no stranger to noise, he was not used to being touched. I reluctantly left him and lay down on the bed. Within seconds I was asleep.

Alan, Locket and Charlie returned from the Embassy in high spirits. The passport was stamped. We were free to leave Romania with Michael. Charlie had enjoyed a high old time in the Embassy reception. One of their plants was now minus a few leaves but otherwise everything had gone smoothly.

When Michael woke, Locket and I took the boys to the swimming pool on the top floor of the hotel, while Alan went back downstairs to the Lufthansa office to see if there was any chance of an earlier flight home. Now there was nothing to stop us leaving Romania, we were desperate to go. It sounds stupid – here we were, staying at the Inter-Continental Hotel, which, although eccentric compared with most international hotels, was very comfortable. We had all the children with us, Michael's passport, and a flight booked for Sunday. I cannot explain the desperation to get home; it was an instinctive thing. Certainly when Alan suggested finding an alternative airline, no one argued with him.

Michael sat contentedly with Locket by the hotel pool while Charlie and I changed and had a swim. It was a splash pool really and very cold, and Charlie did not want to stay in for long. Michael watched, fascinated and incredulous. How could anybody enjoy being in water? We had tea, with juice for the children, and Alan appeared with a shake of the head – Lufthansa was not able to help us, nor was Austrian Airways. Our only chance was to wait until tomorrow morning and see if Tarom could fit us in on the Saturday flight.

Michael's continuing diarrhoea took us back to the hotel room fairly swiftly, where we ordered some spaghetti for the children's tea. Michael ate quite well, but Charlie still ate nothing at all, not a biscuit, or cereal, or fruit, or a rusk. He was in good spirits, if a little sleepy, pale and oddly yellow. I tried not to worry but when I went to take off his nappy for the evening bath he, too, had diarrhoea.

'Romanian squitters', as it is fondly known by most parents who have adopted children from the Romanian orphanages, is like no other squitters in the world – the volume, the liquidity and the smell are in a league all their own. I am sorry in the pages of this book to go into such graphic detail, but any parent of small children can imagine that two children with chronic diarrhoea, in a hotel with limited supplies of nappies and clothes, is not ideal. Luckily, we had a bottle of Dettol. I cut my fingernails almost to the bone and washed, repeatedly, after handling each of them in a desperate effort not to spread it to other members of the family. In this, at least, I was successful.

That first night together, despite the problems of diarrhoea, was a very happy one. Charlie enjoyed a big, deep bath, which Michael watched with interest, then we dumped him in quickly for a wash and dressed them both in pyjamas. We read them stories and then I gave Charlie his bottle, which was the only thing he would still take, and put him to bed. We adjourned to Locket's room with Michael. On his own, with three doting adults, he blossomed, and for the first time we began to see the character he was to become. He was in terrific form, running round the room, oblivious to the tumbles he kept taking, laughing, flirting with us, giving us big cuddles. His walk was rather like a penguin's – in fact, he looked not unlike a penguin, with his tiny little legs and comparatively big body. He loved being tickled and all forms of physical contact. When our supper arrived by room service, he joined in enthusiastically. We were reluctant to put him to bed, he was such good company, but eventually Locket took him to his cot, rocked him and sang to him for a few minutes, and soon he was asleep.

Both boys slept all night but were very disturbed, mostly because of their rumbling stomachs and Michael's restlessness. Not realising, we had covered him with a blanket because with air-conditioning the room was quite cool. Of course, in the orphanage there was no bedding and so he was not used to having anything covering him. He wrestled with the blanket all night until Alan took it away in the early hours of the morning. Charlie and Michael woke at six o'clock, still tired, with terrible nappies and very sore bottoms. Michael also had a very sticky eye, which I had to bathe for some time before he could open it, and the sores on his back, encouraged by the diarrhoea, were red raw. Even so, you would think there was nothing at all wrong with him. He smiled and laughed all through the cleaning-up process, wolfed back a breakfast of scrambled eggs and bread and seemed to have not a care in the world. The question of food worried us a great deal. The traditional way to treat diarrhoea is, of course, starvation, but there was no way, no way at all, we could withhold food from Michael in these circumstances. Even if it was for his own good, the idea of starving a child straight out of an orphanage was unthinkable, particularly as his appetite appeared unaffected.

That morning Locket, Michael and Alan went off to do the rounds of the airlines to see if space had come up on an earlier flight. Charlie and I took a walk round Bucharest. Charlie's lack of food was beginning to tell. He was tired and lethargic, quite happy to sit in his buggy and be pushed, which was not normally his idea of fun. We encountered a demonstration down one of the streets we walked, which frightened me – everyone was so angry – violence was in the air and we returned to the hotel hurriedly. In the lobby we met the rest of the family, who again had experienced no luck with the airlines. On the way up to our rooms we shared a lift with some German businessmen and for the first time we encountered the question, 'Are they brothers?'

'Yes,' said Alan, 'this one is one year old,' he said pointing to Charlie, 'and this one is two,' pointing to Michael. The Germans looked understandably confused, for Michael was half Charlie's size. 'I got that wrong, didn't I?' said Alan, as we stepped out of the lift. 'I should simply have said one was one and one was two and not indicated which was which. Still, we'll learn.'

The rest of the day followed much the same pattern as the previous one, with sleeps for the children, Granny and Christie for lunch, and late afternoon spent at the pool. It was hard work for clearly neither of the children felt well. We were all exhausted and Charlie, the great outdoor man, was wilting under the rarefied atmosphere of hotel life, not to mention the lack of food.

Over lunch with Christie and Granny, I asked them whether there was a park in Bucharest. It transpired that there was indeed a park and we arranged with Christie that on Saturday morning we would all go there early while it was still cool, so that the children would have at least have a little fresh air. Granny's handling of Michael was distressing us considerably. It was impossible to interfere, but she was forcing food down him he really did not want. Spending the following morning in the park gave us the excuse to sidestep lunch and we agreed that we would all come to her flat for tea and to say goodbye.

After spending a short time at the swimming pool that afternoon, we returned to the hotel bedroom and Locket and Charlie fell into a deep sleep. Alan, Michael and I left a note and went off to one of the hotel's many bars for a couple of much-needed gin and tonics. It was the first time that Alan and I had ever been alone with Michael and it was strange to be sitting in the bar with a young son who was not Charlie. Strange, but not uncomfortable, in fact it was very comfortable indeed. He sat between us on the sofa, playing with a toy, happy in our company, us in his. It was not a momentous occasion, nothing dramatic happened, but I suppose it was a bonding experience. We sat there for not much more than half an hour or so, but Alan and I left feeling as if we had achieved something. That night we decided that we should split up Michael and Charlie's sleeping arrangements as they had disturbed each other so much the night before. We put them to bed in our room so that Locket, Alan and I could enjoy a peaceful supper, and then we lifted Charlie's cot through to Locket's room. Locket, Charlie and I spent the night there, so that Charlie would have me with him when he woke in the morning, and Alan slept with Michael. It worked much better, and Saturday morning, we all felt considerably more rested.

By nine o'clock we were in the park, and were astonished by what we found. It was enormous, five, six, perhaps seven times the size of Hyde Park, with a huge lake, tennis courts, children's play areas and a wealth of trees, shrubs and flowers, all very well tended. On the face of it, it sounds idyllic and yet like the rest of Bucharest, it managed to be a weary and run-down place. The whole park suffered, of course, from lack of water. It had a dry, arid, dusty look, which was not surprising, considering the climate, but when coupled with the rust and flaking paint on all the seats, benches and swings, it gave a sense of decay. It was also entirely deserted. Why did the people of Bucharest not come here? Christie seemed unable to explain, but he confirmed that it was free to everyone. The tennis courts, too, were empty. On some there were no nets or the nets were broken, but others were obviously serviceable but unused. The lake was beautiful, until we looked closely and saw that it was little more than a sewage dump. As a slight breeze blew our way we could smell it. Around the lake there were a number of open-air restaurants. Once they had been fine, chalet-type buildings; now they had come to look more like ramshackle garden sheds. We did not stop for a drink or coffee at any of them for fear of being poisoned, but in any event there seemed to be no one about. We had taken the buggy with us – Charlie walked and we pushed Michael. We tried out some of the swings and stopped in the shade to give the boys drinks and biscuits. We could not feel normal in this strange, eerie park but we all felt better for being out in the fresh air and were reluctant to return to the hotel when it came to Charlie's rest-time.

For lunch that day we managed quite well with the hotel room service, with Michael tucking into chicken and potato, though

Charlie as usual ate nothing. After Michael's rest Christie came to fetch us to make our last visit to Granny. Not surprisingly, it was a very emotional occasion. My irritation of the last few days over her handling of Michael vanished. All that mattered now was that her family had been responsible for keeping Michael alive and we were deeply, deeply grateful.

During the afternoon, while Michael had slept, I had sorted out our belongings for the journey home the following day. Much of the children's clothing I had to throw out – it was so hopelessly stained from their constant diarrhoea, and with no proper washing facilities there was nothing I could do with it. I had just enough clothes, waterproof knickers and nappies for the journey home, plus juice, milk and snacks. Everything else, whether it was baby lotion, cotton wool, bubble bath or soap, I had bundled into carrier bags for Granny and her husband. We also had some cigarettes, some brandy and two corsets for Granny, which she had asked me to bring for her from Marks & Spencer. They both seemed very pleased with the gifts.

Granny's husband, whom we had dubbed 'Grandpa', opened a large bottle of plum brandy when we arrived. It was his own home-brew, he assured us proudly. It was delicious but tasted and smelt incredibly strong. 'Will this do us any harm?' Alan asked Christie, in a stage whisper.

He grimaced. 'Two, maybe three glasses and you will be OK. Five glasses and you will be dead.' Neither of us could be entirely sure if he was joking.

We toasted Michael and then Adrian, Marianna and Irena. Granny burst into tears. 'They'll be home soon, won't they?' I asked Christie.

He shook his head. 'I don't think they're ever coming back. Granny spoke to Marianna on the telephone last night. Karen and Alan have offered them a permanent home and will help them to get American citizenship. Granny is sad to be losing Marianna and Adrian but it is Irena who has her heart, she misses the little girl so much.' I went and sat beside Granny and gave her a hug. She wiped her eyes and started speaking rapidly. 'Granny says it is too much heartache, losing Irena and Michael all at once, although she promises she will not cry when we say goodbye to Michael today.'

I left Granny in the kitchen to give Michael tea alone, feeling she might like the time with him. Charlie, in any event, would still eat nothing. He and I went out on to the balcony. He was fascinated by the ancient trams which rocket around the Bucharest streets. For him the noise and bustle of the city, after the quiet of Hampton Gay, was fascinating. We drank some coffee, we took photographs, and we asked Granny and Grandpa whether they would be Michael's official Romanian grandparents. They both cried and, of course, agreed.

Soon it was the children's bedtime and time to go. What do you say to the woman who has probably made the difference between life and death for your son? What do you say to the woman who has cared for him as well as any mother, in the most difficult of circumstances? We all knew it was possible, even probable, that we would never meet again. Granny and Grandpa are not young and Romanians do not live long – their life is too hard.

We hugged and kissed Grandpa and left him upstairs, wiping his eyes. We took the rickety lift for the last time down to Christie's car. I handed Michael to Granny and despite her promises she cried, wiping the tears from her face ferociously. We promised to send them regular parcels of food and clothes to help them. What they wanted most, though, were regular photographs of Michael.

We climbed into the car, Locket and I sitting in the back seat with the boys. As we drove away, Michael suddenly detached himself from my lap and stood up, waving out of the back window to Granny until she was out of sight. Then he sat very still on my lap, silent tears trickling down his face. It was one of the most touching sights I have ever seen. His tears were not the tears of a child but of an adult. There was no doubt that he knew he was saying a very permanent goodbye to her and it made me realise, suddenly, how easy it was to underestimate his understanding. He was a two-year-old trapped in a baby's body, and we would have to be very careful to remember this in future. He had understood the situation far better than we had given him credit for. We should perhaps have prepared him for the parting in some way, or avoided an emotional goodbye altogether. There had been too many sad partings in Michael's short life. We should have been more sensitive to his feelings.

He remained quiet for much of the evening and it was not until we had put Charlie to bed that he became lively once more. That night he was on a real high, roaring round and round the hotel bedroom, laughing, full of fun. He was so different, already, from the little orphanage boy who would sit quietly on anyone's lap, entirely passive. The child was a cheeky scamp, ready for mischief and apparently full of energy. That night we felt we had already made considerable progress, and tomorrow – tomorrow we were going home.

Christie, of course, drove us to the airport the following morning. Both boys' diarrhoea was worse than ever and Charlie had woken with sticky eyes. Michael's eye infection had cleared up almost as soon as I bathed them but Charlie's eyes continued to weep and they were sore and irritated. He even refused his morning bottle of milk and seemed very tired and scratchy. How I longed to be home. The thought of the inevitable delays with the Tarom flight with two small boys, neither of them well, the four-hour flight itself and then more delay at Heathrow with immigration, filled me full of dread. Still, it was the last haul and between the three of us, at least we had plenty of helping hands. I should have known leaving Romania could not possibly be straightforward.

Although we had arrived early at the airport there was already a long queue for the flight to Heathrow. 'Go the manager, Christie,' Alan said, 'explain we have two small children – one just out of an orphanage – and ask whether we can be checked in ahead of the queue.' He handed Christie some lei and cigarettes. Locket and I grinned at one another. In the last few weeks Alan had become quite Romanian. It would never have occurred to him before to jump a queue, being a true Englishman in every sense of the word. Now he saw it as a perfectly normal way to behave. Christie was back in moments, beckoning us, and to our relief we were shown through a side entrance beside the check-in desk, where we waited while Alan presented his tickets.

Moments later, the girl looked up from our tickets. 'You are not on the flight list,' she said. 'You must stay here until I have checked in everyone else to see if we have any free seats for you.'

'What do you mean,' Alan exploded, 'what does the flight list matter – we have valid tickets for today – look!'

She shrugged her shoulders. 'You must wait, I cannot help you.'

'But will we get seats on the plane?' Alan said, desperately.

'I don't know, maybe.'

We could not believe it. We had hung around in Bucharest for three long days waiting for this flight, only to find we were not on it. We looked at Christie, helplessly. 'What do we do?'

'I can go and see the manager,' he said. 'How much money do you have?' We counted it out: about one thousand lei and nearly one hundred dollars. We unloaded it all on to Christie, except for some loose change for coffee, together with our remaining cigarettes.

As luck would have it, the manager who had allowed us to jump the queue had gone off duty and had been replaced by a woman who was not even slightly sympathetic. There was nothing she could do, she assured Christie, we would have to wait. Christie pleaded. Alan went back with him and pleaded again. They waved the money at her, the cigarettes – she did not want to know, we must wait. 'How long?' we asked.

'An hour, maybe two.'

'And if we can't get on the flight?' Alan asked.

'You will have to wait until Wednesday,' was the reply.

We could not wait until Wednesday. I had given away everything, all our food, all our clothes, even our toothpaste. The boys' diarrhoea was so bad they needed to see a doctor quickly, and Charlie had now not eaten for a week. I had also sensed that morning he might be brewing for another fever. Our hotel rooms would have gone and the Inter-Continental was very full.

'Look,' said Alan, seeing my face, 'don't panic. If we can't get on this flight, we'll fly out of Bucharest today, somewhere – Paris, Amsterdam, New York, wherever we can get a flight, whatever the cost, just so long as it is somewhere civilised. We'll work out how to pay for it later.'

'If we could just be somewhere where we could buy some baby food and nappies, where we could see a doctor . . .' I began.

'I know, I know,' said Alan. 'I'll have a look around the airport and see what other flights are leaving Bucharest today.'

While he was gone, Locket put Charlie in the buggy and wrapped him up. By rocking him backwards and forwards he was soon off to sleep. One restless child was a great deal easier to manage.

'Weren't Carol Sarler and her friends coming back on this flight?' Locket said.

'They thought they might be,' I agreed.

'Why don't we look out for them,' I said, 'maybe they'd give us their seats?'

'We can't ask them to do that,' I said, 'but maybe they could take some messages home.' Fran was due to meet the plane and I knew that in the circumstances she would be worried sick if we weren't on it, imagining something had gone wrong with Michael.

Alan returned. 'There is a flight out to Paris, about two hours after ours is due to go. There are no seats on it at the moment, but we could go on standby. There's also a flight to Vienna later this afternoon, we could try that.' He tried a smile, not too successfully. 'You'll never guess who's on this flight.' I shook my head. 'Brian Cavill. Miranda's here, too. They're in the queue, I've just spoken to them.'

'Maybe in a fit of conscience for the way she let us down, she'd offer us her seat?' I suggested.

'I don't think so,' said Alan.

'Is she coming to see Michael?'

'She knows he's here but she didn't suggest it. Do you want to take him to see her?'

I shook my head. 'I think in my current frame of mind I might say something I regret.'

'There she is,' Locket suddenly called. Through the sea of heads we suddenly saw Carol Sarler. 'I'll go and tell her what's happened,' said Locket.

Carol came back with Locket. She hugged Michael. 'What can I do to help?' she said. 'I'd give you my seat but I have to get back to London today.'

'Two things, I think,' said Alan. 'If there are only one or two seats available, what I'd like to do is send Debby and the boys home and Locket and I will get back as best we can. If that happens do you think you could give her a hand with the children?'

'Of course,' said Carol, 'of course we will.' Her kindness had me close to tears. 'Are you being met at the airport?' she asked.

'Yes,' said Alan, 'that's the second thing. If we don't get on this flight, we're going to try for the Paris flight, and failing that the Vienna flight. If I write down the flight numbers and approximate times of arrival, can you ask our driver, Fran, to meet their connection in London. Tell her to contact the British Airways desk at Terminal 2, and if possible we'll get a message to her there to tell her when we'll be arriving.'

'No sooner said than done,' said Carol. 'I'd better join the queue. Good luck.'

After she had gone, Alan and Christie approached the manager again. We had been standing around for over an hour. Charlie had woken up and he was feverish and thirsty. Michael, by contrast, was completely unworried and apparently relaxed. The bustle and noise of the airport did not seem to upset him, nor the atmosphere, which must have been very tense. So long as he was being carried around by either Alan, Locket or I, so long as he had a rusk in his hand, he was happy.

'Things are not looking good,' Alan said, 'it's going to be at least another hour before everyone's checked in. Why don't you take the boys up to the restaurant – at least you can have a coffee and a change of scene and maybe we can persuade them to eat something.'

We had left the hotel sufficiently early that neither of them had had any breakfast. Leaving Christie in charge of our cases and the tickets, we forced our way through the huge crowd and up the stairs to the restaurant. It was full but we were shown through to an open-air restaurant at the back. We sat down. Alan gave me some lei and hurried back to Christie. We waited and waited, no one served us. I got up and asked a waiter. He said he would send someone to see us . . . nothing happened. I asked another waiter, he said he would return to take our order shortly . . . nothing happened. The boys were very restless, Locket looked as exhausted as I felt. At last a man who looked like the head waiter appeared. I got up from the table and went up to him. 'We're very tired and hungry, the children need some breakfast, please could you serve us now?'

He stared at me as though I was crazy. 'This restaurant is closed,' he said, 'you must eat next door.' We had been waiting for half an hour. Wearily, Locket and I got up and carried the boys through into the adjoining restaurant – it was still full and there were people

queuing to sit down. We gave up. Clutching the children and our
baggage, we began forcing our way down the stairs, past the crowds
of people. The heat was oppressive and I realised, suddenly, that I was
crying. It was ridiculous. After all these weeks of struggling to get
Michael out of the orphanage, we had done it. Nothing else mattered,
he was alive and ours. There had been a mess-up with our tickets, that
was all, not the end of the world, but at that moment it seemed as it
we would never get home, as if the children would never be well. When
we reached Alan, he took Michael from me and sat me down on a
suitcase. The queue for the flight was nearly finished. Carol came
through. 'We'll see you in a few minutes, I bet,' she said.

Behind us, standing around, I suddenly saw another couple with a
baby. 'Who are they?' I whispered.

'They're English and that's their adopted child. They're not on the
flight either,' said Alan.

I went over to talk to them and as we began to swap horror stories,
I immediately started to feel better. They were very anxious. They had
entry clearance, they had their daughter's passport and the adoption
papers, but because the Embassy was closed they had not been able to
get the visa stamped on the passport. I silently blessed Bob House. 'We
just couldn't stay in Bucharest another moment, we had to get out. I
suppose there's a risk they'll turn us back at Heathrow but anything's
better than staying there,' said the wife. She was a pretty, blonde girl
in her mid-twenties. I never did get to ask their names but suddenly
my own sense of desperation did not seem so pathetic. They just had
one baby to cope with, who looked well and was only a few months
old, lying placidly in their arms. I had two toddlers, both sick – maybe
I was not so feeble after all.

As the queue dwindled, we realised that there were a number of
other people waiting for standby seats, some of whom clearly did not
have tickets. Alan left us and pressed forward, as close as he could to
the check-in counter. At last the woman turned in his direction, a surge
of people stepped forward. Locket put an arm round my shoulders.
'He'll sort us out I'm sure.'

She was right. Moments later Alan appeared triumphantly with
boarding cards. 'We're on,' he said, 'but only just. They weren't giving
any priority to people with tickets, it was just a question of elbowing
one's way to the front of the queue.'

We were on our way. I hardly dared believe it. We scooped up the
boys and made our way to passport control. Since nothing had been
straightforward, as we queued none of us thought there would be any
chance of getting through without an argument. While we were
waiting, our flight was announced. 'I suppose we could still miss it,'
said Alan, desperately.

A heavily moustached man took our passports. I explained we were adopting Michael. We had the adoption certificate ready. He glanced at us in a disinterested manner, counted us, counted the number of passports and handed them back. If I could have reached him across the counter, I would have given him an enormous hug. We were through, we were on our way.

'To the bar,' said Alan, firmly. We almost ran up the stairs to the bar, clutching children, bags, the buggy, weighed down with posessions. Carol must have seen us coming for by the time we reached the top of the steps, she was pressing cold tins of beer into our hands.

'I must change the boys,' I said. It was an incredible four and a half hours since we had left the hotel. There was nowhere to go, no lavatories. 'Anyone without a strong stomach had better look away,' I said, and there on the floor of the bar I dealt with the two sets of diarrhoea as discretely and as quickly as I could.

Our flight was called again and, terrified of missing it, we all trooped down to the departure area. It was sweltering. Michael was in terrific form, being passed from person to person, smiling, happy. Charlie was friendly but quiet. Carol was travelling back with three people connected with the *Sunday Times Magazine* project. They all took our baggage, so that we had nothing to carry except the children. 'You're all being so kind,' I said.

'It's nothing,' said Carol, 'is there anything else we can do?'

'Yes, reserve us the best seats on the plane.'

'Leave it to me,' she said, 'I'll take my clothes off if necessary.' I don't think she was joking and certainly some half an hour later, when we finally struggled up the steps of the aircraft, she had reserved the best possible seats, right at the front, with leg room and our own table.

Before boarding we had to say goodbye to Christie. We gave him everything we had left as a thank you for all his help. It did not amount to much but I don't think he expected anything. Adrian is a very commercial man but Christie is not and although he had irritated us sometimes, he had been a true friend and he was genuinely fond of both Michael and Charlie. He kissed us all and suddenly, standing there in the airport, he seemed very small and lost. While we were returning to civilisation, we were leaving him with the stark reality of day-to-day life in Romania. Through us, through telephone conversations with his cousin, he had glimpsed another world that he probably will never see. I wished we were like Alan and Karen and had the money to say, 'Come with us, Christie.' He would have done, I know.

'Michael is a lucky boy,' he said to me, 'I know you love him very much.'

'We are also lucky to have him, but then you know that.'

'Yes,' said Christie. 'I like your children, all of them.' He smiled at

Locket. 'You will come and see me again one day, won't you?'

'We promise,' I said. 'It is a promise we intend to keep.' He turned away then but not before we saw the tears in his eyes. 'Thank you, Christie,' I called after him. He half turned and waved and then was lost in the crowd. Christie, like Granny and Grandpa, Adrian and Marianna, Dr Unescu, Miranda Cavill, Dinu Ianculescu and, of course, Nicolae Ivan – they had all brought us to this moment, the moment when at last we were really taking Michael home.

The flight for me is a jumble of impressions. Michael enjoyed it. He was tired, because he was missing his afternoon sleep but elated and very sociable. He still looked awful, with his deathly pale face, his sores, his runny nose, the dark circles under his eyes, his funny little body with its big tummy and tiny legs, his hair shaved in the orphans' cut, but the dead look had completely gone from his eyes. He seemed to be unable to stop smiling. It is ridiculous to say he knew what was happening, but he did. The roar of the jet engines, these people he hardly knew taking him away from everything that was familiar, the strange food and drink he was being given, the collapse of his routine, all this would have uspet a lot of children, most children, but Michael seemed to view it as an exciting opportunity, a new experience. And that has always been his way – he is thirsty for experience of life and, of course, he has much catching up to do. Then we knew something of his suffering, but later we were to learn more. As our knowledge of him and his background increases, it seems even more extraordinary that he has been able to rise above it. But then Michael has style. He flew across Europe with all the confidence of a seasoned traveller. He left his old life without a backward glance, craning his neck for a glimpse of what lay ahead.

At Heathrow, Carol and her chums carried our bags through to passport control and there they found us two trolleys. 'I'll tell your driver you're on your way,' she said.

'I don't know what to say to thank you,' I began.

'It's lovely to see your family complete. A happy ending for one child anyway.' They were gone, and we turned to face immigration.

'Oh no, not another one,' said the man at passport control.

'It's all right,' we said, 'he's legal.'

'I didn't think there was an adoption law in Romania at the moment.'

'There is a new one and we think Michael is the first child out under it.'

'You'd better come with me.'

They took us to a reception area just off baggage handling. 'If they make us wait for long,' I said to Alan, 'I think I might completely freak.'

'You won't have to,' said Alan, 'I'm spoiling for a fight. We shouldn't be held up at all – Michael's passport is as valid as our own.'

A youngish man in a customs and excise uniform came up to us. By now the couple we had met at Bucharest had joined us. 'Deal with these people first,' they said generously, 'we're more complicated and they've got two babies.'

The official examined Michael's passport. 'It's all in order,' he said, in a surprised voice.

'I know,' said Alan, patiently, 'that's what I've just explained at passport control.'

'Still, I think he should have a medical.'

I exploded. I've no idea what I said and if I could remember, it would probably not be repeatable within the pages of this book. All I can recall is that the official went a little pale and said it would be perfectly all right for us to go immediately and no, strictly speaking, a medical was not necessary.

'Wow!' said Locket.

'Impressive,' said Alan.

I didn't know whether to laugh or cry. 'Did I explain the situation properly?' I asked. They confirmed that I had.

Nobody stopped us as we went through customs. I think one look at our exhausted faces would have been enough to deter them. Suddenly we were in the terminal building and there was Fran, tears streaming down her face. Fran crying – Fran, who never allowed anyone to see her feelings. Fran who had not even cried when, as a sixteen-year-old, she had arrived at work one morning to tell me her mother had died in the night. Michael, as if sensing this was someone special, stretched out his arms to her. She stared at him in disbelief and then swept him into a big hug. We were all crying, stumbling along with our trolleys of tatty, soiled luggage. We must have looked a terrible sight but it didn't matter. We were home. We had made it.

13

FIRST IMPRESSIONS

I FIND it hard to describe our feelings that first night as Alan, Locket and I sat round the kitchen table with a bottle of wine, the boys safely asleep in their cots upstairs. We were elated, exhausted, but at that moment the whole experience seemed totally unreal. We had longed to get out of Bucharest, but now we were home we found that Romania still clung to us, we could not shake it off. I think maybe it was then, the very first evening, that Alan and I realised our relationship with Romania had not ended with rescuing Michael. Memories clouded our minds; they still do. I do not believe a day goes by when I do not think of the suffering of the children we left behind. As our relationship with Michael deepens, we gain with it a better understanding of his past and this in turn makes us increasingly frustrated when we think of all the thousands of children who could and should be helped as he has been.

But those feelings came later. That first night we were just aware that we were never going to shake the dust of Romania from our heels, but it did not matter because we had a little piece of Romania upstairs in his cot. For while Michael is going to be brought up as our son, a little English boy, it is also our job to make him proud of his heritage, aware of who he is and where he came from.

Our arrival home had not been without incident. We have three dogs, two cairn terriers and an ancient golden retriever. We had anticipated that Michael would be afraid of the cairns and so had shut them away before taking him out of the car. What we had not anticipated was his fear of cats. He shrieked with terror at the sight of them and his fear did not rest with them – every fluffy toy, however big, however small, sent him into transports of panic. Indeed, the whole house seemed to assault his senses. Trying to look at it through his eyes, I suddenly realised how colourful it was, compared to the drabness of everything in Bucharest. The move from orphanage to hotel, although dramatic in some respects, had not been such a contrast since the hotel was very bleak, decorated in shades of brown and beige.

Luckily I had anticipated some of his reaction and, unlike the riot in Charlie's room, Michael's little bedroom was very uncluttered. Still, while Alan and Locket looked after the boys, I dashed round the house with a dustbin liner, cramming all the cuddly toys into it, except for the few in Charlie's cot.

It has to be said, however, that this initial reaction was very short-lived. We arrived home at three o'clock and by five o'clock Michael had settled in. He had emptied the toy box several times, learnt the layout of the ground floor and, most important of all, the location of the biscuit barrel.

Charlie had gone straight over to see the Reeves. Although he had a very high fever, Anne Reeve reported that he had been ecstatic to be home and had done several laps of honour, at full speed, round the tennis court to celebrate. The Reeves came back with him. We cracked open a bottle of champagne. Michael fell in love with them all, instantly, and I must say it was wonderful to see them. They made us feel normal again.

The next few days passed in a haze. There were endless telephone calls from friends, from desperate would-be parents who were being referred to us now from every quarter – the Home Office, the Foreign Office, Suzy Gale, various adoption agencies – all wanting to know how we had arranged to rescue Michael so quickly. Flowers arrived, as for the birth of a baby, and an endless stream of visitors, who we tried to restrict as best we could. Through it all Michael took everything in his stride. He slept well, he ate well, his only eccentricity being that he had to have some form of food in his hand at all times otherwise he felt insecure, which was very understandable, bearing in mind he had spent so much of his life on the verge of starvation.

Charlie was still a worry. On the Monday morning following our return home, I took the boys to the surgery. It was difficult to get anybody to concentrate on Charlie – everyone was fascinated by Michael, by his extraordinary little penguin walk and his deathly white skin. In the 'fat cat' land of Oxfordshire, nobody had ever seen a case of malnutrition and chronic child neglect before. We were given sample bottles for the boys' diarrhoea, Calpol for Charlie's fever and sent on our way.

Because Michael had not always been in an orphanage we had no idea, of course, what he had experienced of normal living, other than that we assumed he had only ever known city life. On his first morning in England he sat for a good half-hour on the grass, plucking at it, turning it over in his fingers, feeling it, chewing it. Grass was obviously a brand-new experience. A cow lumbered up to the fence. We dashed to pick him up, assuming he would react with terror, as he had with the dogs and cats. Not at all. He waddled up to it and tried to stroke its nose. By the same evening he could moo and by the end of the second day in his new home he had at least a dozen words: cat, dog, tick-tock, cow, tractor, cold, hot, cake and best and most wonderful of all, Mummy and Daddy. It was such a natural thing that I cannot tell you the precise moment he joined Charlie in calling us Mummy and Daddy – it just happened. Perhaps it should have seemed a momentous breakthrough to us, but in our minds, at least, we had been his mother and father from the day we had first met him.

Our days began to have some sort of structure. Charlie still had his walk in his buggy before lunch, which constituted his nap for the day. We tried putting Michael in the buggy but he screamed, and so while Charlie had his walk outside, Michael slept in his cot. He was becoming less easy to put down. As his relationship with us developed, so he wanted to spend time with us rather than sleep. However long it took, though, Alan and I had made a pact. For the time being, at any rate, Michael's days of crying in a cot alone were over. We never left him until he was alseep, whether it was for a nap or at night.

One evening during the first week I tried giving him a bottle of milk at bedtime, as Charlie still had. Michael was used to drinking from an ordinary cup, but while recognising that going back to a bottle was a retrograde step, I thought it might be comforting. Yet, as I held him in my arms and tried to give him his bottle, he seemed to be resisting me, indeed he seemed almost unable to suck. I could not understand it. I left it a few nights and tried again – the same reaction. I laid him in his cot. I do not know what made me do it, but just to see what happened, I handed the bottle to him. Instantly he took it and began to suck earnestly, his eyes closing in apparent bliss. That simple gesture said more about his life than anything else. He did not know how to be held and be given a bottle. He knew only about lying alone in his cot and helping himself to one. Now, six months later, he has his evening bottle cradled in Alan's arms. Yes, in theory a retrograde step for a two-and-a-half-year-old, but to us it seems like a big step forward.

By the middle of Michael's first week at home, I began to feel ill, too, very fluey. I took my temperature one morning and was surprised to find it was 102°. There were no other symptoms of cold or a sore throat, I just ached, felt vaguely sick and kept running high temperatures. I had also caught the conjuctivitis that Michael had passed to Charlie, which meant that I was stumbling round without my contact lenses, which was not easy.

Charlie had improved a little but was still not eating properly and seemed very quiet, as if the stuffing had been knocked out of him. It was difficult to tell whether this was because he felt ill or because of Michael's arrival. The relationship between the boys was still good.

They had their moments, like any brothers, but Michael displayed none of the aggression that we had been led to expect. We were almost waiting for things to go wrong between them but their relationship improved daily. Charlie tended to snatch toys from Michael but this did not seem to matter because Michael never played with a toy long enough to mind it suddenly disappearing. This was one of the more serious aspects likely to affect his future development, as far as I could tell. His complete lack of concentration meant he would flit from object to object, sometimes throwing something down almost before he had picked it up, and moving on to the next thing. I could not imagine him ever sitting still in a classroom. He had obviously never seen a book before. To him it was simply a squarish object for chucking around the room. He could not understand that there were pages to turn, images to look at. He found Charlie's interest in books quite extraordinary. Gradually, though, by starting with Charlie's very first baby books, he began to understand, although he could not sit still long enough to read one.

These, though, were trivial problems. In truth, we had no major ones. Michael is such an easy little boy to love. Even in those early days he was very free with his hugs and kisses. Too free perhaps, for he greeted everyone like a long-lost friend which, while very flattering, was not normal. Everything happened so quickly. By Thursday, 23 August, I had noted in my diary that he was no longer frightened of the cats, and by Saturday the 25th, he was throwing a ball for the cairns and was developing more than a passing friendship with Fran's doberman, Boogy.

On Sunday, I woke feeling very ill but also very happy. It was my forty-third birthday and it was the best I have ever had. Locket gave me four peacocks. I had always wanted peacocks – they suit Hampton Gay. They were young birds and she had bought four to ensure that there was at least one cock amongst them. Murray and Claire came to lunch and gave me a wonderful pair of jazzy baseball boots more suited to an eighteen-year-old. They were just what I needed to ward off the onset of middle-age. My mother came, too, with a much needed new sweater, but Alan's present to me was the best birthday present I will ever have. Alan's present was Michael.

In the preparation of this book I have asked many of our friends and family for their first impressions of Michael. They were all surprised at how small he was and how pale. It was his white skin that shocked them, that and his sores, and his extraordinary shape. My mother saw none of these things on the day she met Michael, which was also my birthday. 'Can I be your Granny?' she asked him, solemnly, as I carried him downstairs to meet her for the first time. He stretched out his arms to her and she dissolved into tears. It was love at first sight, a relationship which has grown and blossomed in the intervening months. Michael now calls her Naughty Gran-Gran, and they are both very pleased with this.

By Monday, when Michael had been home for two weeks, the black cross was still very much on the door. Our illnesses seemed to be on the increase if anything. Despite antibiotics, I still had a very bad fever. Charlie was a little better, though still quiet. We all had conjunctivitis and Michael had come out in an enormous rash of spots on his face, like bad teenagers' acne. Dr Young felt this was caused by the impurities coming out of his system as his skin was exposed to sunlight. Both boys still had appalling diarrhoea and as a result Charlie's bottom was in a terrible state from nappy rash. It was hard work, but the important things were right: we all loved Michael and Michael, it appeared, loved us. We felt a family, we were a family – if only we could be well. The surgery was becoming almost as familiar as our own home but still we could not solve the problem of the diarrhoea. The John Radcliffe Hospital had run four sample tests now, and could find no trace of what the cause could be.

Looking back through Michael's medical records, it appeared he had been in hospital several times with chronic diarrhoea and fever. Indeed, the first occasion had been when he was only nine months old. It was obviously a recurring bug in his system and whatever it was, Charlie now had it, too. We needed to solve it and solve it fast, for all the good food and vitamins we were putting into Michael were of little benefit and Charlie seemed to be fading away before our eyes. I made a fuss at the surgery and they promised to give fresh samples top priority. Rather than run the risk of them getting lost in the system, Alan took them directly to the lab. We waited.

I asked Locket the other day for her impressions of those first few weeks. 'Ghastly,' she said, 'very tense, and all that diarrhoea. I wouldn't have missed it though, I'm glad I didn't go on the choir tour.' On our return from Bucharest, Locket, who is a member of Oxford Girls' Choir, was supposed to be going on a tour of southern Ireland. She had cancelled her place and they had been very understanding, realising that she needed to be around for the first few weeks of her little brother's new life. 'It was such a pity everyone was so ill,' she said.

Yes, it was a pity, but in a strange way it brought us closer together. Our social life was nil. After the rash of people, mostly family, who had wanted to see Michael, we kept everyone away, feeling it was not fair to inflict on them whatever was wrong with us. We closed ranks, stayed at home and concentrated on our various relationships. Charlie's reaction, particularly, was extraordinary. Except very occasionally, when provoked in the extreme, he really did not seem to resent Michael at all. Michael tended to have the lion's share of attention, despite all our efforts to the contrary, yet Charlie accepted the situation very placidly. At a time when he should have enjoyed his mother fussing over him I was dashing between the two of them, but he took it all in his stride.

Finally, on 3 September, Dr Young rang. 'We've found your bug,' he said, 'it's called giardiasis. It's a parasite that gets into the gut. It's mostly a tropical disease, though it is sometimes found in the Mediterranean.'

'Is this what Michael's been suffering from all this time?'

'Without a doubt.'

'And does Charlie have it?'

'Yes, it looks like it.'

'So, what do we do?' I asked, in mounting panic.

'It couldn't be more simple,' he said. 'I'll give you some medicine for them. They have one large dose of 12½ mls a day for three days, at the end of which they're cured.'

'It can't be that easy,' I said.

'It is. It's foul stuff, you'll have a job getting it down them but if you do, all your problems will be over, I promise.'

He was right. The diarrhoea ended with the last dose of medicine. Michael had been suffering from giardiasis for over half his life and thanks to the John Radcliffe Hospital he was cured in just three days.

A fortnight later, I accused Margaret of shrinking his trousers in the wash. 'I haven't,' she insisted. 'If you ask me, it's Michael changing shape, not the trousers. Have you tried measuring him?' We had not measured him since his first day home. We stood him up against the entrance into Alan's office, which is the family measuring post. He had grown a whole one and three-quarter inches in four weeks. We couldn't believe it.

Sitting on the kitchen floor, and still an easy prey to tears, I started to cry. Michael waddled off into the utility room and returned, moments later, with a tissue, which he solemnly handed to me. 'Naughty Mummy,' he said.

14

THE CHRISTENING OF MICHAEL AUREL BURNETT FOWLER

M Y old schoolfriend, Di, became a Marxist while she was at university. When Locket was born and I asked her to be a godmother she looked at me as though I was mad. Fourteen years later, when Charlie was born, I did not dare repeat the request. She had her own son by then, whom she had not christened, yet when she came to see me in hospital I sensed that if I had asked her, she might have accepted. When I told her about Michael she was very supportive and kind. We were supposed to be working on a book together at the time but so caught up was I at trying to bring Michael home that work had taken very much second place. When I plucked up the courage to ask her to be Michael's godmother, her response was simple. 'Thank goodness,' she said, 'I was afraid you weren't going to ask me this time. Yes, of course, I'd love to be.'

We felt the choice of Michael's godparents was very important. He needs a nucleus of friends and family who will always support him and provide much needed security, particularly during the turbulent adolescent years when he is likely to suffer moments of self-doubt and isolation. We were not looking for godparents to set him a moral code for life, we were looking for people who would be good friends. We asked Sally Drummond-Hay to be his other godmother, a true and loyal friend, who acted as a referee for us in the home study report and who is mother of Locket's best childhood friend, Caroline. For godfathers we asked Adam Norton, my own childhood best friend, and John Runacres, Alan's business partner. The christening of course took place in our own little church, here at Hampton Gay. When Charlie was christened, we had opted to have a special service for him, but in Michael's case we felt it would be more appropriate to include his christening as part of one of our normal monthly services, to welcome him into the community. Since October was our Harvest Festival, we decided on the September.

It was a mad scramble of preparation. Anne Reeve arranged beautiful flowers for the church as a wonderful christening present; the local bakery took endless trouble with the christening cake; and the children's shop in Woodstock made Michael a little white shirt and navy trousers for the occasion, because no clothes in traditional sizes fitted him at the time. We invited only the godparents and our immediate family, although of course, we included Margaret and Aunty Vi, our secretary. There were three other very special guests of honour – Kerry, husband Steven and baby Alexander, whose visa had mercifully been extended and who had grown out of all recognition. David Wilcox conducted the service, and we named our new son Michael Aurel Burnett Fowler, keeping his own middle name and adding my father's family name of Burnett.

It was a slightly eccentric but very touching day. The atmosphere was extraordinary and the warmth and good wishes so obviously heartfelt. There was a big turnout at the church. There were many people there we did not know; they had come, it seemed, to see the little Romanian boy from Hampton Gay being christened. They did not seem to have come to gawp with curiosity, however. It felt as though they were there to lend support, to wish us well. David is an unusual vicar in as much as he believes that children should be allowed to do whatever they like in church. Throughout the service, Charlie and Michael wandered about, Michael, of course, with the inevitable rusk in hand. He screamed appropriately when David splashed water on his head, but posed beautifully for the photographs. Looking at them now, I realise how much he had already changed since we had first brought him home. His spots had completely gone and so had his sores, except for one deep one on the back of his head. The sun had brought colour to his hair – formerly a dull, grey mouse, it was now a rich chestnut. The razor-cut hairstyle was growing out and, although he was still very pale, his face had lost the dead-white look and there were no longer dark circles under his eyes. Nonetheless, the contrast between Michael and Adam Norton's two-and-a-half-year-old daughter was enormous. It made me realise what a long way we still had to go.

It was a beautiful day. After the service we had a christening tea in the garden and the children played on a newly acquired climbing frame. Michael wandered freely amongst his guests. I have pictures of him rolling around on the grass, with one of the cats, of him coming down the slide on his godfather's lap, and best of all, one of him up to his elbows in cake – cake at the time was his particular passion.

When the party was over he was, understandably, very difficult to settle to sleep. He was not being naughty or crying, he was on a high and terribly excited. I was so very conscious that night of the extraordinary changes in him. Physically, yes, but much more striking was his attitude to life – the friendly but passive baby of the orphanage days had gone altogether to be replaced by a highly active, highly sociable, highly intelligent little boy. There was no doubt in my mind he was aware that this had been his own special day and he had revelled in it. Now, jumping about in his cot, he simply did not want it to end. It was this love of life that had provided the spark which had kept him alive during his ordeal in the orphanage, and I wondered how much longer he could have hung on before it would have been extinguished completely. The thought now of him being transferred to a home for 'irrecuperables' fills me with such horror that I try desperately to keep it out of my mind. Talking to Alan, we have both found that although we are anxious to put the past behind us all, the awfulness of the situation in which we had found Michael becomes increasingly intolerable. Talking to other parents, we have found they feel the same.

The following night Michael had a nightmare. All children have nightmares, of course, but this was different. His screams were desperate, he trembled from head to foot and, in a warm room, he was ice-cold, so cold that involuntarily I shivered as I held him to me. We have always tried to keep the children out of our bed, except when they're ill, but this was different. We put Michael between us, warmed him and soothed his sobs. It happened the next night and the next, as if all his suffering, all his pain, was draining out of him. We became hollow-eyed from lack of sleep, and so did he, but instinctively we felt it was a vital part of the healing process. Gradually the nightmares became less frequent until now they are very occasional. One day, we feel confident, there will be no more.

Apart from the nightmares, the next couple of weeks were happy ones and various milestones were achieved. We had decided when we brought Michael home that initially we would, as far as possible, always have the boys looked after by two people, so that they would not scrap for the attention of one person. This policy definitely paid off and for quite long periods now one person could look after them without either vying for attention. It was when they were tired or had hurt themselves that things would become tense, particularly for me – both wanted Mummy and Mummy only had one lap and one pair of arms.

Locket was now back at school and we went every day to fetch her. Although Michael is never good in the car – he cannot sit still for long – both the boys enjoy picking up their sister from school. Not only are they very pleased to see her, but they adore the attention they get from all her friends.

One Friday, just over a month after Michael had come home, we embarked on our first major outing, to Granny's for lunch. I was slightly worried as to how Michael would react to an hour's car journey, but it appeared to be no problem. Now both boys were well we began socialising a little more. Charlie has a very special friend called Georgina, whom he adores, and both boys went to visit her. Georgina has gorgeous red, curly hair and is ten days older than Charlie. Michael was very taken with her and again seemed not at all to mind visiting a strange house. Indeed, in many respects he was more confident than Charlie.

During the last week in September we received a telephone call from Dr Magdalena Dragon, who had given Michael his medical examination in Bucharest. At the time she had refused payment and Alan had suggested that if ever she was in England she must come and stay with us. Knowing how difficult it is for Romanians to acquire visas to visit the UK, he had not anticipated that this would happen for some time and he was surprised to hear that she was already in England. She asked whether she and her mother could come and stay for the weekend of 29/30 September. We agreed, of course, but both felt a little reluctant, partly, I think, because we were trying to put the Romanian experience behind us, and partly because we were genuinely concerned that Michael would be unsettled by hearing Romanian spoken. We were very conscious now that he understood most of what we said and so we never spoke of his past in front of him. Nevertheless, this was a debt we owed and we intended to honour it.

I had never met Magdalena Dragon and found her very pleasant. She was a woman in her mid-fifties, her mother somewhere between seventy and eighty. They were wonderful guests who, gratifyingly, enjoyed their food and drink. We took them round Oxford, and showed them something of the Oxfordshire countryside, including Woodstock. Michael, though, was uncomfortable throughout their visit. At first I thought I was imagining it, but Alan sensed it too. He was restless, irritable and very clingy, and it worried me dreadfully as to what he might be thinking – that Magdalena and her mother were going to take him away, perhaps. We asked them not to speak Romanian in front of him, but, of course, they did from time to time. I was glad, to be honest, when they left, though Magdalena had been very interesting on the subject of Romania. As a paediatrician she naturally found the orphanages very distressing, but as she said, in many respects life for the orphans was no harder than life for everyone in Romania. As for the number of abandoned children, she was adamant that it is far greater than is commonly believed – 450,000 is the figure she placed on it and she said she had access to official records. When I told her of Michael and Charlie's giardiasis, she confirmed that this was a common ailment amongst children in

Romania and caused an enormous amount of suffering. Yet the medicine that we had accepted from our GP without question was simply not available. Once the children had the parasite, it remained in their guts and their fever and diarrhoea continued throughout childhood, sapping their energy and greatly diminishing the value of what nourishment they did receive.

All during Magdalena Dragon's visit I was feeling ill again. Margaret had been off sick on the Friday before and on Monday her husband rang in to say she was still unwell. Her symptoms sounded like mine – high fever and nausea. Still, on Monday morning there was no time to consider my ailments for Jane Allan was coming to meet Michael for the first time. Michael and Charlie behaved very well and we brought Jane up-to-date on what had happened to us during the last few weeks. She told us that she would continue to handle our case until Michael's UK adoption could be finalised, which was particularly welcome. Towards the end of her visit I felt increasingly ill and after she had gone I had to subcontract the preparation of lunch to Alan. In the afternoon I took the boys, as usual, to meet Locket from school. The whole journey was an effort and when I got home I managed to struggle through the boys' tea and bedtime routine and then had to collapse in bed myself. When I woke up the following morning I knew I was really ill. I took my temperature – it was 106°. I helped Alan get the boys up and then went back to bed, leaving him to cope with breakfast. Margaret was still ill but Sue Timms, who had been helping us with a little part-time cleaning since Michael had come home, agreed to come in and help us out until Margaret was better.

The next two days passed in a haze, my temperature swinging dramatically between incredible heat and shivering with cold in a matter of minutes. I staggered down to the doctor, who could not imagine what was wrong with me but decided to do a blood test. The boys came to visit me periodically and I tried my best to reassure them but it was an effort even to pick up a glass of water. Alan went to see the Reeves and the two younger girls, Vickie and Karen, agreed to help look after the boys after school each afternoon until I was better. On Wednesday afternoon I noticed that when Alan came up to see me he put on an extra sweater in what was already a hot room. 'You don't feel well either, do you?' I said. He admitted he did not. By that night he too had a raging fever.

The next day, the doctor called to see us both and take fresh blood samples. Neither of us could get out of bed without either feeling or being sick and our temperatures were still swinging up and down, violently out of control. I kept having the most horrible dreams, violent, terrifying dreams, and all the while we kept wondering what on earth was wrong with us. In moments of near-delirium I decided we must have caught AIDS in Romania, which was clearly ludicrous. With the help of Sue and the Reeves we staggered through the rest of the day and that night Margaret telephoned – her blood tests were through, and she had just turned bright yellow. She told Locket, over the telephone, that she had yellow fever. I looked up yellow fever in the *Readers' Digest Home Medical Book* and nearly fainted on the spot. It sounded an absolutely dreadful disease and desperately contagious – it seemed likely that we would infect the whole county.

The next morning I rang the doctor's surgery in a panic. Locket and Margaret had their wires crossed. No, she did not have yellow fever, she had yellow jaundice, a result, they suspected, of having hepatitis. During the next few days the surgery unravelled the mystery. We all had hepatitis A. Because of the incubation period, it appeared that Alan and I had probably caught it on our first trip to Romania and had given it to Charlie, which was why the poor little boy had been so off colour for so many weeks. Margaret, in turn, had probably caught it from Charlie's nappies. Locket and Michael appeared to have escaped, though in all probability Michael will have had it at some stage, for hepatitis A and B effect at least 60 per cent of Romania's population. 'No booze for three months, you'll feel dreadfully ill for three weeks, and tired and depressed for another two months after that,' was the verdict.

Once we knew what was wrong with us it was a great relief, but at the same time we recognised it was going to be a long haul to get us better. Dr Young suggested that we needed a nurse as there was no way we could cope with two toddlers in our condition. On the face of it, this seemed a sensible notion but instinctively we felt it was wrong to bring a stranger into the house, just when Michael was settling in and he and Charlie were doing so well together. The solution came in the form of truly magnificent support from the children's nearest and dearest. Sue worked full-time, coming in every morning at eight-thirty and not leaving until four, when the Reeve children took over. At weekends, the Reeve girls looked after Charlie and Michael in the mornings, and Murray and Claire came both days from two until six. This help was supplemented by Aunty Vi, our secretary, who abandoned her typewriter and came over every weekday afternoon, and Fran, who turned her life upside down so that she could look after the animals, which she did every morning before embarking on a day's work. As soon as Locket was back from school each day, she took over the caring and helped us get the boys to bed. People we hardly knew were incredibly kind. For the first time we got to know Lesley Burt, the mother of a friend of Locket's, married to a doctor and herself a nurse. They had a special interest in Romania and when she heard of our problems she cooked the children the most delicous meals, which I suspect they still miss. Michael's godmother, Sally Drummond-Hay, kept appearing with hot soup and shopping, and all the while, Alan and I continued to be miseries. We turned bright yellow, we kept being sick, we ached from head to foot, it seemed to go on and on. We kept thinking of Charlie – no wonder he had not eaten for weeks. Poor little chap, if only we had known how ill he really was. Adrian Young assured us that Charlie's symptoms would have been very mild compared to ours, but still we felt guilty for not realising what was wrong with him.

Almost to the day three weeks from when we had started to feel ill, we began to get better. More blood tests were taken which showed that our livers were on the mend, although still not right. Dr Young confirmed that the fever and illness I had felt the previous month had all been the build-up for developing hepatitis, as had been Alan's bout of fever in Bucharest. As we emerged slowly, we began to realise that the children had not suffered at all. If anything, our illness had been a good thing. Locket's bond with her brothers was much, much stronger – they adored her and had started to call her Yuggie. Michael and Charlie's relationship was closer, too. Clearly, while their parents were ill they had actually needed one another. They still fought occasionally, but often one would put an arm round the other, particularly if he was hurt or sad. They kissed each other if they had been apart for any length of time, and it was impossible now to give Michael anything – a biscuit, a piece of fruit, a crisp – without him asking for one for 'Chardie' too. Charlie had taken to calling Michael 'Mikey' and I am afraid to say this is a nickname which is starting to stick. In fact, we felt we could at last say with confidence that the boys' relationship was a success, a huge success, and it says a great deal for both of them. If Charlie had not been such an easygoing and generous person, things could have been very different. If Michael had lived up to the reputation of many orphanage children, then they would have fought a great deal. As it was, they genuinely seemed to love one another. We also noticed they had grown up.

On 10 November it was Locket's sixteenth birthday and by then, although tired, we were more or less back to normal. At her request, we all had lunch in Browns restaurant in Oxford. It was Michael's first meal in a restaurant and he loved it. The gap between the two boys had closed considerably while we had been ill and several people asked us if they were twins. At teatime, the Reeves and the Drummond-Hays helped us demolish Locket's birthday cake and with gritted teeth we poured champagne for everyone else, while we toasted her in orange juice. In the evening she went into Oxford with Simon and some friends for dinner, and I indulged in some reminiscing with Alan. What had happened to all those years, how could my baby girl suddenly be so grown up? We toasted her again in orange juice and tonic water and decided that the family had reached a turning-point. We had been though conjunctivitis, giardiasis and hepatitis, intermingled with the usual quantity of coughs and colds, and we had beaten Michael's malnutrition, sores and spots. The boys were growing apace and Locket was very happy, with both her new school year and her social life. It had been a dramatic few months but we had come through it and were closer and stronger for it. We knew that what we had seen in Romania would ensure we never again took our comfortable life for granted. Our experience had shaken us to the core and that was no bad thing. For the first time we felt we could really look forward, that there was no longer any need to glance over our shoulders. Michael was who he was, a real member of the family now. He had found his place, he was well, he was catching up fast. Things could only get better.

15

LEO AND MIRELLA

MICHAEL Fowler was not the only survivor in our family. Leo Mackillop was now stabilised on a complicated cocktail of drugs, which he would need for the next year or so. He was doing well but Lorne and Geraldine were exhausted. Once our various bugs were at last behind us we felt it was safe to ask them to come and spend the weekend, which they did in mid-November. Little did any of us know what a drama, in different ways, that weekend would prove to be for all of us.

Leo had done very well indeed. It was clear that he was still a little on the small side for a three-and-a-half-month-old, but he was such a mature baby, so worldly wise. Indeed, he is such a relaxed, together person that one feels oddly deferential in his presence, knowing what he has suffered in his short life. Michael and Charlie adored him instantly, particularly Michael who is very into babies, calling them 'babbies'. They stroked and cuddled him and made a huge fuss. 'Funny to think they'll all be off to the pub together in a few years,' Lorne said sagely.

On Saturday afternoon we were due to go to an amateur dramatics presentation of *The Nutcracker Suite*, in which Murray's wife Claire had a part. Lorne and Geraldine were very tired and decided to stay behind. Sue came in to look after the boys as Margaret was still off sick and Alan, Locket, Murray and I went along to applaud. When we returned, Lorne met us at the door. 'There's a man been on the telephone from Sicily in response to your letter. I don't speak Italian and he doesn't speak English but we managed to limp through on a little French. He wants you to ring back. I gather he's Michael's sister's adoptive father, is that right?'

He was right. With Ivan's help we had managed to follow not only Christina-Daniella's adoption but also Mirella's. Just ten days before we had received a letter from him, giving us the names and addresses of the two sets of Italian families who had adopted Mirella and Christina-Daniella. We could not believe it. We had been cautiously optimistic about Christina-Daniella's future but had assumed that Mirella was too old for adoption. We were thrilled at the news and still more so when we discovered that both families were living in Sicily and, from their postcodes, seemed to be just outside Palermo. I had immediately written to each of them, enclosing a photograph of Michael and suggesting that while it was obviously important for the children to settle down and establish their own identities within their own new families, it was also very important in our view that the Trifan family should be kept in touch with one another. I said we believed that when the children were older, if they wished to meet then we should make sure that they could do so.

As yet there had been no reply from Christina-Daniella's parents, although the reply from Signor Gabriele, Mirella's adoptive father, was almost by return. We had written the letter in Italian, with the help of a friend of ours, and he had therefore telephoned us assuming we spoke the language. We rang our friend immediately and asked her whether she would ring him and explain that we did not speak Italian but were very pleased to hear from him. She did so and rang us back to say that the Gabrieles were extremely happy to hear from us and would be very pleased for the children to meet whenever we felt it was right for Michael. We were thrilled. Still more extraordinary, it appeared that the Gabrieles had no idea that Christina-Daniella was also in Sicily and had asked for her address. We felt very grateful to Ivan and Adrian for their excellent detective work. Without it, the two sisters could have grown up side by side in Sicily, never knowing that the other was just a few kilometres down the road.

Our relief that the children were all in touch was particularly relevant for, when a child is adopted in Romania, he or she ceases to exist. There is no way that, in the future, the children can go to Romania and establish who they are and where they came from – the records will not be there. It is therefore up to the adoptive parents to keep records of their childrens' past, so that if they wish to know more about their birth families, at least they have a starting-point. In Michael's case, the need to keep a close watch on his sisters had always been a top priority for us, for two reasons. Firstly, if we bring up Michael to be the kind of child and, later, the kind of man that his developing character already suggests he may become, then he will be a very kind and caring person. He is the son of the family and I believe therefore that he will always feel very responsible towards his sisters and will want to ensure that they are happy and well looked after. Secondly, one of the big scourges for adopted children is the feeling of rejection. Ask any adopted child and the thing that most concerns them is *why* their natural parents gave them up. History, no doubt, will relate that many of the women in Romania had no choice but to give up their children. In Michael's case, the fact that not only he but also his sisters were put up for adoption at least proves that he personally was not rejected. The family structure had broken down, however one apportions the blame – Ceauşescu; Michael's father, Vasile for putting the cause of the Revolution before his family; his mother, Lenuta, for not making more of an effort to keep her children; her boyfriend for refusing to make a home for her children . . . Whichever way you look at it, Michael need feel no sense of personal rejection because he knows what happened to him also happened to his sisters.

We went to bed that night feeling very happy. We might still be waiting for a response from Christina-Daniella's parents but at least Mirella's felt exactly as we did. We were awoken at eleven o'clock by Locket. 'There's this woman on the phone, she's a great friend of the Gabrieles, she speaks very good English and she lives next door to them. We've been talking for ages and now she wants to talk to you. It's awful, it seems that Michael had a ghastly babyhood.'

'How do you mean?' I said, still stupid with sleep.

'His mother used to shut them in a room and leave them without food. Mirella's very bitter. You'd better talk to her direct.'

I went to the telephone. The woman introduced herself as a friend and next-door neighbour of the Gabrieles. She spoke excellent English and told me that she herself was of Romanian extraction, although the family had been in Sicily for several generations. Mirella was well, had settled in splendidly with her new family and was putting some of the ugly memories of her past behind her, she told me. When Mirella had first arrived in Italy, she had been very concerned about her little brother and sister. They had been separated when they were put in orphanages and she did not even know if they were alive. The Gabrieles had promised her that they would try and find the little ones, but their first priority was to make Mirella herself strong and well and feel settled into her new life. They had also spent a great deal of money bringing Mirella out of Romania and they explained to her that it would be a year or so before they could afford to go back. My letter arriving as a bolt out of the blue had been an answer to all their prayers. In one stroke they could tell Mirella that her little brother and sister were alive and that both had been adopted. They agonised for some time as to whether they should show Mirella Michael's photograph. In the end they did. Apparently she studied it in silence for a moment or two. He had changed a great deal, and she had not seen him for a year. 'That's my brother,' she said at last, and burst into tears. But happy tears, the woman assured me, she was just so glad that he was alive and safe.

Mirella Trifan's story had not been a happy one. It appeared that she had been very much the little mother to her younger sister and brother. Her father, she said, was very kind and she had loved him very much. It had been her adopted parents painful duty to tell her that he had died, for he had still been in hospital when she had been sent to the orphanage. Her mother, she hated. So far as she was concerned, Lenuta was someone whom she would never see again. She was very bitter. She spoke of being shut in a cupboard, of the three of them being left alone for hours on end without any food. She told the story of a childhood of misery, cruelty and hardship. I let the words wash over me, trying to ward them off – I could not bear to hear them.

'Maybe,' I said, desperately clutching at straws, 'maybe she is exaggerating. It would be very natural after what she has been through to seek sympathy and attention from her new parents.'

'Mirella never lies,' said the woman. 'I know her very well. Sometimes one wishes that she would not speak the truth, for she always says exactly what she thinks, whether it is pleasant or not. I do not think she has exaggerated her childhood misery. I know she has not. She has spoken only the truth.'

She went on to tell me a little more of Mirella. The Gabrieles had managed to bring her out of Romania in early September and had kept her out of school until late October, to give her a chance to settle in. She had learnt to speak Italian in three weeks and had joined school in the correct grade for her age. She was already top of her class. 'She's absolutely brilliant,' the woman told me. 'No one can believe how quickly she has learnt.'

'And is she happy?'

'Very, and now she knows about her brother and sister, her happiness is complete.'

I agreed over the telephone that the Gabrieles would not contact Christina-Daniella's parents until I had received a reply to my letter. I thanked her very much for the trouble she had taken and the enormous cost of the phone call. Then I said goodnight to Locket and went back to Alan. His reaction was exactly the same as mine – one of terrible sadness. Increasingly, as the weeks had gone by and we had come to know Michael better, we had both said how much we wished we had been able to share his babyhood. We felt we had missed out. We loved him so much that inevitably we wished he had been ours from the very beginning. Yet we took comfort from the fact that he had only spent eight months in an orphanage, and that until that time he had been part of a family, one of three children. We knew their life must have been very hard and deprived, but nonetheless, at least as a family unit, we felt there must have been love and comfort, sharing and companionship. In a single stroke our illusions were destroyed. Michael's babyhood sounded a nightmare, but if so why, why had he come through it all so well? Was it because of his father? From the very earliest time, when we first took Michael out into the streets of Bucharest, even while he still lived in the orphanage, we had noticed that he was always attracted to men with beards. His head would swing round sharply to follow a bearded man walking across the street. Even today, if friends come to the house and the man happens to have a beard, Michael is instantly attracted to him. Clearly, then, his father was bearded and clearly he meant a great deal to the little boy. Maybe his father's love was enough to give Michael the strength and courage which he now possesses and will always have. Maybe this is his legacy to his son, for I swear that love is no stranger to Michael. When he came home to us and we loved him, it was not a novelty. He had been loved before, and well.

As on so many other occasions in the past months, we lay in the dark thinking through what we had been told. It is difficult to define why we were so deeply upset. It took us days to come to terms with what we had heard and in some ways we still have not, we are still hoping that when we do one day meet Mirella, she will give us all some crumb of comfort. We shall see.

Charlie woke us early in the morning, early even by his standards. We were bog-eyed through lack of sleep. Going downstairs to make a cup of tea, Alan encountered Lorne making up a feed for Leo. He mentioned that Leo's breathing was a little irregular. It was probably nothing, he assured. By ten o'clock Leo was breathing quickly and shallowly and his colour was bad. We did not mess about. Lorne, Geraldine and Leo, with Locket to show them the way, drove straight to the casualty department at the John Radcliffe Hospital. I stayed behind to look after the boys and to make up feeds and wash Babygros. Whatever was wrong with Leo, it seemed likely that he was in for a stay in hospital.

The John Radcliffe is recognised as having one of the top paediatric units in the country and just recently the hospital has opened a new cardiac wing. It did not take them very long to find what the Brompton Hospital had inexplicably missed – as well as the blocked aorta which had now been repaired, Leo also had a massive hole in the heart and a faulty valve. Once the problem was diagnosed, he was despatched post-haste to the Brompton. Lorne and Locket returned to Hampton Gay to pick up his clothes and milk. Lorne looked strained and very pale; they had thought all Leo's problems were behind him. It seemed as if they were just beginning.

That night Lorne rang from home, having settled his wife and son into the Brompton. The diagnosis had been confirmed, Leo was stable and after a scan the following morning they would be able to tell us what would happen next. I spoke to Geraldine at lunchtime the following day. Leo's condition could be controlled by drugs, probably until he was two, when an operation could be performed. It was felt that repairing the hole would probably be enough and that once the heart was working properly then the valve would sort itself out. 'It's going to be a long haul,' said Geraldine, 'but we'll get there in the end. Leo's a fighter, just like Michael. You, know I couldn't help thinking last night, there's Leo who has benefited from the very best antenatal care with this wretched problem, and there's Michael who had been through every kind of deprivation and yet is as fit as a fiddle.' She sounded more than a little wistful.

I thought about what she had said. Yes, Michael really was as fit as a fiddle. Over the weeks, since that first dramatic bath at the Inter-Continental, his skin had gradually changed from that dead grey to the warm, pink, shiny baby skin we normally take for granted. His eyes had lost their haunted look and they now danced with fun and interest. His sores had all healed up, although I think he will carry some of his scars with him for life. After a great deal of protest, we had persuaded him to have a very quick haircut to trim the ragged edges. Paul, my hairdresser, confirmed that a razor had been used on his hair previously, which was why it was so thin. Now it was thickening up, chestnut brown and glossy. He had also lost the penguin look. His body had thinned down, or perhaps I should say, evened out. He no longer had the pot-belly of the malnourished child and his legs had grown in length and fattened out. He was still not in proportion, but when playing with other children now he no longer looked out of place.

We were invited to a party by Georgina's parents, Sue and Giles. It was a Sunday lunch and all the other guests had young children, which made Alan and I the elder statesmen by some years. Sue and Giles, because they are sensitive people, did not mention Michael's origins to anyone. Several people asked if our boys were twins and we said, 'No, brothers.' Several people commented on the confidence and friendliness of the little one. The temptation to say you should have seen him a few weeks ago was very great but while it is important that Michael is aware of his origins, we do not want them pushed down his throat. People can be so tactless. At a christening several weeks earlier the children had been introduced as, 'Michael, the little boy the Fowlers have adopted from Romania, and Charlie, their real son.' I suppose, inevitably, this sort of blunder is something all of us will have to face in the future. What is vital is that Michael realises that as far as we are concerned, the only difference between them is that he was born in Romania and Charlie in Oxford.

When Jane Allen was preparing her home study report on us, she had given me a number of Social Services booklets on the problems associated with adopting an older child. By 'older' they meant anyone who is not a newborn baby. I had read all the literature she gave me, and that which she recommended me, very carefully. Much of it was not relevant in Michael's case because although he was not a baby, he was very young at the time of adoption. However, there were two recurring themes which did seem relevant. The first was the fact that a damaged child could not be normal until, in some form, the pain had come out. With older children this could take years; with some only a matter of weeks. Undoubtedly Michael is a damaged child. Forget for one moment Mirella's stories of their family life, the fact remains that at eighteen months old he was taken from his family home and placed in an orphanage where conditions were not dissimilar to those of a concentration camp. For comfort, though, he had his older sister, with whom he had always shared a cot. Then, several months later, she, too, had been taken from him, leaving him with no one. These are the bald facts. We read that in most cases the pain manifested itself in the form of aggressive, bad behaviour, excessive clinginess and a variety of other disagreeable symptoms. In Michael's case the only true indication of his awful past (apart from his physical problems) has been his nightmares, which are now so infrequent as to be only a minor problem. Maybe we still have problems ahead of us, yet he seems so settled, so forward-looking, glancing over his shoulder not at all.

The other major problem area is a deprived child's unnatural independence and the need to regress. Children who have been continually let down and neglected develop a hard shell; they have to in order to protect themselves. They are friendly to everyone in an indiscriminate way but show no preferences for their carers. They are sometimes aggressively independent and before they are able to share a normal, close, loving relationship with anyone, it is necesary for them to climb back almost into the womb. They need to go back through the stages of childhood and babyhood. The Social Services booklet quoted many examples of children, perhaps as old as seven or eight, who have gone right back to the stage of having bottles and not being able to walk. Some of these stages would last only a few days or even a few hours, others for several weeks, but it was a necessary part of rehabilitation. Michael, up to a point, has done this. When he falls over now he cries and makes a great deal of fuss, in stark contrast to the early days when he never cried. He used to drink from a cup, now he drinks from a bottle. He used to feed himself, now he quite often likes to be fed. He needed no one, now he cries if I have to go out and does not like being separated from Charlie, even for a few minutes. When Alan is away for a night on business, he is restless and unhappy, and he really suffered when Locket went back to school after the holidays.

Interestingly, much can be seen from our photographs over the months. In purely physical terms the early photographs of him while still in the orphanage show a baby. Now he is a boy, striding around in his jeans, jumper and wellingtons, with his boy's haircut and his rapidly expanding interest in boyish pursuits. But if you look closely at his expression now, in many respects he looks *younger* than he did when we found him. Miraculously, the innocence of childhood has returned. The half-frown which used to play between his eyebrows most of the time in the orphanage has gone, as has the wariness in his eyes. What has happened is that he has shed the responsibility of looking after himself on to us, and the relief is enormous.

One day in mid-December I went to see Carol Cousins, our health visitor, for one of Michael's regular weigh-ins. Carol and I had decided early on that we would do nothing to speed up Michael's rehabilitation but let nature take its course – no special diets, no phsyiotherapy – just so long as he seemed to be moving in the right direction we would not interfere with mother nature's rebuilding programme. As usual, he had put on a considerable amount of weight – two and a half pounds in seven weeks. As I dressed him Carol said, 'If you wait a moment I'll do some sums.' She fiddled around with some graphs for a few minutes. 'I have some good news for you,' she said. 'On his current rate of progress, which seems very steady and stable, it would appear that by his third birthday he will be completely normal.'

'What do you mean, normal?' I asked.

'Average in both height and weight for his age.'

'I don't believe it,' I said. 'That quickly? Then he'll have done it in eleven months.'

'You'll have done it,' Carol corrected 'He's a real credit to you both.'

I shook my head. 'No, we provided the tools, it was Michael who got on with the job.'

I drove away from the doctor's surgery that afternoon with the biggest grin ever. I have always thought of three years old as being a benchmark, the beginning of true childhood. At three, most children can walk and talk, have more or less sorted out potty-training and are altogether thoroughly sociable beings. They have survived babyhood and toddlerhood and are ready to be fully paid-up members of the human race. What Carol's news meant was that Michael would start on real childhood with the slate wiped clean, his past well and truly behind him. I thought back to the morning of his second birthday when I had felt so desperate and miserable for him. Yes, three was going to be better, a lot better. I thanked God for it.

_16_
ELENA

C HRISTMAS Day 1990 could not help but be a very special one for us. We knew that twelve months earlier Michael had been in Orphanage No. 6 and we assumed that Christmas Day was much like Sunday, and he would have spent it cold, lonely, hungry and bewildered. Charlie woke at five, as usual, and tore his way through a stocking full of 'brmm-brmms' with escalating shrieks of delight. He was then persuaded to leave them for a few moments while I changed and dressed him and then he and Alan went downstairs for some serious, manly games. Locket and I made more tea. Granny had joined in the early-morning stocking-opening and had returned to bed. Locket and I were talking when Michael gave us a yell to tell us he was awake. We went to fetch him. He snuggled up in our bed and settled down to his bottle, keeping an eye on the stocking we had placed beside him. After a while, curiosity overcame hunger and he pulled the first parcel out of the stocking and began to unwrap it. In recent weeks he had started to take an interest not only in other people's babies but also in Georgina's dolls, so we had bought him a little doll for Christmas. 'Babby!' he exclaimed as he pulled the doll free of the wrapping and hugged and kissed it. We could not have given him anything better. Clutching Babby in one hand, his bottle of milk in the other, he snuggled down between Locket and me – something which just a few months before he had not known how to do – and in between sucks at his bottle he hummed a tuneless song. For me, it was the highlight of Christmas. Michael was warm, cosy, loved and obviously very, very happy. Locket and I exchanged a smile over his head. There was nothing we needed to say to each other.

Later, over breakfast, the boys compared stocking toys without animosity. In many respects I think the secret of their relationship lies in the fact that they are so different. Charlie is obsessed with anything on wheels and his other idea of fun is digging in the garden. He could not be less interested in Michael's dolls and cuddly toys, or his make-believe games, or complicated building projects. Charlie is the doer,

Michael the thinker. When they make a plan for doing something really bad – breaking out of the garden, climbing up the bookcase, raiding the larder – Michael works out the strategy and Charlie performs the deed. With my hand on my heart I can say that Charlie's life is now infinitely richer and so much more fun for having Michael as his brother. Indeed, if Michael was removed from his life now, it would be a desert. As for Michael, it sounds fanciful, I know, but it feels to us that he was meant to be our child. We fit together.

Christmas was marred for us in just one respect – it appeared that we had lost Christina-Daniella. None of our letters to her adoptive parents had been answered and in desperation, against our English lawyer's advice, we had sent the address to Mirella's parents and asked them to check it out. The news was not good. On the face of it, it appeared both the name and address were bogus. Either Ivan had inadvertently given us the wrong information or, for whatever reason, the adoptive parents had deliberately chosen not to be traced. Another thought began creeping insidiously into our minds – what if she had not been adopted at all? What if Ivan had misread her name? What if she was still in the orphanage? The more we thought about it, the more the idea appalled us. We had been too complacent, we had taken it for granted when Ivan told us both girls had been adopted that all was well with them.

We had been concerned about Christina-Daniella before, of course, but now our concern intensified for it had become much more personal. Michael was a part of us and Christina-Daniella was a part of him. For the first eighteen months of his life she and Michael had been as close as any two human beings could be. They had shared the same cot, every waking and sleeping moment. They had suffered together, lost their home and their parents together, lost their big sister together and finally they had lost each other. We could not let that be a lifetime's loss. Wherever she was, we had to find her.

We telephoned Ivan and he promised that he would recheck the records as soon as the festive season was over. Up to a point, he also allayed our fears about her disappearing altogether. If her adoptive parents had given a bogus address, then apparently the Romanian Government would take a very serious view of the situation, for she was still a Romanian citizen. They would instigate a search immediately, Ivan assured us. 'Do not worry, she will be found,' he said, confidently. We took what comfort we could from his words.

But for the fact that Tarom was on strike, we would have been welcoming one extra member of the family over Christmas. When we finally returned from Romania with Michael, we had actually discouraged Russell and Mitch from trying to press ahead with their adoption for the time being. We had been very aware that Bucharest was in an extremely precarious state. There were demonstrations everywhere and much talk that Christmas – the first anniversary of the revolution – would be the time to spark off another. The general feeling was that President Iliescu had made things worse, if anything. In view of this, we suggested to Russell and Mitch that they should wait a few months, but they decided to risk it. Ivan had vowed to stop handling British adoptions, because they were so difficult, and the British Embassy so awkward, but he agreed to do just one more, for Russell and Mitch. They had expected, like us, a long, harrowing trek round the orphanages, looking for their special child, but in their case the whole process was short-circuited. They had told Ivan that they would prefer a child younger than their daughter, Madi. One day he telephoned them to say that he had found a little girl, who was in fact not in an orphanage but currently with her mother, although she was about to be placed in orphanage care. Russell and Mitch flew out to Romania in early October, took one look at fifteen-month-old Elena and fell in love with her.

Her mother's story was a sad one. She had two children, a son named, strangely enough, Michael, who was then five, and Elena. She lived alone with both the children, who were illegitimate, and while she had the children with her there was, apparently, no hope of her marrying. She had to go out to work every day, sometimes leaving the children alone, and she had reached the point where she could simply no longer cope. In her case, there was no question of trying to persuade her to keep the children. Even if Russell and Mitch had sponsored the family, it would not have solved her problem. She was desperate for a husband and while she had both children this was just not possible. With Ivan's help, the best Russell and Mitch could do was persuade her to continue to look after Elena until they could rush through an adoption. As for Michael, his future seemed uncertain. On the one hand, the mother told Russell and Mitch that she would like the two children adopted together, but then she seemed to change her mind and thought that maybe she would be able to manage Michael on his own. It put them in a very similar situation to the one we had faced with Christina-Daniella. They knew it was not fair on Madi to adopt a brother and a sister, but at the same time they were worried about Michael. In any event the problem was solved for them when the mother decided that she would try to manage with Michael on his own, that one child, particularly a son, did not necessarily wreck her marriage chances.

The adoption process was, on the whole, less traumatic for Russell and Mitch. Elena was in good health and in Romanian terms, at any rate, well cared for. She could walk, was plump and in most respects her development was entirely normal. Although her life had in all probability been a hard one, it had been a great deal better than orphanage life, and the fact that she had thrived so well under her mother's care meant that Russell and Mitch had no real worries about her during the period the adoption was being processed. The law by now was well established and Ivan knew what he was doing. By Christmas Elena was theirs, but thanks to an industrial dispute within Tarom, they had no means of bringing her out of Bucharest.

Eventually, in mid-January, Mitch went alone to collect her, forced to fly Lufthansa at double the air fare. The trip was not without its problems – her luggage was lost, including all the baby equipment she needed to look after Elena, while she waited for a flight home. The handover, which she had been dreading, proved awful. The mother simply passed Elena to Mitch and walked away down the street without a word or any apparent emotion. Mitch had wanted to talk to her, to reassure her, to find out what was going to happen to her son, to ask about Elena's routine, but none of this was possible. Talking about it afterwards, none of us could even guess at how Elena's mother really felt – whether it was a relief or the worst moment of her life. To hand over one's child to a stranger and then walk away – the agony of it. We could not begin to imagine how we ourselves would react.

While Mitch was away, Madi and Russell spent most of their time with us. We fretted and fumed, wondered and worried. Once Elena came home the situation was different, but in many respects more difficult for Russell and Mitch than it had been for us. Our Michael had had nothing when we found him and everything that happened to him from the moment we took him out of the orphanage was a bonus. In Elena's case she was losing both her mother and her brother. The alternative, of course, was an orphanage, and a new life in England had to be better than that, but it would have been foolish for Russell and Mitch not to be anxious as to how she would adapt. They need not have worried. By the time we saw Elena, twenty-four hours after her arrival in the UK, she was already calling Mitch Mummy and seemed to have settled in incredibly well. Like Michael, there was the same independence and the apparent ability to see every new situation as an opportunity rather than as a bewildering experience. She is a most exquisite-looking child, with fair hair and big brown eyes, and apart from an unhealthy pallor, caused by living indoors all the time, she looked very well.

So one little girl was safely home, but another still haunted us – Christina-Daniella. Early in the New Year we telephoned Nicolae Ivan and, good as his word, he had rechecked the records. The name and address of her adoptive parents was as he had given it to us, but he had left out one line. The family were not in Palermo, as the address had suggested, but in a street named Palermo in a district known as Enna. It seemed likely, he assured us, that this would make all the difference to finding the family. Feeling slightly relieved, we decided the best course of action was to ask Mirella's parents to continue the search, since they were on the spot. We telephoned the information through to them, and waited.

Meanwhile, the awful thought of Christina-Daniella being still in the orphanage seemed more and more likely. I had the persistent feeling something was wrong and one evening, Alan, aware of my mounting distress, suggested we talk the problem through. 'If she is still in the orphanage,' I said, tentatively, afraid of his reaction, 'we couldn't leave her there, could we?'

'No,' said Alan without hesitation. 'It would have been wrong to have adopted her and Michael at the same time – that would have been too hard on Charlie and the Trifan children, but now Michael and Charlie are so well adjusted . . .'

The relief was enormous. I realised I was asking a very great deal of Alan even to consider three children under four, but I should have known he could not turn his back on Michael's sister.

'I suppose we should have kept a closer eye on her,' Alan said, after a pause. 'I was never happy about that woman who ran the orphanage. I tell you what, let's at least satisfy ourselves that she's not still there while we wait to hear from Mirella's parents.'

Neither of us could remember the address of Christina-Daniella's orphanage. I, of course, had never been there and Alan had only been there twice briefly. All he could remember was that the orphanage was next door to the house in which Ceauşescu's son had once lived.

We telephoned Adrian in America. Things were not going too well for him. The recession had meant he was still not able to buy a house. He and his family had been living with Karen for six months with all the inevitable pressures that caused. In addition, Marianna was homesick and crying all the time. Still, he was anxious to help and, yes, he did remember the address of the orphanage. Armed with the necessary information we telephoned Christie, who was also pleased to help, and agreed to visit the orphanage the next day.

Again we waited. We had news from Christie first. Christina-Daniella was no longer at the orphanage, but no one knew where she had gone or whether she had been adopted. There was simply no record of her. Next came a call from Mirella's parents – a real body-blow. The new information about the address had only served to provide another dead end. They were confident that no one of the name with which Ivan had provided us existed in Sicily.

Immediately we instructed Ivan to inform the Romanian Government of the problem and to instigate his own search. Christie continued his hunt 'in the field' for the little girl, checking orphanages, bribing officials, asking, asking . . .

So far there is nothing. It is as if she has disappeared off the face of the earth. For Alan and I this unexpected turn of events opens up old scars. We feel so very guilty. We could easily have allowed Adrian to overturn the Italian adoption to which the orphanage principal had alluded. Christina-Daniella could have been ours, reunited with her brother, home, safe . . . Instead, we allowed her to slip through our fingers and now we've lost her, lost her for Michael. In dark moments we wonder at her fate. There has been talk in the Press of child pornography rings taking children out of Romania. Perhaps she is still in an orphanage somewhere, perhaps she has AIDS, perhaps she is dead. The search will continue until we find her – and when we do, we will not make the same mistake again. If she needs a home, then she belongs here with us, with Michael.

Life goes on, and while we wait for news of Christina-Daniella there is much still to celebrate within the family. On the Sunday following Elena's arrival, she was adapting so well that we decided to hold an impromptu family gathering to welcome her. Murray and Claire came as well as Russell, Mitch and their two girls, and Russell and Murray's mother, Sonja.

While everyone had drinks in the sitting room and played with the children, I cooked lunch. I was in the middle of straining the vegetables when Michael came in, pursued by Elena. They walked past me into the playroom, which is an extension of the kitchen. Elena sat down on the carpet and Michael began bringing things to her and carefully naming each one. 'Ball, book, Babby, man, horse, cup . . . car.' He handed her one of Charlie's prized 'brmm-brmms' and she took it reverently. 'Car,' she said, clearly.

Michael was delighted. 'Car,' he agreed, beaming from ear to ear.

I stood watching them, tears pouring down my face. These two little children, who had been through so much, communicating together in what for them was a foreign language. It was almost too much to bear. They were going to be friends, it was easy to see that, and I hope they will draw comfort from one another when inevitably they have doubts and worries about their origins. At least in our family they can never feel the odd one out. We will make mistakes, like all parents, but they will be loved and cherished and cared for to the very best of our ability, for as long as we live.

I thought of the other Romanian children we had come to know and love. Alexander Male: not only was he a big bouncing boy, but he had proved to be the catalyst in his mother's life, changing Kerry seemingly overnight from a dedicated businesswoman to a devoted mother. Little American Emily, in Karen's loving care, had made up for her two months spent clinging to life. Paul and Stacey Vassis now had their little boy safely home, as did Brian and Jo Leeman. Happy endings. But I could not help remembering Caroline Martin, who had really begun it all for us and for the many other families she helped. Emily, her youngest daughter, has AIDS, which was why she was so ill on arrival in England. The test had shown up negative because the disease was still in the incubation stage. And Toby, Caroline's beloved Toby, has suffered from hepatitis B and is likely to remain a carrier for life. And then there is Christina-Daniella . . . What a country, what a world that can cause so much suffering in innocent children. We had been so lucky.

I left my son and my new granddaughter playing happily on the floor together, and went into the sitting room to call the family for lunch.

EPILOGUE:
THE CASE FOR ADOPTION

'LOVE is the same, whichever country it is given in.' So spoke Dr Liliana Bacila, from Orphanage No. 1, in January 1990. It should be, it certainly should be . . .

For some reason I cannot begin to understand, there exists a considerable amount of prejudice and disapproval about adopting a child from another country. The argument seems to have come to a head with the arrival of the Romanian crisis. Individual criticism is everyone's right, but many Social Services in this country have made things very difficult for prospective adoptive parents, in some cases even refusing to conduct home studies at all, for no justified reason. Around the world there are many thousands of couples who would make wonderful parents and who are only stopped from being so because, for whatever reason, they are not able to make a child. Similarly, across the globe, millions of children eke out their miserable lives without love, care or proper food, and with no hope for today and little hope for tomorrow. Surely the sensible, practical, humanitarian answer to this problem is to put the two together and make everyone happy. What does a difference in colour, creed, religion or cultural heritage matter? 'Love is the same, whichever country it is given in.'

If the world, as a whole, is to make any serious strides towards becoming a civilised place, then we have to overcome man's inhumanity to man and stamp out war once and for all. This can only be done by a greater understanding of one another's countries, cultures and thinking processes. Surely the best way this can be achieved is through each other's children. Already we as a family know so much more about Eastern Europe than we would ever have done without Michael, and, of course, our relationship with Romania is only just beginning. I have noticed that those people who are quick to criticise the wisdom of taking a Romanian orphan away from his 'cultural heritage' are usually those people who have never even been to Romania. What cultural heritage can you have living day after day, week after week, month after month, in a stinking cot? In recent months we have spoken to people who have known Romania for much longer than its last, highly publicised year. Talking recently to one relief worker, who has spent years working through the church in Romanian orphanages, he, a mild man, becomes almost hysterical with rage at this argument. He has visited orphanages where the same children have been in the same cots, in the same tiny room, for four or five years, never leaving it. Children who otherwise would be strong in mind, wind and limb are emotional and physical cripples, their lives destroyed before they have begun.

There is also much ignorant criticism of the Romanian people at the present time, because so much of the aid for the orphanages has gone missing. Do-gooders say they will continue to try and help the orphans, but that they are having to do it despite the Romanian people. They criticise their apathetic attitude to the suffering of the children, and say they are too corrupt to be trusted with the aid which has poured into the country. This is all true, but no one asks *why*. Nothing can be done seriously to affect the lives of the abandoned children of Romania until something is done about Romania itself. Romanians are not going to allow the orphanages to become little pockets of luxury while they themselves struggle to survive. Who can blame them? I believe there was no second revolution this Christmas, not through lack of support, nor indeed through the lack of justification for an uprising, but because the people were too dispirited, too tired, too hungry and too cold, to fight any more.

So, where does that leave the children in their suffering? Nowhere, until Romania herself can be helped to recover from her sickness, and that will take years. By then Ceauşescu's children will have died, or grown up into miserable, damaged adults. The quick answer, the only answer in the short term, is adoption. Again, critics will say that Romania is being deprived of the flower of her youth. This is rubbish. The children of Romania's orphanages have no hope of being of service to their country, but I am absolutely certain many of those who are adopted will return to Romania to put something back, to help in some way with the rebuilding of their country. They can only do that if they are well, strong and confident – in other words, if they have had the benefit of happy childhoods.

None of us own our children. Whether we give birth to them or not, they are simply ours on loan. It is our job to raise them as best we can and to teach them to fly. This is what needs to happen to as many of Romania's children as possible. If you have room in your heart, in your home, for a child, then think seriously about the plight of the Romanian children and, if you decide you have something to offer such a child, then fight and kick and scream against the red tape, against the system, as we had to do. And go to Romania, find your special child and give him or her the love that he or she would never have had but for you.

I dedicated this book to the children of Romania because Michael's story was written for them. Equally well, I could have dedicated it to Alan, for without him there is no doubt that Michael would still be in Orphanage No. 4, if he had survived another winter. Yes, I provided the backup support with practical things such as baby clothes and food, and keeping the home fires burning, but it is Alan who clawed his way through the system, who would not accept 'no' for an answer, who freed Michael from his orphanage, who gave us our son, and Russell, Murray, Locket and Charlie their brother.

'You're a very nice man, Mr Fowler, and there are no buts, no buts at all.'

If you would like to make a donation to the scheme to build family foster houses in Romania for orphanage children or to support the Trust's other projects, then please send your donations to:

> The Romanian Orphanage Trust
> PO Box 660
> 32 Queen Victoria Street
> London EC4N 4XX

making your cheque payable to The Romanian Orphanage Trust/The Michael Fowler Appeal.

Alan Fowler has produced a fact sheet giving information on how to begin the process of adopting a child from Romania. If you would like to receive a copy of this, please write enclosing a large stamped addressed envelope to:

> Alan Fowler
> c/o Ebury Press
> Random Century House
> 20 Vauxhall Bridge Road
> London SW1V 2SA